# IDIOT'S GUIDES®

## AS EASY AS IT GETS!

# Baking

by Alexandra Zohn

ALPHA

A member of Penguin Group (USA) Inc.

**ALPHA BOOKS**

Published by Penguin Group (USA) Inc.

Penguin Group (USA) Inc., 375 Hudson Street, New York, New York 10014, USA • Penguin Group (Canada), 90 Eglinton Avenue East, Suite 700, Toronto, Ontario M4P 2Y3, Canada (a division of Pearson Penguin Canada Inc.) • Penguin Books Ltd., 80 Strand, London WC2R 0RL, England • Penguin Ireland, 25 St. Stephen's Green, Dublin 2, Ireland (a division of Penguin Books Ltd.) • Penguin Group (Australia), 250 Camberwell Road, Camberwell, Victoria 3124, Australia (a division of Pearson Australia Group Pty. Ltd.) • Penguin Books India Pvt. Ltd., 11 Community Centre, Panchsheel Park, New Delhi—110 017, India • Penguin Group (NZ), 67 Apollo Drive, Rosedale, North Shore, Auckland 1311, New Zealand (a division of Pearson New Zealand Ltd.) • Penguin Books (South Africa) (Pty.) Ltd., 24 Sturdee Avenue, Rosebank, Johannesburg 2196, South Africa • Penguin Books Ltd., Registered Offices: 80 Strand, London WC2R 0RL, England

IDIOT'S GUIDES and Design are trademarks of Penguin Group (USA) Inc.

International Standard Book Number: 978-1-61564-609-8
Library of Congress Catalog Card Number: 2014935264

16   15   14      8   7   6   5   4   3   2   1

Interpretation of the printing code: The rightmost number of the first series of numbers is the year of the book's printing; the rightmost number of the second series of numbers is the number of the book's printing. For example, a printing code of 14-1 shows that the first printing occurred in 2014.

**Note:** This publication contains the opinions and ideas of its author. It is intended to provide helpful and informative material on the subject matter covered. It is sold with the understanding that the author and publisher are not engaged in rendering professional services in the book. If the reader requires personal assistance or advice, a competent professional should be consulted. The author and publisher specifically disclaim any responsibility for any liability, loss, or risk, personal or otherwise, which is incurred as a consequence, directly or indirectly, of the use and application of any of the contents of this book.

Most Alpha books are available at special quantity discounts for bulk purchases for sales promotions, premiums, fund-raising, or educational use. Special books, or book excerpts, can also be created to fit specific needs. For details, write: Special Markets, Alpha Books, 375 Hudson Street, New York, NY 10014.

**3 3988 10126 4908**

**Publisher:** *Mike Sanders*

**Executive Managing Editor:** *Billy Fields*

**Acquisitions Editor:** *Karyn Gerhard*

**Development Editor:** *Kayla Dugger*

**Production Editor:** *Jana M. Stefanciosa*

**Cover and Book Designer:** *Rebecca Batchelor*

**Indexer:** *Julie Bess*

**Layout:** *Ayanna Lacey*

**Proofreader:** *Tricia Liebig*

# Contents

**Part 1** The Essentials ............................ 3

## 1 Equipment ................................. 5

Utensils ............................................. 6
Machinery ......................................... 10
Baking Pans ....................................... 12
Measuring Tools ................................. 14
Bowls .............................................. 15
Paper, Mats, and Boards ........................ 16
Pastry Bags, Couplers, and Tips ............... 18

## 2 Ingredients and Measuring: A Primer ........ 21

Sweeteners ........................................ 22
Dairy .............................................. 26
Other Fats and Oils .............................. 30
Flours ............................................. 32
Nonwheat Flours ................................. 34
Starches and Jelling Agents ..................... 35
Eggs .............................................. 36
Leavening Agents ................................ 37
Flavoring Agents ................................. 38
Salt ............................................... 41
Nuts .............................................. 42
Edible Decorations .............................. 44
Chocolate and Cocoa ............................ 45
Measuring Basics ................................ 48

## Part 2  Starting Easy:  Cookies . . . . . . . . . . . . . . . . . 53

An Introduction to Cookies . . . . . . . . . . . . . . . . . . . . . . . . . . . . . . . . . . . 54
The Three Basic Mixing Methods for Cookies . . . . . . . . . . . . . . . . 56

### 3 Sheet and Bar Cookies . . . . . . . . . . . . . . . . . . . . . 59

How to Make Pressed Sheet Cookies . . . . . . . . . . . . . . . . . . . . . . . 60
*Shortbread* . . . . . . . . . . . . . . . . . . . . . . . . . . . . . . . . . . . . . . . 62
*Granola Bars* . . . . . . . . . . . . . . . . . . . . . . . . . . . . . . . . . . . . . 64
How to Make Poured Sheet Cookies . . . . . . . . . . . . . . . . . . . . . . 66
*Brownies* . . . . . . . . . . . . . . . . . . . . . . . . . . . . . . . . . . . . . . . . 68
*Blondies* . . . . . . . . . . . . . . . . . . . . . . . . . . . . . . . . . . . . . . . . 70
How to Make Biscotti . . . . . . . . . . . . . . . . . . . . . . . . . . . . . . . . . . . . .72
*Almond-Cranberry Biscotti* . . . . . . . . . . . . . . . . . . . . . . . . . 74

### 4 Dropped and Piped Cookies . . . . . . . . . . . . . . . . 77

How to Make Dropped Cookies . . . . . . . . . . . . . . . . . . . . . . . . . . . 78
*Chocolate Chip Cookies* . . . . . . . . . . . . . . . . . . . . . . . . . . . .80
*Peanut Butter Cookies* . . . . . . . . . . . . . . . . . . . . . . . . . . . . .81
*Oatmeal-Raisin Cookies* . . . . . . . . . . . . . . . . . . . . . . . . . . . 82
*Mexican Wedding Cookies* . . . . . . . . . . . . . . . . . . . . . . . . . 83
Piped Cookies and Piping Basics . . . . . . . . . . . . . . . . . . . . . . . . . 84
*Spritz Cookies* . . . . . . . . . . . . . . . . . . . . . . . . . . . . . . . . . . . . 88

### 5 Rolled-Out and Ice Box Cookies . . . . . . . . . . . . 91

How to Make Rolled-Out Cookies . . . . . . . . . . . . . . . . . . . . . . . . 92
*Gingerbread Cookies* . . . . . . . . . . . . . . . . . . . . . . . . . . . . . . 94
How to Make Ice Box Cookies . . . . . . . . . . . . . . . . . . . . . . . . . . . 96
*Vanilla Cookies* . . . . . . . . . . . . . . . . . . . . . . . . . . . . . . . . . . . 98
*Chocolate Cookies* . . . . . . . . . . . . . . . . . . . . . . . . . . . . . . . 100
How to Make Pinwheel Cookies . . . . . . . . . . . . . . . . . . . . . . . . .102

### 6 Decorating Cookies . . . . . . . . . . . . . . . . . . . . . . . 107

Decorative Toppings . . . . . . . . . . . . . . . . . . . . . . . . . . . . . . . . . . . . 108
How to Adhere Decorative Toppings to Cookies . . . . . . . . . . . . 109
How to Make Royal Icing . . . . . . . . . . . . . . . . . . . . . . . . . . . . . . . . 110
How to Use Royal Icing . . . . . . . . . . . . . . . . . . . . . . . . . . . . . . . . . . .111

**Part 3** Eggs: One Ingredient,
Multiple Functions .................... 115

Egg Basics............................................. 116

## 7 Meringues ........................... 119

How to Make Meringue ............................. 120
How to Make Meringue Cookies.................... 126
*Meringues*......................................128
*French Macarons*............................. 130
How to Make Meringue-Based Cakes .......... 134
*Chocolate Cloud Cake* ......................136
*Pavlova* ................................... 138

## 8 Custards and Mousses..................... 141

How to Make Stovetop Custard.....................142
*Crème Anglaise* ............................. 144
*Pastry Cream* .............................. 146
How to Make Baked Custard ......................148
*New York Cheesecake*........................ 150
*Lemon Bars* ................................154
*Flan* .....................................156
How to Make Mousse ..............................158
*Praline Mousse*............................ 160
*Mascarpone Mousse*.........................162

## 9 Soufflés ........................... 165

How to Make Soufflé...............................166
*Chocolate Soufflé*.......................... 168
*Goat Cheese Soufflé* ....................... 170

## Part 4 Pies, Tarts, and Cakes................... 173

### 10 Pies and Tarts ............................. 175
How to Make a Basic Pie Crust ............................176
Top Crust Variations........................................ 180
   *Apple Pie* ................................................ 188
How to Make a Cracker Crust ..............................192
   *Key Lime Pie* ............................................194
How to Make a Nut Crust ..................................196
   *Fresh Fruit Tart in Almond Crust*...........................200

### 11 Cakes and Cupcakes ......................203
How to Make Layer Cakes Using the Creaming Method.......204
   *Moist Chocolate Cake*....................................206
   *Vanilla Velvet Cake*......................................208
   *Carrot Cake*............................................ 210
   *Molten Chocolate Cake* ..................................212
   *Russian Sour Cream Coffeecake*...........................214
   *Chocoflan* ..............................................216
Adapting Cake Recipes for Cupcakes.......................218

### 12 Cake Decorating........................223
How to Frost a Cake ...................................... 224
How to Decorate a Cake in Simple Ways ................... 226
   *Swiss Meringue Buttercream* .............................. 228
   *Classic American Buttercream* ............................. 228
   *Chocolate Ganache*...................................... 229
   *Whipped Cream*.........................................230
   *Coconut Whipped Cream*.................................230
   *Cream Cheese Frosting*...................................231
   *Fruit Coulis*............................................. 232

**Part 5** Breads . . . . . . . . . . . . . . . . . . . . . . . . . . . . . . .235

13 Quick Breads . . . . . . . . . . . . . . . . . . . . . . . . . . . .237

How to Make Muffins . . . . . . . . . . . . . . . . . . . . . . . . . . . . . . . . 238
*Yogurt Muffins* . . . . . . . . . . . . . . . . . . . . . . . . . . . . . . . . . . .240
*Banana Muffins* . . . . . . . . . . . . . . . . . . . . . . . . . . . . . . . . . .241
How to Make Biscuits and Scones . . . . . . . . . . . . . . . . . . . . . 242
*Biscuits* . . . . . . . . . . . . . . . . . . . . . . . . . . . . . . . . . . . . . . .244
*Oat Scones* . . . . . . . . . . . . . . . . . . . . . . . . . . . . . . . . . . . . 246

14 Yeast-Risen Breads . . . . . . . . . . . . . . . . . . . . . . .249

An Introduction to Yeast-Risen Breads . . . . . . . . . . . . . . . . . . 250
Kneading Bread . . . . . . . . . . . . . . . . . . . . . . . . . . . . . . . . . . . 252
Working with Yeast . . . . . . . . . . . . . . . . . . . . . . . . . . . . . . . . . 254
Freezing Dough . . . . . . . . . . . . . . . . . . . . . . . . . . . . . . . . . . . 256
How to Make Yeast-Risen Bread . . . . . . . . . . . . . . . . . . . . . . 258
*French Bread (Baguette)* . . . . . . . . . . . . . . . . . . . . . . . . . . 262
*Walnut-Raisin Bread* . . . . . . . . . . . . . . . . . . . . . . . . . . . . . 264
*Brioche* . . . . . . . . . . . . . . . . . . . . . . . . . . . . . . . . . . . . . . 266
*Challah* . . . . . . . . . . . . . . . . . . . . . . . . . . . . . . . . . . . . . . 268

Glossary . . . . . . . . . . . . . . . . . . . . . . . . . . . . . . . . .270

Index . . . . . . . . . . . . . . . . . . . . . . . . . . . . . . . . . . . .272

# Introduction

You may have heard that if you want to sell your home, you should bake something with vanilla or cinnamon to entice potential buyers into closing the deal—that it will make them want to keep that place and that scent. There's something magical about sweet baked smells wafting through the kitchen, and consciously or unconsciously, no one can resist them! They silently scream of coziness, love, comfort, joy, family, and happiness. And when the smell is followed by a piece of cake, a crispy cookie, a dollop of whipped cream, a slice of fresh bread, or a tart sliver of pie, all those feelings are evoked to the maximum potency. They turn into smiles, laughter, humming, and even clapping!

Unfortunately, these days—with our busy lives and the abundance of premade goods—the old tradition of homemade treats and everything they represent is slowly vanishing. I hope that with this book, I can inspire you to keep that from happening. I aim to show you how easily it can be done so you shake off any doubts or insecurities and discover the pleasure of baking at home. If you bake with your family or your friends, you can even form special bonds in the process. Or you can just bake by yourself as a creative outlet or a fun project. Whatever the case, if you follow the steps and advice in this book, you'll become a home baker faster than you think. Have fun, and enjoy the sweets of your labor!

## Acknowledgments

This book, as well as everything else in my life, wouldn't have been possible without my mother and my grandmother. They are two incredible, strong women whose baking imbibed every single cell of my body—it created memories, it trained my taste buds, it taught me to fold in meringue, and it took me into the kitchen (a place I decided never to leave). I also want to thank my adored Vitor, Eliana, and Ari, for all their support, patience, understanding, taste-testing, and restraint (especially when I needed to have some goodies left). I love you infinitely, and you inspire me every single moment! Without my friends and the rest of my family I'm nothing, so thank you for sharing, tasting, and having my back. A special thanks to Elisa Strauss for being such an inspiration, for believing in me, and for being my mentor and a wonderful friend. I also want to thank Peggy Grodinsky, because without her encouragement, I'd have never typed a word in English! And thank you to Alpha Books' Karyn and Kayla for your help.

*Editor's acknowledgments:*

Many thanks go to our wonderful photographer, Kotaro Kawashima, for his work on this project; to our stalwart development editor, Kayla Dugger, for bringing all of the pieces together; and to our amazing designer, Becky Batchelor, for making it all look beautiful. Special thanks go to the fantastic chef Janine Desiderio, without whose expertise, skill, and tireless work during a grueling photo shoot, this book would not have come together. —*Karyn Gerhard*

## Special Thanks to the Technical Reviewer

*Idiot's Guides: Baking* was reviewed by an expert who double-checked the accuracy of what you'll learn here, to help us ensure this book gives you everything you need to know about baking. Special thanks are extended to Monita Buchwald.

## Trademarks

*part 1*

# The Essentials

**Chapter 1:** Equipment

**Chapter 2:** Ingredients and Measuring: A Primer

*chapter 1*

# Equipment

Let's face it—most people are afraid of baking, thinking it's an art infused with black magic and a lot of luck. But the deep secrets to successful baking are pretty simple:

1. Equip yourself properly.

2. Use quality ingredients.

3. Measure or weigh ingredients carefully.

4. Stick to the recipes (at least until you get the hang of it).

This chapter covers how to take care of the first point—gathering the right and necessary utensils, machinery, baking pans, supplies, and measuring tools for successful baking. I also talk about equipment that, although not essential, makes the baking process run more smoothly and easily.

# Utensils

**Rolling pin:** A good wood rolling pin is necessary for rolling out any kind of pie or cookie dough. Either a French rolling pin ("stick style") or an American one (rolling on bearings) will do the job, and the longer, the better (ideally 20 inches/50 cm)—this way, you'll be able to cover more surface with each stroke. Choose the one most comfortable for you.

**Cutters:** An assortment of cookie cutter shapes is a great thing to have. However, if you just want a basic, multipurpose cutter that works for cookies, scones, and biscuits, a plain, round, heat-resistant, metal cutter that is 2 to $2^1/_2$ inches (5 to 6 cm) in diameter is a must. If you don't own any cutters, you can substitute them for a glass, cup, or bowl.

## Washing and Drying Your Metal Cutter

To prevent your metal cutter from rusting, dry it completely in a sheet pan in a heated oven for a couple minutes after washing it.

**Cookie scoop:** Also known as a mini ice cream scoop, a cookie scoop has a release mechanism that allows you to produce consistently sized cookies that bake more evenly. Cookie scoops come in different sizes, so choose one according to your desired cookie size.

**Bench scrapers:** These handy tools have many uses in baking, especially when working with dough—they can help you manipulate the dough and scrape off your work surface when you're done. Bench scrapers come in different styles: rectangular metal blades with a thin edge and a handle, often with a ruler stamped on the bottom; or flexible, curved, plastic bowl scrapers. If possible, it's best to have one of each; however, if you need to choose, pick an inexpensive plastic one.

**Pastry brush:** A 1$^1/_2$ -inch (3-cm) pastry brush, either with natural or silicone bristles, is the best tool for brushing butter or other liquids onto doughs and crusts.

**Whisk:** This indispensable tool is great for mixing together lump-free sauces, icings, and batters or for whipping cream and egg whites by hand. Many styles are available on the market, but a large, traditional, balloon, stainless-steel whisk might be the best one to own. Having at least two of them—a long-handled and a small one—is ideal.

**Silicone spatula:** Silicone is a heat-resistant material, so it allows for stirring, scraping, and folding in either cold or hot mixtures. Fairly stiff-bladed spatulas are best. You should consider having at least one large spatula, and if possible, one small spatula.

**Offset spatulas:** With an angled blade and a narrow width, metal offset spatulas are essential for frosting cakes and cupcakes; spreading fillings, doughs, and batters; and removing baked goods from pans, among many other uses. Having at least one short and one long metal offset spatula will make the baking process that much easier.

**Fine-mesh sieve:** A sieve can be used for sifting or dusting ingredients or for straining sauces and fillings. Get a sieve with a strong metal mesh that doesn't stretch or bend and that resists heat (from sauces and so on).

**Vegetable peeler:** Necessary for peeling fruits and vegetables, a good-quality, sturdy, and comfortable vegetable peeler is a great tool to have.

**Microplane zester:** Also known as a rasp grater, this stainless-steel hand-held tool with sharp edges easily removes citrus zest and leaves the bitter pith behind. It can also be used for grating ingredients, such as chocolate, gingerroot, hard cheese, and whole nutmeg.

**Knives:** You don't need to purchase separate knives for baking, but you need to have a good **serrated knife** for slicing crusty baked goods and chopping chocolate, a sharp **paring knife** for more-delicate tasks (such as segmenting and trimming), and a **chef's knife** for making neat slices and cutting and chopping ingredients.

**Oven thermometer:** Chances are you don't get your oven professionally calibrated; therefore, its temperature readings may vary as much as 50°F (10°C) higher or lower than the dial registers. This could severely affect the end product by burning or not baking it through, producing odd textures, and so on. To avoid this in an inexpensive way, I recommend placing an oven thermometer in the oven and checking it when the oven is preheated to make sure it's at the right temperature.

**Instant-read thermometer:** A handheld thermometer is very useful for custards and other preparations—there's nothing more exact. An inexpensive dial face or a digital thermometer (a more-serious financial commitment, but it's faster and easier to read) is strongly recommended.

**Timer:** It's easy to lose track of time while multitasking, so using a timer is an excellent practice. A digital timer is much more accurate than a dial one; you can also use the timer function on your smart phone as an alternative.

**Cooling racks:** Most baked goods need a cooling-down period that allows for air circulation under the pan. Heavy-duty, tight-weave wire racks are best. Get at least one rack—preferably, a rectangular one that fits inside your baking sheet—so you can use it not only for cooling baked goods, but also for icing or glazing cakes or cookies.

## Cooling Rack Alternatives

If you don't own any cooling racks or need more than you own, you can improvise by inverting a muffin pan or an empty cardboard (not plastic) egg container and placing the hot pan on top. Another option is putting the pan on top of two empty cans of the same size.

**Pots and pans:** These are used all the time in baking for everything from cooking custards, to making a water bath, to caramelizing. Good-quality, heavy-duty, stainless-steel pots and pans ensure even cooking. It's good to have at least one saucepan on hand when baking; 3-quart is a good size to have, but you can also use 2- or 4-quart versions.

**Kettle:** Although not indispensable, a kettle is handy when you need hot or boiling water or have to prepare a hot water bath for baking custards or bread. If you don't own one, you can always heat the water in a saucepan.

# Machinery

**Standing mixer:** Although it doesn't come cheap, a good standing mixer is a lifetime investment for pastry making. From kneading bread dough, to whipping meringue, to mixing a cake batter, it is an invaluable tool.

**Handheld mixer:** Because it is relatively inexpensive compared to the standing mixer, a handheld mixer is great for the occasional baker. Although it doesn't allow for a hands-free operation, a handheld mixer basically performs the same tasks as a standing version, with the exception of kneading dough.

**Blender:** A blender is great for puréeing ingredients with high moisture (such as fruit, milk, cream, and eggs) into a pourable mixture, but it's also useful for making sauces or preparing batters. With the new generation of power blenders—which do come with a high price tag—some of the functions of a food processor can be taken over by the blender, such as making nut butters at home.

**Immersion blender:** A handheld ("stick") blender is an inexpensive way of achieving certain functions of blenders, mixers, and food processors for the occasional baker. It can be used in hot or cold mixtures and is great for smoothing sauces and batters. It's very practical and easy to clean, although it doesn't allow for hands-free operation. Some immersion blenders come with special attachments, such as a whisk and blades.

**Food processor:** Great for chopping nuts and making pie doughs and other crusts, a food processor can also slice, grind, grate, and purée. A food processor with a bowl capacity of at least 11 cups is recommended for people who plan to mix dough often.

**Spice or coffee grinder:** This inexpensive machine is helpful for grinding small seeds, herbs, whole spices, and even rice or oats for rice and oat flour. However, it can retain flavors if not cleaned thoroughly. To clean, pulse a few pieces of bread and discard. Keep a separate grinder for coffee grains (if you use any) to avoid the coffee from picking up the flavors of the spices.

**Digital scale:** An inexpensive digital kitchen scale is a life-changing tool in baking. By weighing the ingredients, your recipe will be more accurate and consistent and will clean up much easier, as you'll eliminate the use of many measuring cups. Look for a scale that has an automatic shut-off cycle of at least 4 minutes; an 11-pound (5,000-g) capacity; and a tare feature, so you can zero the scale every time you add a new ingredient. It should also feature weight units in both ounces and grams.

**Cookie press:** This device, which creates consistent cookies every time, consists of a cylinder with a plunger on one end that is used to extrude cookie dough through a small hole at the other end. It has interchangeable perforated disks with different patterns. The cookie press is typically used to press *spritz* or *Spritzgebäck,* the classic German buttery Christmas cookies. It's definitely not an indispensable item for the pastry kitchen (you can only use it with a specific kind of cookie dough), but if you enjoy preparing these delicious cookies often or in large quantities, it's worth it to have one.

# Baking Pans

**Round baking pans:** Two sets of heavy-duty, aluminum, 8-inch (20-cm) and 9-inch (23-cm) diameter pans with, if possible, a 3-inch (7.5-cm) depth are ideal for cake baking. Round cake pans of different sizes are a great addition if you are committed to baking cakes often.

**Square and rectangular baking pans:** An 8-inch (20-cm) square and a 9×13-inch (23×33-cm) heavy-duty aluminum baking pan are great for sheet cookies and sheet cakes.

**Springform pan:** A 9×3-inch (23×7.5-cm) springform pan is an all-purpose pan to bake cakes that would otherwise be impossible to remove from the standard cake pan, such as cheesecakes or some meringue-based cakes.

## Wrapping Springform Pans

Springform pans never seal perfectly, so it's important to wrap their bottoms with foil when baking in a water bath. If not baking in a water bath, always place a springform pan on a baking sheet to avoid possible leakage.

**Rimmed baking sheets:** Also called cookie sheets, sheet pans, sheet trays, half-sheets, or jelly roll pans, the standard 12$^1/_2$×17$^1/_2$-inch (31×44-cm) baking sheet with a $^1/_2$-inch (1.25-cm) rim is a must for baking. The best sheets are the light-colored, heavy-gauge ones, as they conduct heat evenly (avoid the dark-colored ones or nonstick versions, which have a tendency to overbrown baked goods). You should have at least two (preferably up to four) baking sheets to make cookie baking run faster and smoother.

**CHAPTER 1 |** EQUIPMENT

**Muffin pan:** Useful for baking muffins and—when lined with paper cups—cupcakes, muffin pans even work as freezer cake molds. Muffin pans come in different sizes, but the best is standard size (with 12 cavities that each have a $\frac{1}{2}$-cup capacity). If possible, try using a mini muffin pan (usually 2-tablespoon capacity per cavity) for bite-size desserts.

## Substituting for a Muffin Pan

You can currently find self-standing muffin or cupcake molds you can substitute for a muffin pan; some are disposable and others can be washed and reused. Always place those on rimmed baking sheets before filling and baking.

**Bundt pan:** Also known as a tube or kugelhopf pan, a Bundt pan has fluted edges and a tube perforation in the middle that encourages even baking, especially with dense-textured cakes.

**Pie pan:** The standard pie pan is 9 or 10 inches (23 or 25 cm) wide and 2 inches (5 cm) deep (more-shallow ones are not ideal for double-crusted pies). The best option is a tempered-glass (Pyrex) pie pan, which allows for more even browning, because it's see-through and you can view the crust as it bakes. However, metal pie pans also work well and are easy to transport.

**Tart pan:** Fluted and shallow tart pans with removable bottoms are the best option for baking tarts, as the removable bottom makes unmolding a much-easier task. They come in different shapes and sizes, but the most common is a 9-inch (23-cm) round, preferably light-colored. If you can only use a dark-coated tart pan, though, reduce the oven temperature by about 25°F (10°C) to prevent burning.

# Measuring Tools

**Liquid measuring cups:** The best liquid measuring cups are made of tempered glass (Pyrex) and have a spout and graduated measures. I recommend having both a 2-cup (16-oz./480-ml) and an 8-cup (64-oz./2-liter) capacity cups. If you have the storage space, also get a 4-cup (32-oz./1-liter) capacity measuring cup. The larger glass measuring cups can double as a mixing bowl; in fact, some even come with a lid. On the opposite end of the spectrum, when you need to measure small amounts of liquid, you can use mini shot glass measures (about 2-tablespoon capacity measures), which have graduation for volume and measure. Their advantage over a regular measuring spoon set is that you can measure liquids all together up to its capacity; although they're not indispensable, I've found them useful.

## The 8-Cup Liquid Measure

One of my most-used pieces of kitchen equipment is, without a doubt, the 8-cup (64-oz./2-liter) liquid measure. I often use it instead of a mixing bowl, and because it's graduated, I can skip the extra measuring cup when adding ingredients! It's deep and tall, making it the perfect vessel for an immersion blender. It also has a spout that makes it great for pouring liquids, plus it's heat resistant. Mine comes with a cover, so I can even use it to store mixtures in the refrigerator. So I highly suggest getting this measure—it's one of those items you can use over and over.

**Dry measuring cups:** I recommend metal measuring cups with long handles that let you dip, scoop, and level the ingredients. A set usually includes a 1-cup, $1/_2$-cup, $1/_3$-cup, and $1/_4$-cup measures, but they also come in $2/_3$-cup and $3/_4$-cup measures.

**Measuring spoons:** The best measuring spoons have deep bowls that can be easily leveled with the back of a knife. Measuring spoons come in all types of materials, but it's best to stick with metal or anything that is sturdy to prevent them from denting.

# Bowls

A set of stainless-steel mixing bowls with small, medium, large, and extra-large bowls ranging from 1 quart (1 liter) to 6 quarts (6 liters) is incredibly versatile. They can be used for fitting into a saucepan to create a double boiler, for whisking batters, or for mixing dough. Stainless-steel bowls heat up and cool down quickly; however, they can't be used in the microwave and, occasionally, baker's yeast won't proof in them. For those times, you can use your large glass liquid measuring cup or glass mixing bowls.

# Paper, Mats, and Boards

**Parchment paper:** A versatile, nonstick baking paper coated in silicone, parchment paper (either white or brown) can be cut to measure and used to line baking sheets and pans. It prevents baked goods from sticking and makes cleanup easier. You can also sift dry ingredients onto a sheet of parchment paper, and then use the paper to pour it into your bowl. Parchment paper can be used for shaping and wrapping logs of cookie dough or for piping icing or chocolate, and even for cutting out stencils to decorate cakes or cookies. If you can, buy precut 12×16-inch (30×40-cm) sheets of parchment paper to avoid dealing with the more-common (and rather torturous) parchment paper roll. These sheets are available online or at baking supply stores. To store, lay the sheets flat in a rimmed baking sheet. You can trace the bottom of your baking pan with a pencil over the sheet of parchment paper and cut the shape to line the bottom of the pans before baking.

**Silicone mats:** These nonstick, flexible mats come in a variety of shapes and sizes to fit into a baking pan and can withstand temperatures up to 500°F (260°C). However, as opposed to parchment paper, you can't cut on top of the mats or shape them to fit a different pan. And while they are not cheap in price, they can be used and cleaned infinitely.

**Aluminum foil:** Although it's better not to bake on aluminum foil, these malleable tin sheets are very helpful for wrapping, covering, and freezing baked goods.

**Plastic wrap:** With an endless list of uses, clingy plastic wrap is a must-have in the pastry kitchen.

**Cutting board:** A good cutting board is essential for chopping chocolate, slicing butter or fruit, and doing other baking tasks. The best cutting boards for baking and pastry prep are plastic or bamboo. It's better to keep a separate cutting board for sweet/baking ingredients, as other boards used for chopping garlic, onion, and so on might impart undesired flavors. Also, avoid using the same boards for meats and baking ingredients.

**Turntable:** Although not indispensable, a cake-decorating turntable (similar to a lazy Susan, but smaller and with no rim) makes icing cakes evenly much easier, as it allows you to turn the cake from front to back without having to touch it. If you decide to invest in one, make sure it's a sturdy kind that won't flip easily. As an alternative, you can place an inverted round cake pan (that is smaller than the cake) on a lazy Susan and prop the cake on the base of the pan.

**Cake boards:** Precut cake boards in round, square, or half-sheet size are life-changing when frosting or decorating cakes. They provide support during the frosting process and allow for easy transportation from one surface to another, preventing the cake from breaking or collapsing. Choose cake boards that are the same shape as the cake and 1 inch (2.5 cm) larger in size, to give you some room for the frosting. You can find them at specialty baking-supply stores, craft stores, and online. If you need to improvise, cut the sides of a cardboard box or a piece of foam core into the desired size.

**Wooden skewers/toothpicks:** Great cake testers for doneness, skewers and toothpicks can also be used as markers when layering cakes. They come in handy when working in cake decorating details and are helpful for unclogging pastry tips.

# Pastry Bags, Couplers, and Tips

**Pastry bags:** Also called piping bags, these bags are used for piping decorative frosting or icing borders or shapes on cakes, cupcakes, and cookies; shaping meringues or pastries; or filling pastries. There are disposable and reusable bags, and they come in all kinds of sizes and materials. The disposable ones, usually made of plastic (although not eco-friendly), are quite practical and come several to a package, which is good when you are piping different-colored frostings at the same time. If you opt for a reusable bag, go for a flexible one coated inside with plastic to prevent leaking. It's better to use a larger bag, as extra space won't affect the piping process.

## When You Don't Have a Pastry Bag

If you need to improvise, use a zipper-lock freezer bag with a cut-off corner (the freezer kind is thicker than the regular zipper-lock bags and more resistant to the pressure applied by your hands); you can insert a tip or coupler or just use it as is. Another option is cutting a triangle shape of parchment paper and shaping it into a cone, cutting off a tiny tip, and using it for piping very small and detailed decorations. This works best for melted chocolate or royal icing, but it's not the best option for entire cakes or fluffy frostings.

**Couplers:** These plastic tools are made of two pieces: the base (larger part), which is inserted inside a pastry bag before filling the bag with frosting; and the pastry tip, which is fitted over the base (from the outside) and secured by screwing the coupler ring on. Couplers allow for switching pastry tips while using the same pastry bag and frosting. To change the tip, just unscrew and remove the ring, change the tip, and secure it into place with the same ring.

**Pastry tips:** With a wide array of shapes and sizes, pastry tips allow you to decorate cakes, cupcakes, and cookies with different designs, effects, and textures. It takes some practice to learn how to pipe evenly, but the more you do it, the better you will be at it. A basic set of pastry tips (I prefer metal ones) is a good place to start.

## Types of Pastry Tips

| Style | How It's Used |
|---|---|
| Plain and round | The most commonly used tip, it can be used to fill, make beads or dots, pipe borders, outline, write, and do lattice work. |
| Open-star | This type of tip is great for creating stars, ruffles, rosettes, ropes, and zigzags. |
| Closed-star | You can use this tip to make rosettes and flower and shell designs. |
| Petit-four | Like the closed-star tip, you can create flower and shell designs with this. You can also use this tip to make outlines and borders on your baked good. |
| Basket-weave | As the name implies, this tip can help you create a basket-weave design. You can also use it to make ribbons, stripes, and lattice weaves and to ice large surfaces. |
| Petal | If you guessed this tip is used for flower designs, you're right! You can create roses, carnations pansies, daisies, and so on with this tip. You can also use it to make ribbons, bows, and garlands. |
| Specialty | From hair tips to heart tips, these are tips beyond the norm you can use to make unique designs. |

# chapter 2

# Ingredients and Measuring: A Primer

The traditional baking pantry consists of flours, dairy products, sugars, eggs, fats (mostly butter), and often leaveners (such as baking powder and baking soda). There is also a great diversity of flavoring agents from chocolate, to liquors, to spices, and even to teas.

With the development of technology, the influence of international cuisines—plus trends and other factors—has led the pantry to grow to include variations of the original ingredients you know and brand-new products with which you're unfamiliar. This wide variety of baking ingredients can be overwhelming, which is why, in this chapter, I explain them and how they can be used.

But having the appropriate ingredients is only the first step. Baking is based on the chemical reactions of the ingredients, so the proportions have to be watched carefully to achieve the desired outcome. Just think about it: you could bake cookies, a cake, and bread using the exact same ingredients, with the difference being only how much of each ingredient is used. When there's heat involved, there's no improvising, so careful measuring—or even better, weighing—is indispensable before the baking takes place.

# Sweeteners

As the name states, these are ingredients that add sweetness to food. They can add tenderness and color to baked products, retain moisture (improving shelf life), and provide food for yeast.

## White Sugars

**Sugar:** Sugars are classified by the size of their grains, although the names of the granulation may vary depending on the manufacturer. This is the term used for refined sugar derived from sugarcane or beets, chemically known as sucrose.

**Granulated sugar:** Also called *table sugar*, it's the most commonly used white sugar.

**Superfine (caster) sugar:** Finer than granulated sugar, superfine sugar dissolves quite easily into liquids, batters, meringues, or doughs and can be substituted 1:1 for granulated sugar. You can make your own by pulsing granulated sugar in a clean spice or coffee grinder.

**Confectioners' sugar (powdered, 10X, or icing sugar):** This sugar is ground into a powder and mixed with about 3 percent of a starch (usually corn) to prevent caking. It's great for making a variety of icings and can be dusted on cakes or cookies for an attractive finish. Confectioners' sugar should be sifted before adding it to a mixture.

**Decorator's (sanding) sugar:** This coarse sugar, which comes in many different colors, is used for coating cookies, cakes, and other decorated goods. Due to its coarseness, it's not practical to mix into doughs or batters.

# Brown and Unrefined Sugars

**Brown sugar:** This is refined sugar mixed with molasses. **Light (golden) brown sugar** has a mild molasses flavor, while **dark brown sugar** is more intense. It can be used 1:1 in place of granulated sugar when a caramel-molasses flavor is desired and when a finished product of a darker color is not objectionable. Brown sugar should be kept in an airtight container to prevent it from drying and hardening. If it hardens, it can be softened by placing it in the microwave with a piece of fresh bread for 30 seconds.

**Natural cane sugar (unrefined sugar):** Slightly coarser, darker, and less refined than granulated sugar, it can still be used interchangeably with granulated.

**Evaporated cane juice (whole cane sugar or sucanat):** This is a juice extracted from sugarcane by mechanical processes, heated, and cooled until small, brown, grainy crystals are formed. This minimally processed sweetener contains much of the molasses that would otherwise be removed in the refining process, giving it a strong flavor while retaining some of the nutrients present in sugarcane. Evaporated cane juice can be substituted 1:1 for granulated sugar when the caramel-molasses flavor is desired and when a finished product of a darker color is not objectionable. It's recommended for use in chocolate, caramel, and coffee-flavored recipes.

**Turbinado:** This coarse, raw, unrefined sugar with light molasses flavor and color can be substituted 1:1 for brown sugar.

**Demerara:** Also known as natural brown sugar, demerara is raw and unrefined and has small, amber-colored crystals with molasses flavor. Demerara can be substituted 1:1 for light brown sugar.

**Muscovado:** A raw, unrefined, dark brown sugar with slightly coarser granulation and a more assertive molasses flavor than brown sugar. Muscovado can be substituted 1:1 for dark brown sugar or evaporated cane juice.

# Nectars, Syrups, and Non-Cane-Derived Sweeteners

**Liquid and nonsugar sweeteners:** Liquid sweeteners can't be substituted 1:1 for sugar in recipes, as their degree of sweetness should be considered, and the total amount of liquid ingredients in the recipe should be reduced to compensate for the moisture provided by the nectars and syrups. A rule of thumb is to reduce the total liquids (milk, water, eggs, juice, and so on) in a recipe by $^1/_4$ when using a liquid sweetener (such as maple syrup or honey), but it's not a foolproof method.

**Molasses:** A byproduct of sugar refinement, this dark, thick, sticky syrup adds a slightly spicy and acidic flavor, dark color, and moisture to baked goods. Molasses is used as an additional flavoring, acidifying, and color ingredient, but it doesn't impart enough sweetness to be used all by itself.

**Honey:** Made by honey bees from flower nectar, this liquid, viscous sweetener is one and a half times sweeter than sugar, so it's important to adjust the measurements when substituting it for sugar in a recipe. Honey never spoils; if it crystallizes, it can be heated to return it to its liquid consistency. Darker honeys tend to be stronger-tasting than light-colored honeys, but each type has a distinctive flavor and scent.

**Pure maple syrup:** Originally extracted from the sap of maple trees, this amber-colored, silky nectar has a distinctive caramel flavor and is a lovely sweetener for baking and drizzling over goods. It comes in different grades that vary depending on where the syrup was produced—usually A has a milder flavor, while B is stronger. Choose according to your own preference; however, always use "pure" maple syrup and avoid "pancake syrup," which is completely artificial.

**Date syrup:** Also known as *silan,* this Middle Eastern sweetener is made by cooking dates in water. With a strong caramel flavor and about $^1/_4$ less sweet than sugar, it can substituted 1:1 for maple syrup.

**Agave nectar:** Extracted from the blue agave plant from Mexico, agave nectar is one and a half times sweeter than sugar and has a clean, pleasant flavor. The darker kinds have a stronger caramel taste. I prefer raw agave nectar, which is less processed; however, I advise using it sparingly, as excessive consumption has raised some health concerns about it.

**Corn syrup:** Made by converting cornstarch into simpler compounds, corn syrup helps products retain moisture and is useful when making icings and candy. It has a mild flavor and is less sweet than sugar. If color is not an issue in a recipe, light and dark corn syrup can be used interchangeably.

**Coconut palm nectar and sugar:** Made from the sap of the coconut plant—the sugar is the evaporated form of the nectar—both have a lovely caramel flavor that harmonizes well with chocolate, caramel, and nuts. Because they have a very low glycemic index, they are good options for people with blood sugar issues. Coconut palm nectar can be used interchangeably with other liquid sweeteners. Coconut palm sugar can be substituted 1:1 for brown sugar, although it doesn't absorb moisture as much and burns more easily.

**Sugar alcohols:** Able to be substituted 1:1 for sugar, sugar alcohols dissolve well and can be used for baking. They cause no blood sugar imbalances, may help prevent cavities, have 50 percent less calories than sugar, and have a long shelf life. However, they are not safe for animals and may cause digestive distress in some people. The most widely available (in specialty shops) is xylitol, which tastes and looks very similar to sugar.

**Stevia:** The only sweetener that doesn't have a real impact in blood sugar, this basically calorie-free South American plant extract is many, many times sweeter than sugar, so a tiny bit goes a long way. Baking with it is tricky, as you need to find a substitute for the bulk of sugar you are removing from the recipe when using stevia; however, there are currently some products on the market that are a combination of stevia and another sweetener that can help.

# Dairy

Milk, butter, and cream are ubiquitous in the pastry kitchen, as they contribute to the texture, flavor, and color of baked goods. Dairy products absorb the odors from other refrigerated foods, so keep them well sealed to protect them from smelling like last night's dinner. Because they are perishable, always check their expiration date before using.

## Milk and Cream

Most recipes call for **whole milk,** which comes from the cow (around 3.5 percent fat content) and has nothing removed or added except vitamin D. If you're substituting **skim milk** (0 to 0.5 percent fat) or **low-fat milk** (1 to 2 percent fat) for whole milk, the product may be less rich, but generally, the recipe should work.

**Condensed milk:** This canned milk, from which about 60 percent of the water has been removed, is heavily sweetened with sugar.

**Evaporated milk:** This canned milk, from which about 60 percent of the water has been removed, has a cooked, boiled-milk flavor.

**Dried milk or milk solids:** Made from whole or nonfat milk (which has a longer shelf life), this milk powder is sometimes added to enhance the flavor and texture in baked goods.

### Nondairy Milk Alternatives

If you or anyone you're baking for suffers from milk intolerances, sensitivities, or allergies, you can find many kinds of milk substitutes on the market. The most common ones are soy, almond (and other nuts), hemp seed, rice, oat, and coconut milks. They can be substituted 1:1 and will usually work well in place of cow's milk, although the flavor of the product might change slightly depending on the kind of milk alternative. I prefer to use the unsweetened varieties, as often many milk substitutes are overly sweet.

**Heavy cream (whipping cream):** Cream with a fat content between 30 and 40 percent—the higher the fat content, the easier to whip and the more stable it is after whipping. Although ultrapasteurized heavy cream has a longer shelf life, it doesn't whip as well as pasteurized cream. Authentic heavy cream should have no additives.

**Half-and-half:** This is equal parts milk and cream and has a fat content of 10 to 15 percent. It provides baked goods with richness, but it doesn't whip.

## Cultured Dairy Products

**Buttermilk:** Made of milk soured by bacteria, buttermilk contains no butter, but is named that because it traditionally used to be the liquid left after churning butter. It provides recipes with moisture, acidity, and creaminess.

**Yogurt:** Made with milk cultured by special strands of bacteria, yogurt has a thick, custardlike consistency. Sold plain or sweetened and flavored, it provides recipes with moisture, acidity, and creaminess. Greek yogurt is made by straining regular yogurt; it contains less moisture and has a thicker consistency than regular yogurt. Greek yogurt can be used as a substitute for sour cream in many recipes.

**Sour cream:** Made of fresh cream that has been fermented by the addition of bacteria that produce lactic acid, sour cream has a thick consistency and a slightly tangy flavor, with a fat content around 18 percent. It can be found in whole, low-fat, and nonfat versions. Sour cream provides recipes with moisture, acidity, and creaminess.

## Cheese

**Cream cheese:** This is a soft, mild, rich, spreadable, and slightly sour cheese made from cow's milk. Cream cheese is used for cheesecakes, icings, and in some rich pastry and cookie doughs.

**Mascarpone:** A delicate, Italian cream cheese made of cream coagulated by the addition of acid, mascarpone can be used instead of American cream cheese or heavy cream.

**Ricotta:** Another Italian mild-tasting cheese with a low fat content, ricotta can be used as a filling or for baking, among other products, Italian-style cheesecake.

## Butter

Fresh butter contains about 80 percent fat (or even higher in European-style butters), 15 percent water, and 5 percent milk solids. Besides imparting the benefits of its fat content into baked goods (tenderizing and enriching), butter gives them a desirable flavor and a melt-in-your-mouth quality. Butter is available salted and unsalted. Unsalted butter is more perishable but has a fresher, sweeter taste and is the one preferred for baking. If you're using salted butter, the amount of salt used in the recipe should be altered accordingly. Butter is usually sold in 4-ounce (120-g) sticks or 1-pound (480-g) bricks; for measuring purposes, it's easiest to use sticks.

### How to Melt Butter

You can melt butter effectively by following one of the following methods:

- **Stovetop:** You can melt butter in a heavy saucepan on the stovetop or in the top of a double boiler over medium-low or medium heat. (Never use high heat, as butter burns easily.) Remove the butter from the heat when it's about $^3/_4$ melted, and then stir with a heat-resistant spatula until it's completely melted.

- **Microwave:** Cut butter into small pieces, place it in a heat-proof glass bowl, and cover the bowl loosely with a paper towel. Place it in the microwave and melt on medium-low (30 percent) power or defrost, checking every 10 to 15 seconds until it's almost melted but a few small solid pieces remain. Remove from the microwave and stir with a heat-resistant spatula until it's completely melted.

# How to Clarify Butter

Clarifying butter removes the moisture (water) and milk solids, which allows the butter to withstand higher temperatures for a longer time without smoking (burning). You can clarify butter as follows:

1. Cut unsalted butter into cubes and melt it in a heavy-duty saucepan over very low heat. Simmer gently until the foam rises to the top of the melted butter. (Be careful, as the butter may splatter a bit.) The bubbles are the butter's water content boiling off, and the white residue is the milk solids separating out from the butterfat and water.

2. When the butter stops splattering and no more foam seems to be rising to the surface, remove it from the heat and skim off the foam with a spoon or ladle (it's okay if a bit remains). You can reserve the removed milk solids for topping pancakes, popcorn, vegetables, or rice. *NOTE: If you keep cooking the butter until it browns slightly and emits a pleasant, nutty aroma, you'll end up with brown butter or beurre noisette (which you can use with or without skimming the foam). Brown butter can be used in baking in place of regular butter and gives a delicious, nutlike taste and smell to baked goods.*

3. Line a sieve with two layers of cheesecloth and set the strainer over a heat-proof container. Carefully pour the warm butterfat through the lined sieve and into the container, leaving behind any solids from the bottom of the pan.

Clarified butter can be covered and kept refrigerated for up to 6 months. No time? You can purchase prepared ghee, which is an Indian version of clarified butter.

# Other Fats and Oils

In general, the functions of fat and oil in baking are to tenderize and provide a soft texture; add moisture, richness, and flavor; and lengthen the shelf life of the produce. When used as creaming agents, fat and oil help in the leavening process and give pie dough and pastries a flaky quality. Although butter is the most widely used fat in baking, other fats and oils are commonly used in recipes.

**Shortening:** The name comes from its ability to shorten the gluten strands and tenderize the product. Any fat is capable of shortening, but the term is mostly applied to solid fats that are usually white and flavorless. While shortening is almost 100 percent fat and solid at room temperature, it's very soft and easy to cream, making it great for baking flaky products and for creaming. Suitable for vegetarians, it's mainly made by the industrial process of hydrogenating vegetable oils. Unfortunately, the process of hydrogenation converts the fats into trans-fats, which are quite detrimental to your health. Therefore, I recommend only using trans-fat-free shortening.

**Lard and other rendered fats:** The rendered fat of hogs, lard is very plastic and great to use when making a flaky pie crust. Since the introduction of shortening (which is cheaper and much more stable), though, it hasn't been that widely used in baking. Other rendered fats—such as chicken, goose, and duck rendered fats—can all be used instead of shortening.

**Margarine and vegan butter substitutes:** These substitutes are all industrially manufactured products usually obtained through hydrogenation of vegetable oils. They have a similar composition to butter in terms of fat (80 to 85 percent), moisture (10 to 15 percent), and solid content (5 percent, which is usually salt), so they can be used in place of butter when the latter is not suitable. Most margarines may contain trans-fats, which you should avoid; however, if you want to use it, opt for a trans-fat-free version. Also note that these products are often salted, so you may have to omit or adjust the salt in the recipe (which is usually written for unsalted butter) accordingly.

**Neutral-tasting oils:** Oils are liquid fats derived from plants. They spread through batters or doughs too thoroughly and shorten the gluten too much, so people prefer not to use this fat for pastries. However, you can use them to make some kinds of breads, moist cakes, and quick breads with great success. Some neutral-tasting oils that won't impart undesired flavors to baked goods and have a high smoking point (withstand high temperatures) are grape seed, safflower, sunflower seed, avocado, canola, and vegetable oils. If possible, purchase oils labeled "expeller pressed," as they don't have any additives.

**Coconut oil:** This oil, extracted from the coconut fruit, behaves a bit more like butter than oil, as it's solid at room temperature but melts above 75°F (24°C). If you use it in a solid state, it's works as a natural alternative to margarine and is great for making flaky doughs and cakes. Coconut oil used to have quite an unhealthy reputation, but the latest trends and advocates have been suggesting the opposite, leading to coconut oil increasingly being stocked on store shelves. The virgin and extra-virgin kinds—which are the least processed—are said to have the most benefit; however, they impart a strong, sweet, and characteristic coconut flavor. When you don't want that characteristic flavor, you can use the refined, expeller-pressed version.

**Olive oil:** This delicious Mediterranean oil has a very characteristic flavor that may not always be desired. Extra-virgin olive oil burns easily due to its low smoke point, so you shouldn't use it for frying or for baking at very high temperatures.

**Nonstick cooking spray:** Although some purists don't like it, you can use nonstick cooking oil spray for greasing pans. You can also spray it on a knife before slicing or in liquid measuring cups right before measuring (such as honey, molasses, or syrups) to prevent sticky liquids or ingredients from adhering to them.

# Flours

Flour is a powder made by grinding cereal grains or other nuts, legumes, seeds, or roots that's used to provide bulk and structure in recipes. The most commonly used flour in baking is wheat flour. The most important characteristic of wheat flour is its protein content, which is what determines its different flavors. Usually in the form of gluten, the protein content depends on the type of wheat, its growing conditions, and the milling process.

**All-purpose flour:** A blend of hard-wheat and soft-wheat flours, all-purpose flour is a fine-textured flour with an average protein content of 5 to 7 percent. It's the most widely available and used flour by home bakers.

**Cake flour:** This is a very fine, smooth, and completely white flour made from soft wheat with a protein content of 3 to 5 percent. Cake flour is used for delicate cakes and goods that require a low gluten content.

**Pastry flour:** This is a low-gluten flour that contains 4 to 6 percent protein. Pastry flour can be used to make pie doughs and some cookies and tender muffins.

**Bread flour:** Made of hard wheat, it's often referred to as "high-gluten flour," as it contains at least 12 percent protein. Bread flour is slightly coarser than all-purpose flour and provides preparations with a strong structure, making it ideal for preparing breads and puff pastry. However, if you can't find it, you can substitute it 1:1 for all-purpose flour.

**Self-rising flour:** A flour with baking powder and salt already added, self-rising flour is traditionally milled from soft, low-protein wheat. However, it can only be used in recipes that specifically call for self-rising flour. To make self-rising flour at home, whisk together thoroughly 1 cup pastry flour (or all-purpose flour, though the product might be less tender) with $1^1/_2$ teaspoons baking powder and $^1/_4$ teaspoon salt.

**Whole-wheat flour:** This flour still contains the bran (fiber) and the germ of the wheat berry. It contains more nutrients than white flour and gives a chewier, coarser texture to baked goods. Mostly used in breads and quick breads, whole-wheat flour can substitute 1:1 for between $^1/_4$ or $^1/_2$ of the white flour in a recipe (as using 100 percent whole-wheat flour could produce a very dense good). Another type of whole-wheat flour is white whole-wheat flour, which comes from a different kind of wheat but is still made by grinding the whole grain. Lighter and milder-tasting, the end product with white whole-wheat flour is more similar to one made with white flour; however, it should often still be used in combination with white flour for best results. Because whole-wheat flour has a shorter shelf life than other flours, keep it refrigerated to avoid rancidity.

**Spelt flour:** A cousin to wheat, spelt is an ancient grain with a deep nutlike flavor and a high nutritious profile. It offers a broader spectrum of nutrients compared to many of its more inbred cousins in the wheat family. Although spelt does contain gluten, it does not seem to cause sensitivities in many people who are intolerant of wheat (although it's not recommended for people with celiac disease). You can find both white and whole spelt flours in health-food stores year-round. White spelt flour can be substituted 1:1 for all-purpose flour, while whole spelt flour can be used instead of whole-wheat flour—and sometimes, even in place for white flour.

## What Is Bleached Flour?

When flour is first milled, it needs to age a bit—with the help of oxygen—in order for the gluten to mature and make the proteins stronger and more elastic. This natural aging process—which changes the color of flour from yellowish to white—is long, expensive, and inconsistent. Therefore, at the beginning of the twentieth century, millers started adding chemicals (such as potassium bromate or bleaches like benzoyl peroxide and chlorine dioxide) to speed up and control the process and to imitate the whiteness of naturally aged flour, producing what's known as *bleached flour*. Although bleaching hasn't been brought into question medically, it does produce flour with a somewhat chemical flavor.

# Nonwheat Flours

As mentioned previously, flour is made by grinding grains, nuts, legumes, seeds, or roots into a powder—so the flour you use doesn't have to be all wheat. With an increase of people staying away from gluten—the main protein in wheat and other grains that's responsible for the structure and elasticity of baked goods (indispensable in bread making)—more and more people are turning to nonwheat flours and flour mixes for baking. The following table shows you which nonwheat flours do or do not have gluten.

| Flour | With Gluten | Without Gluten | Flour | With Gluten | Without Gluten |
|---|---|---|---|---|---|
| *Grain-derived:* | | | *Nut-derived:* | | |
| Barley | X | | Almond | | X |
| Rice (brown or white) | | X | Hazelnut (filbert) | | X |
| Corn (meal*, flour, and polenta grits) | | X | Coconut | | X |
| | | | Chestnut | | X |
| Oats | | X* | *Root-derived:* | | |
| Rye | X | | Arrowroot | | X |
| Sorghum | | X | Tapioca | | X |
| Kamut | X | | Potato | | X |
| *Seed-derived:* | | | Sweet potato | | X |
| Quinoa | | X | *Legume-derived:* | | |
| Millet | | X | Fava bean | | X |
| Buckwheat | | X | Garbanzo bean | | X |
| Flaxseed | | X | Green pea | | X |
| Amaranth | | X | Soy | | X |
| Teff | | X | White bean | | X** |

\* Oats need to be purchased "gluten free," as some oat flour may be cross-contaminated with gluten-containing grains.

\*\*The term meal is used for products that are not as finely ground as flour.

# Starches and Jelling Agents

Starchy flours can be used to thicken fillings and sauces. Gelatin is capable of jelling, which means it forms a gel with liquids, making them thicker and changing their texture.

## Starches

**Cornstarch:** This is made from the interior part of corn kernels. When thickening hot liquids (and to prevent lumps), dissolve cornstarch in a small amount of cold liquid (called *slurry*), and then add it to the heated liquid. Continued heating reverses cornstarch's thickening properties.

**Tapioca starch (flour):** Made from the root of the South American cassava plant, tapioca starch thickens quickly at a low temperature and retains its consistency when frozen. When used as a thickener, tapioca flour becomes a clear, glossy gel, and its neutral taste won't compete with the other flavors in a recipe. Use 2 tablespoons tapioca flour for each 1 tablespoon cornstarch when substituting. Note that although tapioca pearls come from the same root, they can't be used interchangeably with tapioca starch as thickeners in recipes.

**Arrowroot starch (flour and powder):** Made from the root of a rainforest herb, arrowroot starch can be used as a 1:1 substitute for cornstarch. It has no flavor and is the easiest starch to digest. It's best used at the end of the cooking, just before boiling, as continued heating reverses its thickening properties. To use, dissolve it in a small amount of cold liquid (called *slurry*), and then add it to the hot liquid.

## Gelatin

Derived from collagen and commonly used in creams and mousses, a water-soluble protein extracted from animal connective tissue, gelatin melts to a liquid when heated and solidifies when cooled again. Together with water or liquid, it forms a semi-solid gel. Powdered gelatin is the most widely available form; make sure you get plain powdered gelatin and not a flavored gelatin dessert for baking. To use, sprinkle powdered gelatin over cold water to soften. Once softened, add the mixture into hot ingredients (or heated with other ingredients) until it dissolves, and then chill until it sets.

# Eggs

Eggs are one of the basic ingredients for baking. They are produced by free-range (uncaged) chickens or by animals raised and fed organically, while others are produced by battery chickens. If you purchase your eggs in a grocery store, their containers should be labeled accordingly; if you get them at the farmer's market, the farmer can explain his or her practices. You can use them interchangeably in recipes, although some bakers have strong preferences for a certain kind. The color of the shell is determined by the breed of the chicken. There are three main colors: white, brown, and even blue-green. Although the color of the shell doesn't affect the flavor, what the animals are fed does change the color of the yolk—and, some experts claim, the taste as well.

Because they're perishable, refrigerate eggs in their containers or cartons on the top shelf (not in the door, where the temperature is too high for proper storage) so they don't absorb unwanted odors; they can be kept this way for up to 1 month. You can even freeze separated eggs. Egg whites can be frozen in an airtight container for up to 1 year. Egg yolks must be mixed with a pinch of salt or $\frac{1}{2}$ teaspoon sugar per yolk before being frozen up to a couple months; if sugar is used, it should be subtracted from the total amount in the recipe.

**Liquid egg whites:** If you're concerned about using raw egg whites, you can find pasteurized egg white cartons in most grocery stores. However, depending on the brand, they sometimes don't whip as well and might be too thin. If you decide to purchase these, make sure the label lists egg whites as their only ingredient, as ones that contain additives may not have the protein structure needed to capture air and increase volume for good whipping.

**Egg sizes:** In increasing order, eggs come in small, medium, large, extra-large, and jumbo. Large eggs are the standard in most recipes (unless specified); however, if you have any other size, here's how you can substitute them for large ones in a recipe:

| Number of Large Eggs | 1 | 2 | 3 | 4 | 5 | 6 |
|---|---|---|---|---|---|---|
| Small | 1 | 3 | 4 | 5 | 7 | 8 |
| Medium | 1 | 2 | 3 | 5 | 6 | 7 |
| Extra-large | 1 | 2 | 3 | 4 | 4 | 5 |
| Jumbo | 1 | 2 | 2 | 3 | 4 | 5 |

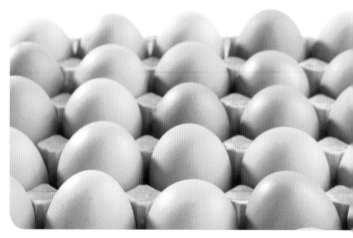

# Leavening Agents

Leavening is the production or incorporation of gases in baked products to increase volume and develop shape and texture. It's important to measure leaveners carefully, as the amount can either make or break the final product.

## Yeast

This microorganism ferments sugars—producing carbon dioxide gas and alcohol—and gives yeasted baked goods flavor. The release of gas produces the leavening action in breads and rolls. Baker's yeast is available in compressed form (or fresh yeast), which is sold refrigerated; granulated active dry, which is the most widely available; and quick-acting dry (fast-rising, instant, or quick-rise), which comes in a powder that doesn't need hydrating. Quick-acting dry yeast is stronger than active dry yeast, so follow the instructions on the package if you decide to use this kind.

When substituting dry and fresh yeast: 1 (0.25-oz./7-g) package active dry yeast ($2\frac{1}{4}$ teaspoons) equals 1 packed tablespoon (0.75-oz./22-g) compressed fresh yeast. For other calculations, you need 1.4 times the volume of packed fresh yeast to replace active dry in a recipe.

When activating yeast in warm water and sugar, it should make bubbles. If it doesn't, the yeast might have died and can no longer be used.

## Chemical Leaveners

Chemical leaveners release gases produced by chemical reactions.

**Baking soda:** The chemical sodium bicarbonate, this reacts when moisture and an acid are present. Products leavened with baking soda must be baked immediately after the dry and moist ingredients have been mixed, as the chemical reaction starts then; if it's not, the gases will escape and the leavening power will be lost. Some acidic ingredients that react with baking soda are honey, molasses, cream of tartar, vinegar, buttermilk, sour cream and yogurt, fruit juices and purées, and chocolate. Baking soda loses potency after some time; to test whether it's still fresh, add a bit of baking soda to vinegar (it should make bubbles).

**Baking powder:** This is made of a mixture of baking soda, acid, and starch. The most commonly used type is double-acting baking powder, which is activated by moisture and heat. This allows mixtures to stand for a longer time before being baked than products leavened with baking soda. To test whether it's still fresh, add a bit of baking powder to boiling water (it should make bubbles).

# Flavoring Agents

Here's where the endless possibilities of baking start. You can use the same basic recipes but vary or add spices, herbs, liquors, extracts, fruits, zests, and so on to get a whole new kind of baked good. Flavoring agents give you the option of adapting dishes to the seasons or making something you crave at a certain time without risking the outcome.

## Spices and Herbs

**Herbs:** Culinary herbs are the fresh or dried leafy-green parts of a plant. Dried herbs, which lose their potency with time, are stronger in flavor than fresh and are often more bitter. Therefore, a couple teaspoons dry herbs are equivalent to a couple tablespoons fresh herbs.

**Spices:** Usually dried, they are a product from any part of a plant other than the leaves, including seeds, berries, bark, roots, and fruits. They can be found whole or ground; ground spices lose their flavor faster than whole. To store them, keep them tightly sealed in a cool, dark, dry place for no longer than 6 months or freeze them for a longer shelf life. A little amount of spice has great flavor potency, so use between $\frac{1}{4}$ teaspoon to 1 teaspoon in a recipe, depending on taste and type of spice. Spices should be added to the fats when creaming, as the fat-soluble flavoring compounds in the spices will dissolve better. They can also be toasted by heating them in a small, dry skillet over medium-high heat and stirring or shaking the pan until the spices become one shade darker and you can start smelling the slightly toasty aroma. Once that has happened, you immediately transfer them to a bowl and use them when you're ready. Two spices you'll come across quite a bit are vanilla and the zest of citrus fruits:

> **Vanilla:** This is perhaps the most important spice in the pastry kitchen. Inside each pod are thousands of vanilla beans, which carry the beloved flavor into desserts. Vanilla can come from Madagascar (Bourbon), Mexico, or Tahiti; although they can be used interchangeably, they do have distinct flavors. To use them, you split the vanilla beans lengthwise and scrape out the seeds; you can then add the seeds directly to the recipe. The scraped pods can be placed in a jar with sugar to infuse the sweetener with vanilla, which you can use in cookies and other recipes. Vanilla beans are expensive, so 1 scraped vanilla bean can be substituted for 2 teaspoons of pure vanilla extract.

> **Zest:** This is the outer colored layer of the skin of citrus fruits. It can be removed by zesting, grating, or peeling and can be frozen for later use. It's easier to obtain zest from an unpeeled, uncut fruit. Also, be careful to leave the bitter white pith underneath the zest behind.

# The Most-Commonly Used Herbs and Spices in Baking

**Herbs for sweets and bread:**

- Lavender: Perfumed flavor and aroma
- Mint: Intensely flavored and fresh-tasting; goes well with chocolate and fruit and cuts through richness
- Rosemary: Strong and piney; goes well with honey and citrus
- Verbena: Lemony scent and flavor; available mostly at farmer's markets or in dried form

**Herbs for bread:**

- Basil: Highly aromatic, with a robust licorice flavor
- Chives: Oniony flavor; milder than scallions
- Dill: Sweet and pungent
- Fennel: Mild licorice flavor
- Sage: Pinelike flavor, with more lemony and eucalyptus notes than rosemary
- Scallions: Onion flavor
- Thyme: Pungent and woodsy

**Spices:**

- Allspice: Smells like a mixture of cinnamon, nutmeg, and clove; best used in fall spice mixes
- Anise: Sweet licorice flavor
- Cardamom: Warm, aromatic spice from India; great in baked goods when combined with clove and cinnamon
- Chili: Hot and spicy; combines well with chocolate and citrus, giving them a kick
- Cinnamon: Milder, floral flavor from the bark of Ceylon; spicy-sweet flavor from the bark of cassia cinnamon
- Cloves: Sweet and warming flavor
- Ginger: Nicely pungent; can be found fresh, dried and ground, candied, or juiced
- Mace: From the same plant as nutmeg, but more subtle and delicate
- Nutmeg: Sweet and pungent flavor
- Saffron: Subtle but distinct floral flavor and aroma; gives foods a bright yellow color
- Star anise: Sweet licorice flavor; can be used to infuse custards
- Vanilla: Succulent flavor; from the dried pod of an orchid plant
- Zest: Highly concentrated in citrus flavor; contains many essential oils

**Extracts:** These are concentrated aromatic liquids obtained through distillation or infusion of plants. During or after extraction, the flavor or essence is placed into a liquid base (usually alcohol), potentially with other ingredients (as in the case of vanilla or almond extract). Flavorings in general may be natural or artificial. The former tend to come with a higher price tag but are of higher quality and better flavor; because flavorings are used in such small quantities, it's worth it to invest in the natural ones. The most concentrated forms of flavors come from flavor oils—specifically essential oils, which are the aromatic oils extracted from the ingredient itself. Essential oils have a flavor that is pure, clear-tasting, and as intense as it gets. Health-food stores and online businesses sell a huge variety of herb, fruit, and spice essential oils; read their labels before using. You can substitute oils for extracts, but you only need a few drops of oil in place of a teaspoon of extract. To prevent flavor oils from going rancid, refrigerate them.

## Other Flavoring Agents

**Fruit:** Fruit gives a sweetness, texture, flavor, acidity, and color to many preparations. Many different forms of fruit can be used in baking, such as fresh, dried, frozen, canned, preserved, and candied.

**Liqueurs:** Sweet alcohols—either fruit, nut, chocolate, mint, or coffee flavored—can be useful flavoring ingredients for baking. Some examples where liqueurs work best are buttercream and other frostings and soufflés and custards.

## Oils, Extracts, and Flavors—What's the Difference?

Oils are the most concentrated form of flavor, while extracts are mixes of flavor oils and a liquid (usually alcohol) and sometimes other ingredients. "Flavor" is a vague term that may refer to natural extracts or artificial compounds. Always read the ingredient label to find out what kind each specific bottle of oil, extract, or flavor contains. I recommend only using natural oils and extracts.

# Salt

Besides being a seasoning, a flavor enhancer, and a natural preservative, salt improves the texture of bread by strengthening the gluten structure and making it more stretchable. It also inhibits the growth of yeast, which helps control the fermentation process (this is why salt should never be added directly to the water in which yeast is being activated).

## Types of Salt

- **Sea salt:** Obtained by evaporating seawater, this salt comes in coarse and fine grains. Each kind of sea salt contains different minerals and is distinctively flavored depending on its origin. I use fine sea salt for all my baking.
- **Kosher salt:** This coarse salt, which comes either from the sea or the earth, is made without additives. Its name comes from its use in the preparation of meat according to Jewish dietary guidelines. It doesn't dissolve as easily into doughs and batters as fine salt; however, it's good for topping finished products that benefit from salt flakes.
- **Rock salt:** Large, chunky, nonuniform salt crystals with a grayish color that are used in old-fashioned ice cream making.
- **Table salt:** Refined salt mined from underground salt deposits, this contains more sodium chloride (97 to 99 percent) than sea salt. Unless specified, this is the kind of salt called for throughout this book.
- **Exotic salts:** Used in baking mainly as finishing salts (sprinkling a dish at the end, right before serving), they add an interesting visual effect and texture. *Himalayan salt* is a white, pink, or red salt hand-mined from ancient sea salt deposits in Pakistan that's rich in minerals; it is believed to be one of the purest salts available. *Hawaiian sea salt* is a red (with volcanic clay) or black (with charcoal), fine- or coarse-grained sea salt that's full of trace minerals. *Celtic sea salt* is a coarse sea salt raked after salt crystals have sunk to the bottom of the ponds. Moist, granular, and chunky, it can be used for baking or as a finishing salt. To add a special touch to a baked good, you can also use salts with a variety of different flavorings, including truffles, lemon, herbs, vanilla, and so on.

# Nuts

Nuts provide nice flavor, texture, and presentation to baked goods. They can be purchased raw, roasted, salted, shelled, skinned, broken, or chopped; some are even ground into flour. However, the best way is to buy them in bulk, whole and in raw form (except slivered and sliced almonds, which should be purchased in that form), and chop them as needed to keep them fresh longer. You can store nuts either in the fridge or freezer to avoid their natural oils from becoming rancid. The following are some common things you can do with nuts in baking:

- **Toasting nuts:** To develop their flavor optimally, toasting nuts before you use them is recommended. Place them on a baking sheet lined with parchment paper in a 350°F (180°C) preheated oven and bake for 5 to 15 minutes or until they smell toasty and are a shade darker. If you're toasting unpeeled hazelnuts, cool them thoroughly, and then rub them together in a tea towel until most of the skins flake off.

- **Chopping nuts:** To chop nuts by hand, grasp the handle of a large, sharp chef's or serrated knife and place your other hand over the tip, and then carefully rock the blade across the nuts until the pieces are the desired size. If you need to chop 1 cup nuts or more, pulsing them in a food processor is best. Coarsely chopped nut pieces should be about $1/3$ inch (7 mm), while finely chopped nut pieces should be about $1/8$ inch (2 mm).

- **Making homemade nut flour:** To make nut flour at home, in a food processor with a blade that's completely dry and cool, grind room-temperature nuts until finely ground, scraping the sides and corners of the processor bowl with a chopstick from time to time. Don't overprocess or you will end up with nut butter.

## Nut Varieties

- Almonds
- Brazil nuts
- Cashews
- Chestnuts (must be cooked)
- Coconut (used mostly in dried form and available sweetened and unsweetened and in flour, grains, flakes, chips, and shreds)
- Hazelnuts (best if toasted and peeled before using)

- Macadamia nuts
- Peanuts (technically a legume, but has the culinary uses of a nut)
- Pecans
- Pine nuts
- Pistachios
- Walnuts (raw walnuts might add a bitter flavor, so toast them to remove)

**Nut butters:** These are made by grinding nuts and most seeds to a spreadable consistency, which is achieved by their high oil content. Their name comes from the fact that they are spreadable like butter, but they don't contain any actual butter. Nut butters can be used as cookie sandwich fillings (such as macarons) and to flavor cookies, cakes, buttercreams, and other frostings. To make them at home, place either raw or toasted nuts into a food processor and grind until very finely chopped, scraping down the sides with a chopstick and blending to your desired consistency; 1 cup yields $^2/_3$ cup butter. For extra-smooth nut butter, you may need to add a tablespoon of neutral-flavored oil (see "Neutral-Tasting Oils" in this chapter). You can also add sweeteners to taste and even some spices or melted chocolate.

**Nut pastes:** These are nut products usually blended with different amounts of sugar. The most common are almond paste, which is made of $^2/_3$ ground almonds and $^1/_3$ sugar (often used in cakes, pastries, cookies, and fillings); marzipan, which is sweetened almond paste used in decorative and confectionary work; and praline paste, which is made from hazelnuts (and sometimes almonds) and caramelized sugar ground to either a smooth or coarse paste. Nut pastes are used as delectable flavorings for icings, fillings, pastries, and creams. Usually sold in cans, they can be purchased online or in specialty stores.

# Edible Decorations

Cakes, cupcakes, and cookies can be attractively decorated with an abundance of specialty products.

**Food coloring:** Available in liquid, powder, and gel forms, food coloring is usually made with synthetic, nontoxic substances (although some natural, plant-derived liquid and powder food colorings are available in health-food stores and online). The most commonly available is **liquid food coloring,** which is useful when just a little color is needed; however, it can't be used in chocolate. If you'd like one for chocolate that also creates stronger, more saturated colors, use **gel food coloring;** this type doesn't alter the consistency of the product as much. **Powdered food colors** are also suitable for chocolate and can be even more intense; however, they're very messy to use.

## Food Coloring Caution

In general, food color intensifies as it sits, so take this into account when trying to achieve a particular hue.

**Food color markers** are a type of food coloring that's useful for writing, drawing, or adding details; however, they aren't recommended for coloring the whole surface of a product. These must be used on dry, edible surfaces, such as dried royal icing or rolled fondant. **Food color sprays** are good for full-surface coloring and are suitable for using on frostings. If you decide to use color sprays, make sure you cover your work surface and have your workspace well ventilated.

A more innovative form of powder nontoxic food coloring is **luster dust.** Available in metallic, pearl, matte, and glitter finishes, it's painted with a brush on dried royal icing or on fondant. To use, combine about 1 teaspoon luster dust with a few drops lemon extract or vodka to obtain the consistency of thin paint (you might have to add a few more drops later, as the alcohol evaporates rather quickly, but add only a bit at a time). You then paint designs and let it dry for a few minutes.

**Rolled fondant:** A sugar and shortening–based product with doughlike consistency, rolled fondant is used for covering cakes, cupcakes, or cookies, giving them a smooth surface. It can also be cut out into shapes and adhered to baked goods as decorations. Unless predyed, fondant is white; it can be colored with gels, sprayed, or painted using the food coloring products described previously. For consistency purposes, I recommend store-bought fondant.

# Chocolate and Cocoa

Real chocolate comes from cacao beans, or the seeds in the pods of the tropical cacao tree, which are roasted (unless it's raw chocolate) to develop flavor. Once cooled, the beans are cracked open and separated from the shell until just the interior meat of the bean, called the *nib,* remains. The nibs are then ground and turned into chocolate liquor (which has no alcohol), while most of the cocoa butter (the fat in the nibs) is separated. Chocolate liquor is the main ingredient in all chocolate products; its content determines the chocolate mass or cacao content of the final product. In further processing, the cooled chocolate liquor is ground into powder and mixed with cocoa butter, sugar, milk or cream, and flavoring agents. Finally, through conching (continuous wavelike kneading), this mixture turns into smooth chocolate.

The process varies from manufacturer to manufacturer, so the final product is unique based on the region where the nibs come from; the roasting, grinding, and conching processes; the proportion of chocolate liquor; and the added ingredients. As long as it's real chocolate, you can use any brand for the type of chocolate you want, so look for the kind you like the most.

## Types of Chocolate, Based on Their Chocolate Liquor Content

| Name | Percent of Chocolate Liquor | Description |
| --- | --- | --- |
| Unsweetened cocoa powder | 100 | This is made by grinding chocolate liquor even further to release more cacao butter, while the remaining chocolate liquor is pressed, dried, and pulverized. If processed with alkali to neutralize the naturally occurring acid, it's called *Dutch-processed cocoa,* which is more subtle-tasting than nonalkalized (or natural) cocoa. Preference is the only deciding factor about which one to use. In general, cocoa has the most intense chocolate flavor of all. Widely for baking, it should be sifted to remove any lumps before adding it to a batter. |
| Unsweetened (bitter or baking) chocolate | 99 | With no sugar added, it's very intense and adds a pure chocolate flavor. Used in baking along with a high amount of sweetener, it can be purchased in bricks or paillettes (coins). |
| Bittersweet chocolate | 50 to 80 | This has intense flavor with a hint of sweetness—the higher the chocolate liquor content, the more intense the flavor. It can be purchased in bricks or paillettes (coins). |

| Name | Percent of Chocolate Liquor | Description |
| --- | --- | --- |
| Semisweet chocolate | 35 to 50 | This has a weak chocolate flavor, making it good to use together with unsweetened chocolate. It can be purchased in bricks or paillettes (coins). |
| Milk chocolate | 10 to 30 | This is very sweet, with about 15 percent made of milk solids. It pairs well with caramel and can be purchased in bricks or paillettes (coins). |
| Chocolate chips | Variable | For best results, make sure the first ingredient listed in the label is "chocolate"; otherwise, these morsels might be mostly palm oil or shortening and sugar, with too little chocolate liquor. |
| White chocolate | 0 | While not technically accepted as chocolate, it's made of cacao butter plus sugar, vanilla, and often milk solids. It has a rich, sweet flavor that many people enjoy and goes particularly well with berries and other sour flavors. Able to be dyed and used for decorations in place of icing, it can be purchased in bricks or paillettes (coins). |

*Note that all chocolate liquor does contain some cacao butter, which remains after the grinding process during manufacturing.*

## How to Chop Chocolate

Place the chocolate on a cutting board. Place a serrated knife at one side or corner of the chocolate. Using one hand to hold the handle and your other hand to put pressure straight down (rather than side to side), push the knife through the chocolate and work your way in toward the center. Make sure to use just the part of the blade closest to the handle for maximum force. The chocolate should break and flake, making it perfect for melting or adding into doughs or batters.

## How to Melt Chocolate

Chopped chocolate can be melted either on the stovetop or in the microwave. When melting make sure the chocolate avoids direct contact with moisture—meaning your boards, knife, bowl, and spatulas should be completely dry—so it doesn't seize.

- **Stovetop:** You can use a double boiler or make your own water bath. To make your own, fill a saucepan halfway with hot water and place it over low heat. Place the chopped chocolate in a heat-proof bowl and fit it securely over the saucepan. Stir the chocolate gently with a silicone spatula until it melts. Remove bowl from the saucepan and wipe the bottom of the bowl dry (to make sure condensation doesn't get into your chocolate mixture when pouring).

- **Microwave:** Place the chopped chocolate in a microwave-safe bowl (preferably tempered glass) and microwave at 50 percent power for 2 minutes; stir. Continue heating at 30-second intervals until melted, always stirring in between. The chocolate is finished heating when most but not all of it is melted; stir until completely melted. Make sure you keep an eye on it, as it's easy to scorch the chocolate by overheating it.

## Storing Chocolate

Store chocolate well wrapped and airtight in a cool, dry place (60°F to 65°F [15°C to 18°C]); however, make sure not to refrigerate it. Keep chocolate away from foods with strong odors, so it doesn't absorb them. Good-quality chocolate with a high chocolate liquor content has a very long shelf life and ages just like wine.

## Seized Chocolate: Can It Be Saved?

If water does come in contact with your melted chocolate, it can seize, turning dry and pasty and becoming unworkable. To fix it, add some cream, oil, or butter (the fat should bring the mixture back into balance) and stir until smooth and creamy. If it doesn't work, add more heavy cream and use the mixture as a ganache instead of plain melted chocolate—at least it won't go to waste!

Chocolate can also seize if it gets too hot and scorches. To fix this, it's best to heat it gently over a water bath or in 20-second increments in the microwave, stirring occasionally.

# Measuring Basics

As I mentioned earlier, precision in measuring the ingredients is essential in baking. When measuring, *don't use dry and liquid measures (cups) interchangeably.* Use the proper tool to ensure as much precision as possible, as well as the right method.

## Dry Measure

If you ask two or more people to carefully measure a cup of flour, and you then weigh their results, you might notice that some 1-cup flours are 4 ounces (120 g), while others are up to 6 ounces (180 g); this depends on how much the flour was compacted while measuring. To minimize the margin of error as much as possible, when measuring flour, sugar, and other dry ingredients, don't shake, tap, or press the measuring cup to settle it—instead, sweep it level with a straightedge, such as the back of a spatula or knife. You can use either one of the following methods to fill up a dry measuring tool:

- **Dip and sweep:** Fluff up the dry ingredient in the sack or canister with a spatula to loosen it slightly. Dip the dry measuring cup into the dry ingredient, filling it gently above the top, and level it.

- **Lightly spooning:** Use a spoon to place the dry ingredient lightly into the cup and level it.

These methods are used for measuring flours and most types of sugar (except packed brown sugar, which should be packed in tightly and pressed down using the back of a slightly smaller measuring cup).

## Liquid Measure

To measure milk, oil, honey, syrup, water, juice, or any other kind of liquid, you use a liquid measure. Simply place the liquid measuring cup on a flat surface (don't hold it with the other hand) and pour in the ingredient. Bring your eye down to the measure—not the measure up to your eye—to make sure the meniscus (curved upper surface of the water) hits the mark of the desired measure. Make sure you also use the appropriate size of measuring cup—for example, an 8-cup-capacity liquid measuring cup is not calibrated to measure $1/4$ cup liquid.

## Sifting

Sifting removes lumps and distributes (but doesn't really mix) ingredients that are sifted together. It also aerates the flour, allowing it to mix more easily into batters, which is important for batters that might deflate or toughen from excess mixing. You can buy a sifter, but a sieve does the job just as well and can be used for other purposes.

Presifted flour still needs to be sifted if the recipe calls for sifting, as sifting before packaging doesn't keep the flour from compacting in between its production and the time it makes it to your pantry. Sifted flour weighs 20 to 25 percent less per cup than unsifted; therefore, it's important to note what a recipe asks for the following:

- If the recipe says "1 cup (or other amount) sifted flour," you should sift the flour before you measure it, lightly spoon it into a dry measuring cup, and sweep it level without shaking or tapping.

- If the recipe says "1 cup (or other amount) of flour, sifted," you should measure the flour first with a dry measuring cup using the dip-and-sweep method and then sift it without shaking or tapping. The purpose of sifting after measuring is only to aerate the flour and remove lumps. This is also the case when a recipe calls for sifting ingredients together, such as flour, baking powder, and baking soda. They can all be sifted after you measure them into a bowl or onto a sheet of parchment paper for easy lifting and addition into mixtures and for easy cleanup.

## Weighing

If there was only one technique I could teach you in this book, I would choose how to use digital scale to weigh your ingredients for baking hands-down. Weight is the most absolute and precise way of adding the right amounts of ingredients. Four ounces (120 g) is 4 ounces (120 g)—it doesn't change based on how lightly or heavily you add the confectioner's sugar into the measuring cup or if you sifted the flour first or last. Weighing also eliminates almost completely the need of multiple measuring cups in different sizes, making cleanup even faster.

When weighing, you pretty much use one bowl and keep taring (zeroing) the scale as you add each ingredient. Many scales allow for either weighing in grams or ounces; unfortunately, just a few cookbooks and publications use weight units in their recipes. However, it's slowly getting there, which is great news. In baking, there's no better way of achieving good results than weighing.

# How to Use a Digital Scale

1. Have all the ingredients in the recipe on the work surface (most digital scales have an automatic shut-off cycle, so if you take too long, it may go off while you are weighing).

2. Turn on the scale.

3. Select weight units (if offered by the scale's model).

4. Place the mixing bowl on the scale's platform.

5. Press the tare ("zero") button to reset the displayed weight on the scale back to zero.

6. Add the first ingredient in the weight it's called for.

7. Press the tare ("zero") button to reset the displayed weight on the scale back to zero.

8. Add the next ingredient and tare again, repeating until all your ingredients are weighed. Make sure the total weight of the mixture and the bowl doesn't exceed the capacity of the scale (which should be stated in the user's manual).

9. Ta da! You're done! To clean the scale, just wipe it off.

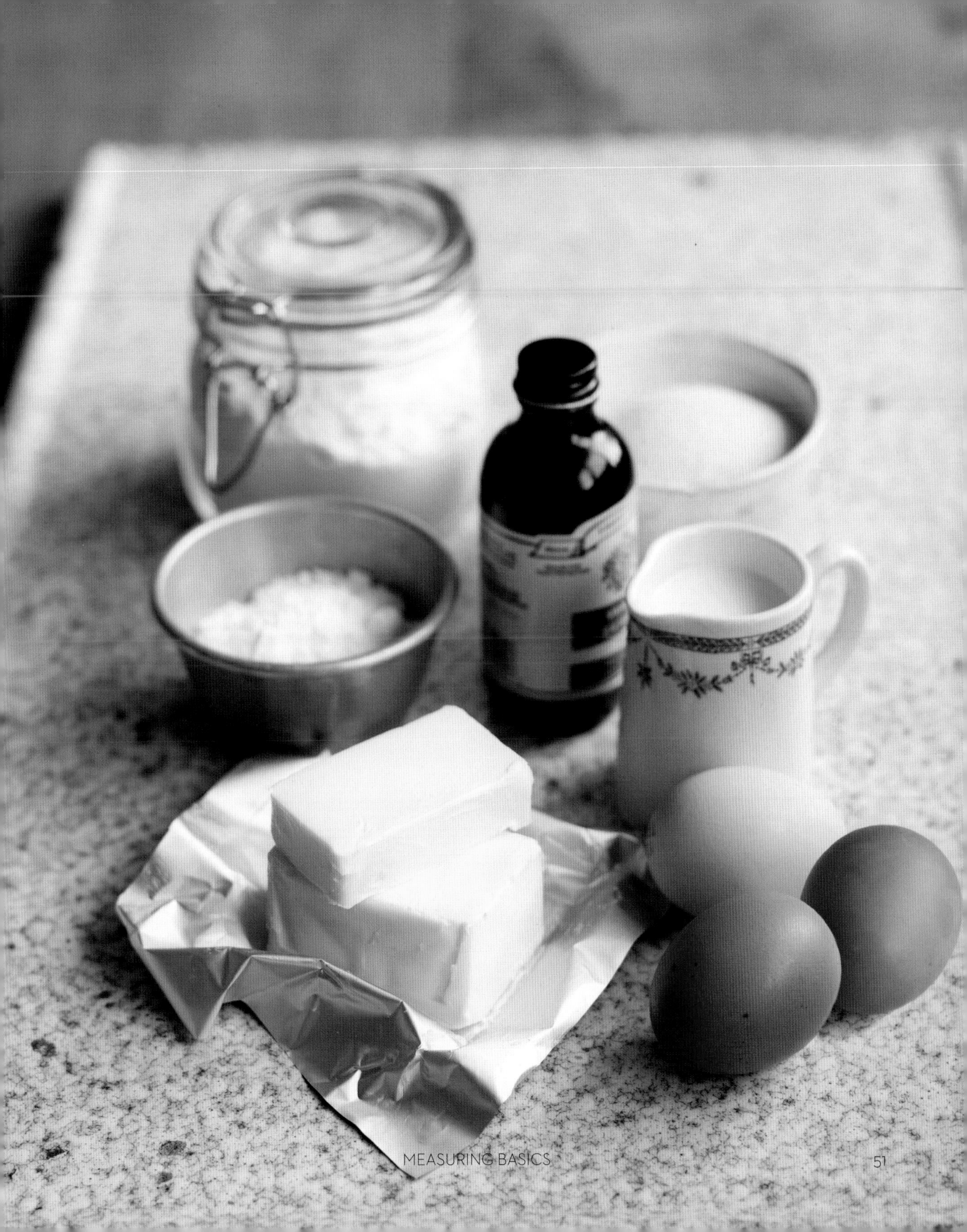

*part 2*

# Starting Easy: Cookies

**Chapter 3:** Sheet and Bar Cookies

**Chapter 4:** Dropped and Piped Cookies

**Chapter 5:** Rolled-Out and Ice Box Cookies

**Chapter 6:** Decorating Cookies

# An Introduction to Cookies

The word *cookie* comes from the Dutch word *koekje* or *koekie*, which means "little cake." In the United States and Canada, that's exactly what a cookie is—a small, baked treat that's usually made with the classic baking quartet of flour, eggs, sugar, and butter (or another fat). In Europe and other countries, these are commonly referred to as *biscuits* (not to be confused with the American biscuit, which is a quick bread).

Cookies come in an infinite variety of flavors, sizes, textures, and shapes. Some are crisp, while others are chewy or moist; some are thin and delicate, while others are thick and fudgy; some come in slices, while others are cut out into fun shapes, decorated artistically, or made into balls. So what makes a cookie a cookie isn't exact.

However, I can definitely say that despite all the options and varieties, cookie baking is a good place to start for the novice baker. In general, it's very easy to put a cookie dough together. What makes the biggest difference in the final product is the way the cookies are formed. There are many methods to form cookies, and most of them are quite simple. The following are the different types of cookies I'll cover in this part.

## Sheet Cookies and Biscotti

Sheet cookies are made by spreading a mixture (either dough or batter) into a sheet pan—hence their name. Some are doughs pressed into the pan (pressed sheet cookies), while others are batters poured in the pan (poured sheet cookies). Often, toppings are added to sheet cookies before the pan goes into the oven. Once baking is completed, the cookie sheet is unmolded, frosted or drizzled (if applicable), and cut into pieces. Some examples of sheet cookies are brownies, blondies, shortbread, fruit squares, granola bars, pecan bars, and lemon bars.

You may hear sheet cookies sometimes called *bars,* which has nothing to do with the method of baking—it's simply due to the fact that the final product is cut into bar shapes (although the proper designation would still be sheet cookies).

Biscotti are made by mixing cookie dough and dividing it into portions. Each portion is shaped into a long, narrow cylinder and baked. After the cylinders are baked—and usually while they are still warm—they are sliced crosswise into bars. Those sliced bars are then put back onto baking sheets and into the oven again for a second baking, so the cookies dry and crisp even further. This very hard, barely risen cookie was for centuries a staple food of soldiers and sailors (since the time of the Romans), as their low humidity kept them from spoiling for long periods of time. This is still useful in present times, as this type of cookie keeps well for up to several weeks.

## Dropped and Piped Cookies

Dropped and piped cookies are made from soft doughs. Dropped cookies are formed by dropping the dough onto the pan with a spoon or a scoop, while piped cookie dough (also known as bagged or pressed dough) is forced through a pastry bag. Some examples of dropped cookies are chocolate chip, oatmeal raisin, and peanut butter cookies. The most typical example of a piped cookie is the buttery spritz cookie.

## Rolled-Out and Ice Box Cookies

Rolled-out (or simply "rolled") cookies are made by rolling out stiff dough with a rolling pin and then cutting it out into cookies, most often with cookie cutters. Although this method can be a bit more labor intensive than others, it allows for making cookies in a huge variety of shapes that become a canvas for further decoration—the possibilities are endless! They're great for holiday treats or any other special occasion, such as a baby shower, a wedding, or a birthday. Gingerbread cookies are the classic example of rolled-out cookies, but many recipes for dough might yield good results when the rolled-out technique is applied to them.

Ice box cookies can be made from the same dough as rolled-out or other cookie methods. This method refers to rolling the cookie dough into logs that are stored in the refrigerator or freezer. The cylinders are then sliced into cookie rounds and baked as needed. This method allows you to mix once and have freshly baked cookies available anytime. Some examples of ice box bookies are vanilla and chocolate cookies.

# The Three Basic Mixing Methods for Cookies

Although each cookie recipe is different and should be followed as written, there are three general ways to incorporate the ingredients when making a cookie dough or batter.

## *Creaming*

Most cookie recipes use this method. The fat (butter, shortening, and so on), sugar, salt, and spices are mixed together first until they are creamy (the amount of mixing will depend on how aerated you need the final product to be). The eggs are then added and mixed until blended. Finally, the flour and leavening are mixed in until just combined (overmixing is not recommended).

### Creaming Butter

When creaming butter, it must be softened to room temperature (not melted, unless the recipe specifies it) in order for it to combine with the other ingredients and cream properly. A room-temperature stick of butter should still hold a shape but should not be cold or completely firm. If you don't have time to bring butter to room temperature, you can cut cold butter into very small pieces with a bench scraper and set aside. By the time you've preheated the oven, assembled the equipment, and measured the other ingredients, your butter will be soft enough to be creamed.

## One Stage

As its name states, all the ingredients are mixed at once, in one bowl.

## Sponge

The sponge method produces a delicate batter that is usually piped (bagged) into cookies. For this method, the eggs and sugar are whipped to the desired stage (soft peaks for egg whites, and thick and light for whole eggs or egg yolks), with a spongelike consistency (hence the name), and then the other ingredients are folded into the batter. The trick to this method is to not overmix the batter, which will deflate the eggs and give you flat cookies.

# chapter 3

# Sheet and Bar Cookies

*Sheet cookies* are made by spreading a mixture (either dough or batter) into a prepared pan—often, a sheet pan. Doughs (which are less liquid) are pressed into the pan, while batters are poured in.

Sometimes, sheet cookies are called "bars," not because they are made using a bar cookie method, but because the final product is cut into bar shapes (although the proper designation would still be sheet cookies). Other names by which sheet cookies are known are "tray bakes" or "slices." Some examples of sheet cookies are brownies, blondies, shortbread, fruit squares, granola bars, pecan bars, and lemon bars.

*Bar cookies* are made by mixing cookie dough and dividing it into portions. Each portion is then shaped into a long, narrow cylinder. After the cylinders are baked—and usually while they are still warm—they are sliced crosswise into bars.

This very hard, barely risen cookie was a staple food of soldiers and sailors for centuries, as their low humidity kept them from spoiling for long periods of time. This longevity is still useful in the present time, allowing the cookie to keep well for up to several weeks. The most common example of a bar cookie is biscotti, but mandelbrot (or mandelbread) is also considered a bar cookie.

# How to Make Pressed Sheet Cookies

The basic difference between pressed and poured sheet cookies is the batter—poured sheet cookies have a pourable mixture, while pressed sheet cookies are made with a sturdy dough that is pressed into the pan. Here are the basic techniques and tips for making great pressed sheet cookies.

Even when recipes call for greasing the pan first the overhang is still used.

**Line the pan.** The easiest way to get sheet cookies out of the pan is by lining it with parchment paper, cut with a 1- to 2-inch (2.5- to 5-cm) overhang. These "handles" allow you to lift the entire sheet out in one piece.

**Cream the fats.** The fats (such as butter) and sugars are creamed in a standing mixer until the mixture is completely incorporated. Be sure to check the recipe to see what stage of creaming is needed. Eggs, salt, and vanilla are also incorporated at this stage.

**Add the dry ingredients.** Dry ingredients (flour, salt, and so on) are whisked together in a separate bowl, then added to the butter mixture. Don't overmix—stir just until the ingredients are combined. Overmixing will give you tough cookies.

Set the timer for the minimum baking time to avoid overbaking.

**Press and bake.** Press the dough into the pan, making sure it is evenly distributed. If you don't, you could have burned edges and a middle that isn't baked all the way through! Bake as directed. Cookies are done when they are golden and slightly firm to the touch.

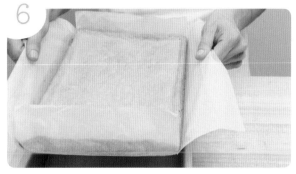

**Cool.** It's important to always cool sheet cookies on a wire rack. This allows air to get to the bottom of the pan and stop the baking process. If you set it directly on a counter, it traps the heat and could overbake your cookies into a dry—or even burnt—state!

**Remove.** Here is where the overhang comes in handy. Once the cookies are cool, just gently pull the overhangs to lift the sheet and transfer it to a rack or board. If your overhang only covers two sides, run an offset spatula or knife around the uncovered sides to loosen the cookie.

## Pressing the Dough

 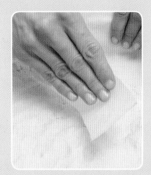

There are a number of ways to press dough into a pan effectively and save your hands from getting sticky. You can use the back of a measuring cup (as in the left image) or place a piece of parchment paper on top of the dough and press it out that way (as in the right image). Be sure to remove the parchment paper before baking, though! If the dough is not too sticky, a silicone or an offset spatula will suffice to do the job.

# Shortbread

It doesn't get more minimalist than shortbread in the pastry world. These Scottish confections—with their unadorned crumbly, buttery sweetness—are traditionally made with just flour, butter, and sugar. This particular recipe calls for some cornstarch or rice flour, which make the cookies extra tender.

## INGREDIENTS

2 sticks (8 oz./240 g) unsalted butter, cut into
    ½-in. (1-cm) cubes
⅔ cup (5 oz./150 g) granulated sugar
1 tsp. pure vanilla extract
¼ tsp. salt
1 ¾ cups (8 ¾ oz./260 g) all-purpose flour, sifted
¼ cup (1 ⅓ oz./40 g) cornstarch or rice flour, sifted

## EQUIPMENT

9×13-in. (23×33-cm) baking pan
Parchment paper
Standing mixer fitted with paddle attachment
Silicone spatula
Small offset spatula or spoon
Bench scraper
Toothpick or skewer or fork
Cooling rack
Cutting board
Sharp knife
Plastic wrap (optional)

1. Line the bottom of a baking pan with parchment paper, leaving an overhang. Set aside.

2. In the bowl of a standing mixer, combine butter, sugar, vanilla extract, and salt, and cream on medium speed until dough is pale yellow, about 2 minutes. Turn the mixer off and scrape down the bowl with a silicone spatula.

3. With the mixer off, add all-purpose flour and cornstarch. Turn on the machine to low speed, and mix just until flour is completely incorporated and dough comes together. Turn off the mixer and scrape the bowl once more.

4. Transfer dough to the prepared pan. Using the back of an offset spatula (or your palms and fingers), press dough firmly into the pan, making sure it is pressed uniformly all over the pan. Smooth it out with the back of the offset spatula.

5. Place the pan in the refrigerator and chill for 20 minutes or until firm.

6. Preheat the oven to 325°F (180°C).

7. Using a bench scraper, score chilled dough into 20 equally sized rectangles and prick decoratively all over with a toothpick.

8. Bake shortbread until golden, 35 to 40 minutes. Remove from the oven and allow to cool in the pan for 20 minutes.

9. Grasping the overhangs of the parchment, carefully remove shortbread from the pan and transfer to a cooling rack to cool completely.

10. Place shortbread on a cutting board and cut where the score marks are with a sharp knife. Shortbread can be stored in an airtight container for up to 2 weeks or double-wrapped in plastic wrap and frozen for up to 3 months.

**Variations:** Shortbread can alternatively be baked in a round 10-inch (25-cm) springform pan. If you decide to do this, score the shortbread into wedges instead of rectangles. The baking time will be the same.

## Why Chill the Dough?

Some pressed cookie recipes, such as shortbread, call for the dough to be chilled before you bake it. This is more common in recipes with a high proportion of fat, as when butter melts in the oven, it produces steam, which gives the cookie an airy, flaky consistency. Once the dough is chilled, it is then scored to allow for the steam to come out. You can use a toothpick, knife, skewer, or fork to score the top of the cookie in any pattern you like!

# Granola Bars

makes **12 to 16** bars

Even if you immediately associate granola with healthy, wholesome food, granola bars are still a type of sheet cookie. They are easy to make at home, and you can customize them as you please. This granola is made up of oats, nuts and seeds, and dried fruit, with maple syrup binding them all together.

## INGREDIENTS

Nonstick cooking spray

2 cups (7 oz./210 g) rolled oats

1 cup (5 oz./150 g) raw almonds

1/2 cup (2 oz./60 g) hulled pumpkin seeds

1/2 cup (2 oz./60 g) shelled sunflower seeds

3 TB. seeds, such as sesame, poppy, flax, chia, or hemp

1/4 cup (2 oz./60 g) extra-virgin olive oil

3/4 cup (81/4 oz./250 g) pure maple syrup

11/2 tsp. pure vanilla extract

1 tsp. ground cinnamon

1/2 tsp. salt

1/2 cup (21/2 oz./75 g) pitted dates, chopped

1/2 cup (2 oz./60 g) dried cranberries

## EQUIPMENT

Rimmed baking sheet

9×13-in. (23×33-cm) baking pan

Parchment paper

Medium saucepan

Whisk

Large heat-proof mixing bowl

Silicone spatula or wooden spoon

Cooling rack

Sharp knife

Cutting board

Serrated knife

1. Preheat the oven to 350°F (180°C). Line a baking sheet with parchment paper and set aside. Line a baking pan with parchment, leaving an overhang, and spray with nonstick cooking spray. Set aside.

2. Toss rolled oats, almonds, pumpkin seeds, sunflower seeds, and seeds on the prepared baking sheet and bake until lightly browned, about 10 to 12 minutes.

3. While oat mixture toasts, place extra-virgin olive oil, maple syrup, vanilla extract, cinnamon, and salt in a medium saucepan, and bring to a boil over medium-high heat, about 3 minutes. Lower the heat, and whisk constantly for 2 more minutes.

4. Remove oat mixture from the oven and transfer to a large bowl (save the parchment paper). Pour in maple mixture (it will sizzle) and mix with a silicone spatula until oats, nuts, and seeds are evenly coated with syrup. Add dates and cranberries, and stir well.

5. Spoon granola mixture into the prepared baking pan. Place the reserved parchment paper on top and use it to spread and press granola evenly and tightly in the pan. Remove and discard that parchment.

6. Bake granola until light golden brown, 25 to 30 minutes (add 10 more minutes if you want crunchier bars). Remove from the oven and place on a cooling rack to cool and set completely, about 2 hours.

7. Once cool, run a sharp knife around the edges of the pan. Lift granola by pulling up on the parchment overhang. Transfer granola to a cutting board and, using a serrated knife, cut into bars of desired size. Serve or store. These bars keep well in an airtight container for about 2 weeks.

**Variations:** Replace the almonds with any other kind of nut or a combination of nuts—just make sure it's equal to 1 cup (5 oz./150 g). The dates and cranberries can also be replaced with equal amounts of chopped dried apricots, apples, coconut, cherries, or any dried fruit.

# How to Make Poured Sheet Cookies

Poured sheet cookies, such as brownies and blondies, are a great cross between a cookie and a cake and are easy to put together. Most recipes are put together in one bowl, poured into a baking pan, and voilà! Here are some basic guidelines and tips for making any kind of poured sheet cookie.

Even when recipes call for greasing the pan first the overhang is still applicable.

**Line the pan.** The easiest way to get sheet cookies out of the pan is by lining it with parchment paper, cut with a 1- to 2-inch (2.5- to 5-cm) overhang. These "handles" allow you to lift the entire sheet out in one piece.

**Melt the fats.** In order to get a smooth, pourable mixture, you first melt the fats (such as butter) and any other ingredients your recipe calls for in a bowl over a pan of simmering water, called a "water bath." Don't let the water touch the bottom of the bowl or get into the mixture, or it could turn into a hard lump (or *seize*) and be totally unusable.

**Put it all together.** The butter mixture is whisked into the sugars. Next, the dry ingredients are first whisked together in a separate bowl, and then added. Don't overmix—stir just until the ingredients are combined. Overmixing will make your cookies come out tough and rubbery.

**Pour and smooth.** The most important thing about pouring your batter is that you evenly spread the batter into the corners of the pan and smooth the top—otherwise, you'll end up with lopsided or unevenly baked cookies.

**Bake.** When baking sheet cookies, it's always best to set the timer for the minimum baking time to avoid overbaking. This will give you a moist, fudgy cookie. The longer you bake, the more cakelike they get.

**Cool.** It's important to always cool sheet cookies on a wire rack. This allows air to get to the bottom of the pan and stop the baking process. If you set it directly on a counter, it traps the heat and could overbake your cookies into a dry—or even burnt—state!

## When Is It Done?

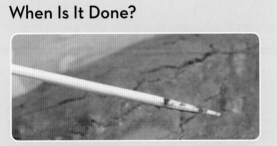

The best way to tell if a sheet cookie is done is by using a toothpick. Insert the toothpick into the middle of the cookie; if it comes out with some crumbs on it, it's done. However, if it comes out with some uncooked batter on it, it's still got a few minutes to go.

## Freeze!

If you're not serving cookies right away, double-wrap the uncut sheet in plastic wrap and freeze it. They will keep moist longer, and frozen sheet cookies are easier and neater to cut.

**Remove.** Here is where the overhang comes in handy. Once the cookies are cool, just gently pull the overhangs to lift the sheet out and transfer it to a rack or board. If your overhang only covers two sides, run an offset spatula or knife around the uncovered sides to loosen the cookie. Don't try to remove your sheet before it has completely cooled—you'll end up with a mound of crumbles!

# Brownies

These chocolatey wonders with a paper-thin, sugary crust and a rich, moist center are the typical example of a sheet cookie. Make these treats for your next get-together, and watch them disappear!

## INGREDIENTS

7 oz. (210 g) best-quality bittersweet chocolate, chopped

1 stick (4 oz./120 g) unsalted butter, softened (plus more for greasing the pan)

3 TB. cocoa powder

3 large eggs

1 cup (5 oz./150 g) light or dark brown sugar, firmly packed

1½ tsp. pure vanilla extract

½ tsp. salt

¾ cup (3 oz./90 g) all-purpose flour

## EQUIPMENT

8-in. (20-cm) square baking pan

Parchment paper

Small saucepan

Medium heat-proof mixing bowl

Silicone spatula *or* wooden spoon

Large mixing bowl

Whisk

Toothpick or cake tester

Cooling rack

Offset spatula *or* knife

Cutting board

Sharp knife

1. Preheat the oven to 350°F (180°C). Grease a baking pan with butter and line it with parchment paper, leaving an overhang. Set aside.

2. Fill a small saucepan with about 2 inches (5 cm) water, and bring to a simmer over low heat.

3. Place bittersweet chocolate, butter, and cocoa powder in a medium bowl and set it on top of the pan with the simmering water. Stir mixture occasionally with a silicone spatula until it melts and is completely combined. Set aside to cool.

4. In a large bowl, whisk together eggs, light brown sugar, vanilla extract, and salt until combined. Slowly whisk chocolate mixture into egg mixture. Switch back to the spatula and stir in all-purpose flour until combined.

5. Pour batter into the prepared pan, spreading into the corners and smoothing on top with an offset spatula.

6. Bake until slightly puffed and a thin crust has formed on top, about 35 to 40 minutes. A toothpick inserted in the center should come out with some moist crumbs attached (but no batter). Transfer the pan to a cooling rack to cool completely, about 2 hours.

7. Run a clean offset spatula around the edges of the pan. Lift brownie sheet by pulling up on the parchment overhang, and place on a cutting board. With a sharp knife, cut brownies into 2-inch (5-cm) squares. Brownies can be stored at room temperature in an airtight container for 3 to 4 days.

## Storage Tips

To keep your brownies fresher, store them between layers of parchment paper, and place a slice of bread in the container. The bread will absorb the excess moisture and keep the brownies soft.

Brownies don't do well refrigerated, but they freeze quite well. If you're not serving the brownies right away, double-wrap the entire uncut sheet in plastic wrap and freeze until ready to use. Make sure the brownies are completely cool first!

**Variations:** Fold in $1\frac{1}{2}$ cups (6 oz./180 g) coarsely chopped nuts of your choice (walnuts, pecans, macadamias, hazelnuts, almonds, and so on), shredded coconut, or chocolate chunks or chips right after adding the all-purpose flour in step 4.

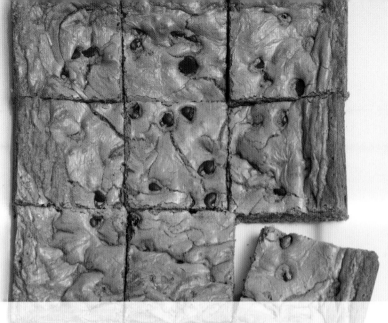

# Blondies

The perfect marriage of a brownie and a chocolate chip cookie, blondies have a lovely chewiness and butterscotch flavor that is enhanced with the addition of chocolate chips or chunks at the very end of the mixing process.

## INGREDIENTS

1 stick (4 oz./120 g) unsalted butter
1 cup (4³⁄₈ oz./125 g) all-purpose flour
¹⁄₂ tsp. baking soda
¹⁄₈ tsp. salt
³⁄₄ cup (6¹⁄₄ oz./200 g) dark brown sugar, firmly packed

2 tsp. pure vanilla extract
1 large egg
¹⁄₃ cup (2¹⁄₂ oz./75 g) chocolate chips

## EQUIPMENT

8-in. (20-cm) square baking pan
Parchment paper
Small saucepan
Large heat-proof mixing bowl
Silicone spatula
Sieve

Whisk
Cooling rack
Cutting board
Sharp knife
Plastic wrap (optional)

1. Preheat the oven to 350°F (180°C). Line a baking pan with parchment paper, leaving an overhang. Set aside.

2. With a sieve, sift together all-purpose flour, baking soda, and salt onto a clean piece of parchment paper. Set aside.

3. Fill a small saucepan with about 2 inches (5 cm) water, and bring to a simmer over low heat.

4. Place butter in a large bowl and set over the saucepan. Stir occasionally with a silicone spatula until butter melts. Move the bowl off the simmering water and add in dark brown sugar and vanilla extract. Whisk together until incorporated. Whisk in egg.

5. Carefully lift the parchment paper with flour mixture and add to butter mixture, whisking just until incorporated. Switch back to the spatula and mix in chocolate chips.

6. Turn batter into the prepared pan, smoothing top with the spatula.

7. Bake until top is cracked and feels slightly firm to the touch (like a thin crust), 20 to 25 minutes. Remove and set on a cooling rack to cool completely, about 40 minutes.

8. Remove blondies from the pan by lifting up on the parchment overhang, and transfer to a cutting board. Use a sharp knife to cut into bars. Blondies can be stored in an airtight container for 3 days or double-wrapped in plastic wrap and frozen for up to 3 months.

**Variations:** Take your blondies up a notch by adding $1/3$ cup ($2^1/_2$ oz./75 g) toasted chopped nuts, white chocolate chips, or shredded coconut along with—or instead of—the chocolate chips.

# How to Make Biscotti

The word *biscotti* (plural) or *biscotto* (singular) originates from the Latin word *biscoctus,* meaning "twice baked." This relates to how it's made—the dough is shaped into logs and baked before being sliced into bars and baked again. The result is an oblong, crispy, and dry cookie that can be stored for a long time. Here are the basic steps for making biscotti.

**Mix the fats and sugars.** Start by combining your fats (oil), sugar, and any kind of extracts until well mixed. Eggs are added at this point as well.

**Add the dry ingredients.** Still using the whisk, add in the dry ingredients. It's important not to overwhisk— you only want to beat until just combined. Overmixing at this stage will produce flat, hard cookies.

**Fold in the nuts.** Most biscotti recipes call for additions, such as nuts, dried fruits, and chocolate. Fold in these ingredients using a silicone spatula—don't whisk. Remember, you want to stir the batter as little as possible while still getting everything incorporated.

## How Should the Batter Look?

This is what your batter should look like when the wet and dry ingredients are incorporated.

4

Dust your hands with flour to prevent the dough from sticking to them.

5

Putting the baking sheet on a cooling rack helps stop the baking process.

**Make the logs.** Most biscotti recipes make two logs, so you will halve the dough. Biscotti dough is very loose—more like a batter—so shaping the logs is about patting them into shape, not rolling. Don't worry if the shapes are not perfect! The logs will spread when baked, so be sure to space them about 3 inches (7.5 cm) apart.

**Bake and cool.** Biscotti go through two rounds of baking—first when uncut, and then when cut. In the first round of baking, the logs are done when they are golden and just beginning to crack on top. You then remove them from the oven and cool them on the baking sheet.

6

A serrated knife works best.

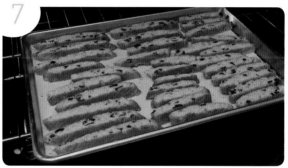

7

**Cut the cookies.** Once the logs have cooled a bit, they are cut into ½-inch (1-cm) diagonal strips and put back onto the baking sheet, cut sides up. The cookies are done expanding at this point, so they can be put close together.

**Bake again.** The second round of baking is done at a lower temperature, which gives the cookies their crisp, crumbly texture. The cookies are done when the cut edges are crisp and golden brown. They are then transferred to a wire rack to cool completely.

Biscotti keep well stored at room temperature in an airtight container for up to 2 weeks. They can also be double-wrapped in plastic wrap and frozen for up to 3 months.

# Almond-Cranberry Biscotti

makes about **36** cookies

The almonds, the very low fat and liquid content, and the double-baking process give these biscotti an extremely satisfying crunch, balanced by the addition of the slightly chewy and sweet-and-sour dried cranberries.

## INGREDIENTS

1 cup (3 oz./90 g) sliced almonds

¼ cup (1¾ oz./55 g) neutral-tasting oil (see "Other Fats and Oils" in Chapter 2)

¾ cup (5¼ oz./160 g) granulated sugar

2 tsp. pure vanilla extract

½ tsp. almond extract

2 large eggs

1¾ cups (7½ oz./225 g) all-purpose flour

¼ tsp. salt

1 tsp. baking powder

½ cup (2 oz./60 g) dried cranberries

## EQUIPMENT

Rimmed baking sheet

Parchment paper

Large mixing bowl

Whisk

Silicone spatula or wooden spoon

Cooling rack

Cutting board

Large offset spatula

Sharp knife, preferably serrated

1. Preheat the oven to 300°F (150°C). Line a rimmed baking sheet with parchment paper.

2. Place almonds on the prepared sheet and bake until they are slightly toasted (a shade darker), about 7 minutes. Remove from the oven and let cool.

3. In a large bowl, whisk together neutral-tasting oil, sugar, vanilla extract, and almond extract until well mixed. Whisk in eggs. Add in all-purpose flour, salt, and baking powder, whisking until just combined. Switch to a silicone spatula and incorporate cranberries and toasted almonds; dough will be sticky. (Set aside the parchment-lined baking sheet for baking biscotti.)

4. With wet or floured hands, halve dough and form two logs, each 12 inches long and 2 inches wide (30×5 cm). Place logs about 3 inches (7.5 cm) apart on the prepared baking sheet.

5. Bake until logs are golden and just beginning to crack on top, about 35 minutes. Remove from the oven and place the baking sheet on a cooling rack for 10 minutes.

6. Reduce the oven temperature to 275°F (140°C). Use an offset spatula to transfer logs to a cutting board. With a sharp knife, cut each loaf diagonally into $1/2$-inch (1-cm) thick slices. Lay slices back on the parchment-lined baking sheet cut side up, and return to the oven.

7. Bake until crisp and golden brown on the edges, about 10 minutes. Transfer biscotti to a cooling rack and cool completely or serve warm. Biscotti keep well stored at room temperature in an airtight container for up to 2 weeks.

## Biscotti Ideas

Biscotti are a very versatile cookie. Here are some things you can do:

- Substitute the almonds with pistachios or hazelnuts.

- Add $1/4$ cup ($1^1/2$ oz./45 g) chocolate chips (white, dark, or both).

- Replace the dried cranberries with chopped dried apricots, dried cherries, or raisins.

- Add the zest of 1 orange at the end of step 2 (when the cranberries are added).

For a gluten-free option, you can substitute the all-purpose flour with $1^3/4$ cups ($5^3/4$ oz./170 g) certified gluten-free oat flour.

You can also dunk your biscotti in chocolate. Just melt a few ounces of your favorite chocolate, dunk the edge or the bottom of the biscotti, place on a sheet lined with parchment, and chill to set.

*chapter 4*

# Dropped and Piped Cookies

*Dropped (or drop) cookies* are made from a relatively soft dough that is dropped by spoonfuls or with a mini ice cream scoop onto a baking sheet. During baking, the mounds of dough usually spread and flatten. Chocolate chip cookies, oatmeal cookies, peanut butter cookies, molasses cookies, and snickerdoodles are examples of drop cookies. These cookies can be served individually or sandwiched with frosting spread in between.

*Piped cookies,* also known as *bagged* or *pressed cookies,* are made from soft doughs or batters that can be forced through a pastry (piping) bag or a cookie press and onto a prepared baking sheet. Some are decorated with toppings right before baking, while others are decorated and filled or sandwiched once baked and cooled. French macaroons, coconut macaroons, meringues, and spritz cookies are all examples of piped cookies.

# How to Make Dropped Cookies

Dropped cookies are some of the easiest cookies to make. You simply mix the ingredients together—usually all in one bowl—and drop portions of the dough (hence the name) onto a baking sheet. For beginning bakers, making dropped cookies is a great place to start; here's how.

Beat until fluffy for light and chewy cookies.

**Cream the fats.** Dropped cookies have a dense batter, so most recipes use the creaming method. The fats (such as butter) and sugars are creamed in a standing mixer until light and fluffy. Salt and vanilla are also incorporated at this stage.

**Add the eggs.** Eggs are always added one at a time and mixed well after each addition. Never add all of the eggs at once, as too much liquid added into the fat at one time might not get incorporated properly.

**Add the dry ingredients.** All of the dry ingredients (flour, salt, and so on) are first whisked together in a separate bowl, and then added to the butter mixture. Don't overmix—stir just until the ingredients are combined. Overmixing will give you tough cookies.

## Cracking Eggs

If you're new at cracking eggs, it's best to first crack them into a small bowl and check for pieces of shell before pouring them into the cookie batter.

**Add the mix-ins.** Mix-ins such as chocolate chips, chopped nuts, and dried fruits are folded into the dough by hand with a silicone spatula. This prevents overmixing the cookie dough.

**Drop and bake.** Cookies can be dropped onto the sheet using two spoons (one to scoop up the dough and the other to scrape it onto the sheet) or using a mini ice cream scoop, which makes more uniform cookies. Because drop cookies expand, space them 1½ inches (3.75 cm) apart.

## Freezing the Dough

If you'd like to bake the cookies later, you can freeze the dropped dough on the baking sheet for about 1 hour or until firm, and then transfer the balls to zipper-lock bags and freeze them for up to 1 month. Once ready to bake, follow the recipe instructions without thawing but lengthen the baking time by a few minutes.

**Cool and remove.** Cookies are done when they are golden brown on the bottom and the middles have set. Cool cookies on a wire rack; this allows air to get to the bottom of the pan and stop the baking process. If you need to reuse the baking sheets, slide the parchment onto the cooling rack; however, be sure to cool the sheets before using again, or the dough will start melting.

Dropped cookies can be stored at room temperature in an airtight container for up to 3 days or double-wrapped in plastic wrap and frozen for up to 1 month.

# Chocolate Chip Cookies

makes about **60** cookies

It's said that in 1930, Ruth Graves Wakefield substituted broken pieces of semisweet chocolate for baker's chocolate in her cookie recipe, thinking they would melt. They didn't, and the iconic chocolate chip cookie was born.

## INGREDIENTS

2¼ cups (9½ oz./285 g) all-purpose flour
1 tsp. baking soda
2 sticks (8 oz./240 g) unsalted butter, softened
1 cup (7½ oz./225 g) light brown sugar, firmly
   packed
1 tsp. pure vanilla extract
1 tsp. salt
3 large eggs
About 1 cup (5 oz./150 g) mini chocolate chips
1 cup (4 oz./120 g) chopped walnuts or other nuts
   (optional)

## EQUIPMENT

2 rimmed baking sheets
Parchment paper
Standing mixer fitted with paddle attachment *or*
   handheld mixer and bowl
Medium mixing bowl *or* 8-cup-capacity liquid
   measuring cup
Whisk
Silicone spatula
Cookie scoop (mini ice cream scoop) *or* 2 spoons
2 cooling racks
Plastic wrap (optional)

1. Evenly space two oven racks toward the center of the oven and preheat the oven to 375°F (190°C). Line the baking sheets with parchment paper. Set aside.

2. In a medium bowl, whisk together all-purpose flour and baking soda. Set aside.

3. In the bowl of a standing mixer, cream together butter, light brown sugar, vanilla extract, and salt on medium speed until light and fluffy. Add eggs one at a time, mixing after each addition, until incorporated. Add flour mixture to batter and beat on low speed until just combined. Turn off the mixer and stir in mini chocolate chips and chopped walnuts (if using) with a silicone spatula.

4. Scoop tablespoonfuls of cookie dough onto the prepared baking sheets, spacing about 1½ inches (3.75 cm) apart.

5. Bake until golden brown, 10 to 12 minutes, rotating the baking sheets from top to bottom and back to front halfway through. Remove from the oven and let cool on the sheets for 10 minutes.

6. Slide the parchment with cookies onto cooling racks and let cool completely, about 30 minutes. Line the cooled baking sheets with new parchment paper and repeat the process with remaining cookie dough. Cookies can be stored in an airtight container at room temperature for up to 3 days or double-wrapped in plastic wrap and frozen for up to 3 months.

# Peanut Butter Cookies

makes about **36** cookies

These delicious cookies typically sport a crosshatch pattern not only to enhance their aesthetics but to flatten down the dough and ensure even cooking. When it comes to ingredients, some recipes call for butter (which makes the cookies crisp), while others call for shortening or a combination of the two (which makes a chewier cookie).

## INGREDIENTS

$\frac{1}{2}$ cup ($3\frac{2}{3}$ oz./110 g) nonhydrogenated vegetable shortening

1 cup ($9\frac{1}{2}$ oz./285 g) chunky peanut butter

1 cup ($7\frac{1}{2}$ oz./225 g) light brown sugar, firmly packed

$\frac{1}{2}$ tsp. salt

$\frac{1}{2}$ tsp. pure vanilla extract

1 large egg

$1\frac{1}{2}$ cups ($6\frac{1}{3}$ oz./190 g) all-purpose flour

$\frac{1}{2}$ tsp. baking soda

## EQUIPMENT

2 rimmed baking sheets

Parchment paper

Standing mixer fitted with paddle attachment or large mixing bowl and silicone spatula

Silicone spatula

Mini ice cream scoop or 2 spoons

Fork

Small bowl of cold water

2 cooling racks

Plastic wrap (optional)

1. Evenly space two oven racks toward the center of the oven and preheat the oven to 375°F (190°C). Line the rimmed baking sheets with parchment paper. Set aside.

2. In the bowl of a standing mixer, cream together vegetable shortening, peanut butter, light brown sugar, salt, and vanilla extract at medium speed until light and fluffy. Beat in egg, mixing until incorporated. Add all-purpose flour and baking soda and mix with the silicone spatula until just combined.

3. Drop cookies onto the prepared baking sheets, or use your hands to roll tablespoonfuls of dough into balls. Place balls on the sheet $1\frac{1}{2}$ inches (3.75 cm) apart.

4. Dip a fork into cold water and press the fork into each ball. Rotate the fork 90 degrees and press into the balls once more to make a crosshatch pattern.

5. Bake until golden, 8 to 10 minutes, switching the baking sheets from top to bottom and back to front halfway through. Remove from the oven and cool on the baking sheets about 5 minutes.

6. Slide the parchment with cookies onto cooling racks and let cool completely, about 30 minutes. Line the cooled baking sheets with new parchment paper and repeat the process with remaining cookie dough. Cookies can be stored in an airtight container at room temperature for up to 3 days or double-wrapped in plastic wrap and frozen for up to 3 months.

# Oatmeal-Raisin Cookies

makes about **36** cookies

Nicely scented with spices, slightly sweetened, and with the comforting qualities of oatmeal, the only thing these versatile dropped cookies need is a glass of milk. Most recipes call for butter, but this recipe uses a neutral oil to let the other flavors shine.

## INGREDIENTS

1¾ cups (6 oz./180 g) rolled oats (not instant or quick-cooking)

¾ cup (3 oz./90 g) all-purpose flour

1 tsp. ground cinnamon

¼ tsp. ground nutmeg

½ tsp. baking soda

½ cup (4 oz./120 g) neutral-tasting oil (see "Other Fats and Oils" in Chapter 2)

⅓ cup (2½ oz./75 g) dark brown sugar, firmly packed

⅓ cup (2¼ oz./70 g) granulated sugar

½ tsp. salt

½ tsp. pure vanilla extract

1 large egg

½ cup (2½ oz./75 g) raisins (optional)

## EQUIPMENT

2 rimmed baking sheets

Parchment paper

Medium mixing bowl or 8-cup-capacity liquid measuring cup

Whisk

Large mixing bowl

Silicone spatula

Mini ice cream scoop or 2 spoons

Measuring cup

2 cooling racks

Plastic wrap (optional)

1. Evenly space two oven racks toward the center of the oven and preheat the oven to 350°F (180°C). Line the rimmed baking sheets with parchment paper. Set aside.

2. In a medium bowl, whisk together rolled oats, all-purpose flour, cinnamon, nutmeg, and baking soda until combined. Set aside.

3. Using the same whisk, in a large bowl, mix together neutral-tasting oil, dark brown sugar, sugar, salt, and vanilla extract until incorporated. Whisk in egg until well combined.

4. Switch to a silicone spatula and stir oat mixture into oil mixture until just combined; avoid overmixing. Stir in raisins.

5. Scoop tablespoonfuls of cookie dough onto the prepared baking sheets, spacing about 2 inches (5 cm) apart. Flatten dough mounds with the bottom of a measuring cup.

6. Bake until golden, 8 to 10 minutes, switching the baking sheets from top to bottom and back to front halfway through. Remove from the oven and cool on the baking sheets about 5 minutes.

7. Slide the parchment with cookies onto cooling racks and let cool completely, about 30 minutes. Line the cooled baking sheets with new parchment paper and repeat the process with remaining cookie dough. Cookies can be stored in an airtight container at room temperature for up to 3 days or double-wrapped in plastic wrap and frozen for up to 3 months.

# Mexican Wedding Cookies

makes about **36** cookies

Growing up in Mexico, I knew these cookies as *polvorones,* or "dust." This is because when you bite into them, they dissolve into a delicate whisper of nuts, butter, and just a tiny hint of sweetness.

## INGREDIENTS

1³⁄₄ sticks (4³⁄₄ oz./140 g) unsalted butter, softened
1¹⁄₄ cups (5.5 oz./155 g) confectioner's sugar
2 tsp. pure vanilla extract
¹⁄₈ tsp. salt
2 cups (8¹⁄₂ oz./255 g) all-purpose flour
1 cup (3¹⁄₂ oz./105 g) almond or other nut flour
1 tsp. water, at room temperature

## EQUIPMENT

Standing mixer fitted with paddle attachment or
    handheld mixer and bowl
Medium mixing bowl *or* 8-cup-capacity liquid
    measuring cup
Sieve *or* sifter
Silicone spatula
Plastic wrap
2 rimmed baking sheets
Parchment paper
2 cooling racks
Plastic wrap (optional)

1. In the bowl of a standing mixer, cream butter, ¹⁄₄ cup confectioner's sugar, vanilla extract, and salt at medium speed until light and fluffy.

2. In a medium bowl, sift all-purpose flour. Stir flour into butter mixture at low speed. Add almond flour and water and mix until a dough forms. Scrape the sides of the bowl with a silicone spatula. Cover the bowl with plastic wrap and refrigerate for at least 1 hour.

3. Evenly space two oven racks toward the center of the oven and preheat the oven to 400°F (200°C). Line the rimmed baking sheets with parchment paper. Set aside.

4. Using your hands, roll tablespoonfuls of dough into balls, and place on the sheet 1¹⁄₂ inches (3.75 cm) apart. If dough becomes sticky, refrigerate it for 10 minutes.

5. Bake until lightly golden, 10 to 12 minutes, switching the baking sheets from top to bottom and back to front halfway through.

6. Place the baking sheets on cooling racks. Use a sieve to dust cookies generously with remaining 1 cup confectioner's sugar. Cool on the baking sheets about 10 minutes.

7. Slide the parchment with cookies onto cooling racks and let cool completely, about 30 minutes. Line the cooled baking sheets with new parchment paper and repeat the process with remaining cookie dough. Cookies can be stored in an airtight container at room temperature for up to 3 days or double-wrapped in plastic wrap and frozen for up to 3 months.

# Piped Cookies and Piping Basics

Piped cookies, also known as bagged or pressed cookies, are made of dough soft enough to be forced through a pastry bag but stiff enough to hold its shape. Before you make piped cookies, though, you need to know how to work with a piping bag! This can look intimidating, but it's not—once you get the hang of it, you'll be using piping bags for everything! So let's look at the basics.

**What you'll need:** In addition to the piping bag, couplers, and tip, you'll need scissors, a tall glass, and a rubber band (optional).

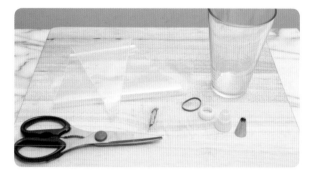

## Assembling the Bag

Unscrew the ring from coupler base. Drop the coupler base, narrow end first, into the piping bag and push it down as far as you can. If your bag doesn't have a perforation, mark (with a pen or pencil) a spot that is about ¼ inch (5 mm) below the bottom screw thread of the coupler.

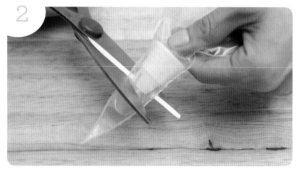

Cut an opening at the mark with sharp scissors, making sure the cut is completely even so small pieces of plastic don't go into the frosting.

Push the coupler base down through the opening without pushing too hard so the bag doesn't rip. You don't want the whole coupler to come through the opening—the bag should still be covering the threads of the screw part.

Place your desired pastry tip over the end of the coupler base's end to fit tightly.

## Filling the Bag

Secure the pastry tip by screwing on the ring over the tip until it locks.

Make a large cuff by folding the top of the bag down and out.

Place the bag in a tall glass and stretch the cuff over the rim of the glass.

With a silicone spatula, transfer the dough into the bag. Fill the bag only to where the cuff starts forming (don't overfill or it may turn into a messy experience, with batter coming out of the top).

Because air bubbles interrupt the flow of the batter, you want to try to get rid of as many as you can. Unfold the cuff; lay the bag on a flat surface; and, using a bench scraper (or even your hand), gently force the dough down toward the tip.

Twist the end of the bag closed, just above the filling. If you're a beginner piper, use a rubber band to hold the twist in place. As you become more experienced, you can just twist the end closed and fold it over, holding it closed with the palm of your hand.

Now that your bag is ready, it's time to pipe those cookies!

Cookies can be piped into any form—just make sure the cookies on each pan are approximately the same size so they bake evenly.

**Hold the bag and pipe.** To hold a pastry bag correctly, your dominant hand (the one you use to write) is around the top of the bag, holding the twist and doing the squeezing (with even, gentle pressure) to force the batter out. Push mainly with the palm of your dominant hand, rather than squeezing with your fingers, to generate even pressure. The other hand is there to guide the pastry tip (yes, it is counterintuitive, but as you practice, you'll see how this is the best way of doing it, because it allows you much more control).

**Add any finishing touches and bake.** Decorate the cookies with candied fruit, sprinkles, nuts, or decorator's sugars, if desired. Bake the cookies until slightly golden and the dough feels set to the touch.

## Cookie Presses

Another great way to make spritz cookies is to use a cookie press. Cookie presses have small disks at the bottom with decorative shapes cut out of them; the dough is pressed through these plates to make everything from hearts, to trees, to even dogs! There are old-school presses that are hand-cranked, but the easiest are the "gun" style presses—you just place the disk you want in the bottom, fill the barrel, and squeeze the trigger for perfect cookies every time.

# Spritz Cookies

Few cookies evoke nostalgia like spritz cookies. The name comes from the German word *spritzen,* meaning "to squirt," because the dough is "squirted" through a piping bag or cookie press. They are a great holiday project and allow a lot of room for easy creativity with the decorations. Family members of all ages can join in the kitchen helping out and celebrating with these buttery and delicate cookies lightly scented with vanilla and almond extracts.

## INGREDIENTS

1 cup (8 oz./240 g) unsalted butter, softened
½ cup plus 2 TB. (2⅕ oz./75 g) confectioner's sugar
2 tsp. pure vanilla extract
½ tsp. almond extract
¼ tsp. salt

1 large egg
2¼ cups (8¾ oz./295 g) all-purpose flour
Candied fruit, nuts, colored sprinkles, chips, or colored sugars (for decoration)

## EQUIPMENT

2 rimmed baking sheets
Parchment paper
Standing mixer fitted with paddle attachment
Silicone spatula

Piping bag fitted with large star tip or cookie press (optional)
2 cooling racks
Medium offset spatula
Plastic wrap (optional)

1. Evenly space two oven racks toward the center of the oven and preheat the oven to 350°F (180°C). Line the baking sheets with parchment paper. Set aside.

2. In the bowl of a standing mixer, cream butter, confectioner's sugar, vanilla extract, almond extract, and salt at medium speed until light and fluffy. Add egg and beat until incorporated. Stir in all-purpose flour on low speed until just combined.

3. With a silicone spatula, scrape the mixing bowl and transfer dough into the prepared piping bag. Hold the piping bag almost perpendicular to the prepared sheet, with the tip almost touching the parchment; squeeze the bag; and pipe your desired shapes leaving a 1-inch (2.5-cm) space between cookies. Decorate cookies with candied fruit, nuts, colored sprinkles, chips, or colored sugars.

4. Bake cookies until slightly golden and dough feels set to the touch, about 10 minutes, switching the baking sheets from top to bottom and back to front halfway through the baking time. (Doneness will depend on size and shape of cookie.)

5. Cool cookies on baking sheets about 5 minutes. Slide parchment with cookies onto cooling racks and let cool completely, about 30 minutes. Line the cooled baking sheets with new parchment paper and repeat the process with remaining cookie dough. Cookies can be stored in an airtight container at room temperature for 3 days or double-wrapped in plastic wrap and frozen for up to 3 months.

## Decorating Ideas

Instead of decorating the cookies with sprinkles or fruit, try dipping the ends in melted chocolate. Or, for a festive look, try tinting the cookie dough with food coloring—just add a few drops of your favorite color to the dough and gently knead the color throughout.

**Variations:** To make *spiced spritz cookies,* add 1 teaspoon cinnamon, $1/2$ teaspoon ground nutmeg, and $1/4$ teaspoon ground allspice to the all-purpose flour before pouring it in. To make *butterscotch spritz cookies,* exchange the sugar in the recipe with brown sugar. To make *lemon spritz cookies,* exchange the almond extract with lemon extract and add 1 tablespoon lemon zest. To make *peppermint spritz cookies,* exchange the almond extract with $1/4$ to $1/2$ teaspoon peppermint extract.

# Rolled-Out and Ice Box Cookies

*Rolled-out cookies* are made from a stiffer dough that is rolled out, chilled, and cut into shapes with cookie cutters. Although a bit more labor-intensive than other methods for forming cookies, this one allows you to make cookies in a great variety of shapes with seasonal motifs or specific themes. Gingerbread men (or any other shapes) are an example of a rolled-out cookie.

*Ice box cookies,* also called *refrigerator cookies,* are formed through a method in which the dough is mixed and shaped into cylinders or logs. These cylinders are wrapped (usually in parchment paper or plastic wrap) and stored in either the fridge or freezer (hence their name). The dough is then sliced and baked as cookies are needed.

This method can be used for a huge variety of cookie doughs and allows you to always have freshly baked cookies on hand without having to whip up a new batch of dough every time. You can also use this method to make cookies with different designs using doughs in contrasting colors, such as pinwheel or bull's-eye cookies.

# How to Make Rolled-Out Cookies

When making rolled-out cookies, use dough without any elements that would disrupt their uniformity (such as chips, nuts, or dried fruit) or with too much leavening, as the cookies should maintain their shape after they are cut and baked. The secret to achieving thin, crisp cookies suitable for decorating is rolling out the dough to an even thickness from edge to edge. It takes some practice to get it right, but the following steps help you make the job easier and more precise.

The paper layers also make it easy to transport the dough to and from the freezer.

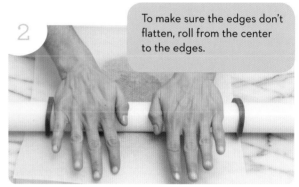

To make sure the edges don't flatten, roll from the center to the edges.

**Portion the dough.** Dividing your dough into four equal portions allows you to have a manageable amount of dough to roll. By then placing each portion in between two pieces of parchment paper or sturdy plastic wrap, the dough won't stick to the work surface or rolling pin and won't require additional flour (which could toughen the cookies).

**Roll the dough.** To get the cookies to the thin, crisp state you need, use a rolling pin to roll out each portion of dough ¼ to ⅛ inch (6 to 3 mm) thick. Positioning the rolling pin in the center of the dough and rolling it away from you flattens the first half of the dough.

## Rolling Equipment

If the rolling process seems overwhelming, don't get discouraged! There are a couple utensils on the market that can help in the even-rolling department:

**Rolling pin bands or rings:** Available in sets of assorted sizes, these keep the rolling pin at a precise distance from the dough. Simply select a pair for the desired thickness and place them on opposite ends of the rolling pin.

**Rolling strips:** Also sold in assorted sets of different thicknesses, you place these same-size strips on each side of the dough and roll the dough flat over them.

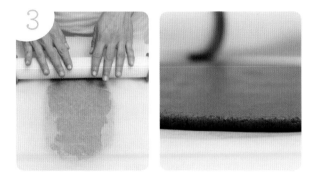

**Continue rolling the dough.** As you continue rolling, make sure you use even pressure on the rolling pin so the cookies bake evenly. Repositioning the pin in the center of the dough and rolling toward you flattens the other half of the dough. To get the desired thinness, rotate the dough 90 degrees and repeat until you achieve it.

**Freeze.** Freezing the rolled-out dough portions in parchment sandwiches stacked on a baking sheet makes them firmer and easier to cut out and handle. While the dough chills, you can preheat the oven and prepare the baking sheets for the rest of the process.

Transfer the cookies (while still cold) with an offset spatula.

Decorate the cookies only when completely cooled; otherwise, the icing will melt.

**Cut the cookies.** Dipping the cutter in flour prevents the dough from sticking and makes a neater cut. Make each cut as close as possible to the next one so you have fewer scraps. If the dough becomes too warm to handle, you can refrigerate or freeze it.

**Transfer and bake.** Don't forget to space the cookies as you place them on the baking sheet; they'll expand during baking. The color of rolled-out cookies aren't an accurate measure of doneness, so bake—switching the baking sheets from top to bottom and back to front halfway through—until the dough barely retains an indentation in the center when gently touched with your finger.

**Cool.** Cool on a wire cooling rack so air gets to the bottom of the sheets and stops the baking process. If you need the baking sheets to keep baking more cookies, you can slide the parchment with cookies onto the cooling rack. These cookies can be served, stored, or frozen once completely cooled.

With any remaining scraps, you can repeat the rolling-out and baking process.

# Gingerbread Cookies

*makes about **72** 2.5-in. (6.5-cm) cookies*

Gingerbread cookies are one of the best options for rolling, cutting in an endless variety of shapes, and decorating, because they are smooth and sturdy. The spice combination can be adapted to your liking, although ginger and molasses are the keynote flavors in this type of cookie.

## INGREDIENTS

3 cups (15 oz./450 g) all-purpose flour
3/4 cup (51/4 oz./155 g) dark brown
    sugar, firmly packed
1/4 tsp. baking soda
21/2 tsp. ground cinnamon
2 tsp. ground ginger
1/2 tsp. ground cloves
1/2 tsp. ground allspice
1/2 tsp. salt

1/4 tsp. ground black pepper
1 cup (8 oz.) nonhydrogenated
    shortening
3/4 cup (9 oz./270 g) unsulphured
    molasses
2 TB. water, milk, or rum
1 batch Royal Icing (see "How to Make
    Royal Icing" in Chapter 6)

## EQUIPMENT

Standing mixer fitted with paddle
    attachment
Bench scraper
Parchment paper
Rolling pin
Rolling pin stripes, bands, or rings
    (optional)

3 rimmed baking sheets
Cookie cutters
Small mixing bowl filled with flour
Medium offset spatula
3 cooling racks
Plastic wrap (optional)

1. In the bowl of a standing mixer, stir together all-purpose flour, dark brown sugar, baking soda, cinnamon, ginger, cloves, allspice, salt, and black pepper on low speed until combined, about 30 seconds. Stop the mixer, add in shortening, and mix on medium speed until mixture is sandy, about 90 seconds.

2. Reduce speed to low and, with the mixer running, gradually add molasses and water. Mix until dough is evenly moistened, about 20 seconds. Increase speed to medium and mix until well combined and dough forms, about 10 seconds. Avoid overmixing, as dough could yield tough cookies.

3. With a bench scraper, divide dough into 4 portions of approximately equal size. Working with 1 portion at a time, place dough in between 2 12×16-inch (30×40-cm) pieces of parchment paper.

4. With a rolling pin fitted with rolling pin stripes, bands, or rings (if using), roll out each portion of dough $\frac{1}{4}$- to $\frac{1}{8}$-inch (6- to 3-mm) thick. Transfer dough, still between the parchment, onto a rimmed baking sheet.

5. Repeat the process with the other portions of dough and stack them on the baking sheet. Place in the freezer or refrigerator to chill until firm, about 20 minutes for the freezer and 1 hour for the refrigerator.

6. Evenly space two oven racks toward the center of the oven and preheat the oven to 325°F (170°C). Line two rimmed baking sheets with parchment paper. Set aside.

7. Remove 1 dough sheet from the freezer, place on a work surface, and peel off top parchment paper. Dip a cookie cutter into flour and press into dough to cut cookies. Make each cut as close as possible to the next one.

8. Transfer cut shapes to the prepared baking sheets with an offset spatula, leaving 1 inch (2.5 cm) in between cookies. Repeat with remaining dough until the baking sheets are full. Set aside dough scraps.

9. Bake cookies until dough barely retains an indentation in the center when gently touched with a finger, 12 to 15 minutes. Switch the baking sheets from top to bottom and rotate them back to front halfway through the baking time.

10. Cool cookies on the baking sheets about 5 minutes. Slide the parchment with cookies onto cooling racks and let cool completely, about 30 minutes. Reroll all scraps together and repeat cutting until all dough is used. Line the cooled baking sheets with new parchment paper and repeat the process with remaining cookie dough.

11. Remove cooled cookies from parchment with the offset spatula. Decorate with Royal Icing (see "How to Use Royal Icing" in Chapter 6). Cookies can be stored in an airtight container at room temperature for 3 days or double-wrapped in plastic wrap and frozen for up to 3 months.

## Before Decorating

If you're decorating the gingerbread cookies, make sure they are completely cooled first.

# How to Make Ice Box Cookies

The term *ice box cookies*—which are also known as refrigerator or slice-and-bake cookies—doesn't really comprise a specific kind of cookie, but refers to the way many doughs can be shaped into long cylinders, stored in the refrigerator (or freezer), sliced, and baked when needed. The slices could even be rolled into balls to make shaped cookies, guaranteeing equal size and even baking.

Learning how to make ice box cookies allows you to mix the dough when you have some extra time, store it, and use it when you want it. You don't even have to bake a whole batch of cookies at once, and you'll always have fresh-from-the-oven cookies.

Don't make them too big, or they can break or lose shape.

If the dough is too sticky, refrigerate or freeze it for a few minutes.

**Divide and shape.** Divide the dough into equal portions to make it easier to handle and store. Working with each portion separately, pat the dough into a log on a sheet of parchment paper. The thickness of the log should depend on the desired cookie diameter (although in many recipes, the cookies spread while baking, so the diameter of the cylinder might not be the exact size of the baked cookie).

## Shaping the Dough

To shape the dough into a crisp, long, and narrow cylinder, press a bench scraper or ruler against the edge of the parchment-wrapped dough.

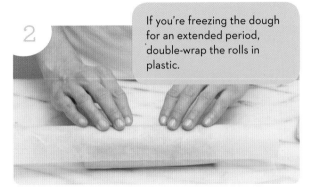

2

If you're freezing the dough for an extended period, double-wrap the rolls in plastic.

3

**Wrap it up.** Position the log on the edge of the parchment paper and roll the paper tightly around the dough. Wrapping the dough as tightly as possible protects it against air damage. Twist the ends of the parchment paper, making sure they are completely covered.

**Chill.** Refrigerate or freeze the wrapped dough until firm (at least 2 hours, but preferably overnight). Don't refrigerate the dough for more than 2 days; if the cookies will be baked more than 2 days later, freeze the dough. To help the logs keep their rounded shape while chilling, insert the dough into empty paper-towel tubes and secure them with a rubber band.

4

Make sure the rounds are sliced to the same thickness to ensure even baking.

5

Make sure to leave enough space between the cookies, because some do expand while baking.

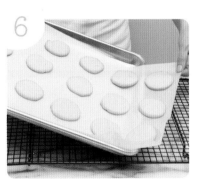

6

**Cut the cookies.** Unwrap the dough and slice it into rounds with a sharp knife. Rotate the log ⅛ turn after every slice to prevent one side of the log from flattening. If the dough softens too much, making it difficult to slice, freeze it for a couple minutes. This method can also be used for cutting thicker portions of dough of equal thickness and then rolling them into balls; this ensures ball-shaped cookies of equal size.

**Pan and bake.** Use an offset spatula to transfer the cookies to the prepared sheet. Bake, rotating the baking sheets front to back and top to bottom halfway through the baking time to ensure even baking, as the oven temperature varies on each spot.

**Cool.** Place the cookies, still on baking sheets, on cooling racks for about 5 minutes. Slide the parchment with the cookies onto wire cooling racks and let cool completely. Remove cooled cookies from the parchment with the offset spatula.

# Vanilla Cookies

makes about **36** cookies

This is an all-purpose butter cookie that you will be glad to keep safely stored in your fridge or freezer for when unexpected guests pop in or you desire a sweet treat. They are also very versatile and can be flavored in all sorts of ways. With this delicious dough ready to go in your freezer, a freshly baked cookie is always 15 minutes away!

## INGREDIENTS

1³/₄ sticks (7 oz./210 g) unsalted butter, softened
¹/₂ cup (2 oz./62.5 g) confectioner's sugar
1 tsp. pure vanilla extract
¹/₂ tsp. salt
2 large egg yolks
2 cups (8¹/₂ oz./260 g) all-purpose flour

## EQUIPMENT

Standing mixer fitted with paddle attachment or large mixing bowl and silicone
    spatula
Silicone spatula
Parchment paper
Empty paper-towel tubes (optional but highly recommended)
Plastic wrap (optional)
2 rimmed baking sheets
Cutting board
Sharp knife or bench scraper
2 cooling racks

1. In the bowl of a standing mixer, cream butter, confectioner's sugar, vanilla extract, and salt on low speed until light and fluffy, about 1 to $1\frac{1}{2}$ minutes. Scrape the sides of the bowl with a silicone spatula. Add egg yolks and beat on low until incorporated.

2. Scrape down the bowl. Add all-purpose flour and mix on low speed until dough forms and is well mixed, about 25 to 30 seconds (avoid overmixing).

3. Halve dough and place each piece on a sheet of parchment paper. Working with each portion separately, shape dough into a 2-inch (5-cm) diameter log. (If the dough is too sticky to do this, chill for 10 minutes.) Position log on the edge of the parchment paper and roll the paper tightly around it. Twist the ends of the parchment paper, making sure dough is completely covered. Insert parchment-wrapped cookie dough into empty paper-towel tubes (if using).

4. Refrigerate wrapped dough until firm, at least 2 hours up to 2 days, or freeze. Dough can also be double-wrapped in plastic wrap and frozen at this point as well.

5. Evenly space two oven racks toward the center of the oven and preheat the oven to 350°F (180°C). Line rimmed baking sheets with parchment paper and set aside.

6. Unwrap a chilled log and place on a cutting board. Using a sharp knife, slice log into $\frac{1}{4}$-inch (6-mm) thick rounds, rotating $\frac{1}{8}$ turn after every slice. If dough softens too much, put it back in the freezer for a couple minutes. Place cookie slices on the prepared baking sheets, spacing them 1 inch (2.5 cm) apart.

7. Bake until edges start to brown slightly, 10 to 12 minutes, rotating the baking sheets front to back and top to bottom halfway through the baking time.

8. Cool cookies on the baking sheets about 5 minutes. Slide the parchment with cookies onto cooling racks and let cool completely, about 30 minutes. Cookies can be stored at room temperature for 3 days or double-wrapped in plastic wrap and frozen for up to 3 months.

**Variations:** For different flavors, mix the zest of 1 lemon, lime, or orange into the dough together with the egg yolks. You can also substitute vanilla extract with the seeds of a vanilla bean for a concentrated vanilla flavor. To make delicious sandwich cookies, put dulce de leche, Nutella, chocolate ganache, fruit fillings, or even peanut butter between two cookies! You can even give these cookies extra flair by drizzling melted chocolate on them.

# Chocolate Cookies

makes about **36** cookies

The dough has a similar texture to the vanilla cookie, which is an advantage when combining them into pinwheel, checkerboard, or marbled cookies. By itself, this recipe is the ultimate chocolate cookie recipe!

## INGREDIENTS

1³/₄ cups (7¹/₃ oz./225 g) all-purpose flour

¹/₄ cup (³/₄ oz./20 g) unsweetened cocoa powder

1³/₄ sticks (7 oz./210 g) unsalted butter, softened

¹/₂ cup (2 oz./62.5 g) confectioner's sugar

1 tsp. pure vanilla extract

¹/₂ tsp. salt

2 large egg yolks

2 oz. (60 g) semisweet chocolate, melted (see "Chocolate and Cocoa" in Chapter 2) and cooled

## EQUIPMENT

Sieve or sifter

Medium mixing bowl or 8-cup-capacity liquid measuring cup

Standing mixer fitted with paddle attachment or large mixing bowl and silicone spatula

Silicone spatula

Parchment paper

Empty paper-towel tubes (optional but highly recommended)

Plastic wrap (optional)

2 rimmed baking sheets

Cutting board

Sharp knife or bench scraper

2 cooling racks

1. With a sieve, sift together all-purpose flour and cocoa powder into a medium bowl. Set aside.

2. In the bowl of a standing mixer, cream butter, confectioner's sugar, vanilla extract, and salt on low speed until light and fluffy, about 1 to 1½ minutes. Scrape the sides of the bowl with a silicone spatula. Add egg yolks and melted semisweet chocolate and beat on low until incorporated.

3. Scrape down the bowl. Add flour mixture and mix on low speed until dough forms and is well mixed, about 25 to 30 seconds (don't overmix).

4. Halve dough and place each piece on a sheet of parchment paper. Working with each portion separately, shape dough into a 2-inch (5-cm) diameter log. (If dough is too sticky to do this, chill for 10 minutes.) Position log on the edge of the parchment paper and roll the paper tightly around it. Twist the ends of the parchment paper, making sure dough is completely covered. Insert parchment-wrapped cookie dough into empty paper-towel tubes (if using).

5. Refrigerate wrapped dough until firm, at least 2 hours up to 2 days. Dough can also be double-wrapped in plastic wrap and frozen at this point as well.

6. Evenly space two oven racks toward the center of the oven and preheat the oven to 350°F (180°C). Line the rimmed baking sheets with parchment paper and set aside.

7. Unwrap a chilled log and place on a cutting board. Using a sharp knife, slice log into ¼-inch (6-mm) thick rounds, rotating ⅛ turn after every slice. If dough softens too much, put it back in the freezer for a couple minutes. Place cookie slices on prepared baking sheets, spacing them 1 inch (2.5 cm) apart.

8. Bake until edges start to brown slightly, 10 to 12 minutes, rotating the baking sheets front to back and top to bottom halfway through the baking time.

9. Cool cookies on the baking sheets about 5 minutes. Slide the parchment with cookies onto cooling racks and let cool completely, about 30 minutes. Cookies can be stored at room temperature for 3 days or double-wrapped in plastic wrap and frozen for up to 3 months.

**Variations:** You can create a delicious salted chocolate cookie by sprinkling a few salt flakes on top of the cookies before baking. You can also make chocolate caramel sandwiches by putting dulce de leche between two cookies.

# How to Make Pinwheel Cookies

Icebox cookies can be rolled into logs that produce cookies with two-color designs. The following are some simple techniques for making pinwheel cookies.

**Roll out and prep the dough.** Roll out the Vanilla Cookie dough (see the recipe in this chapter) in between 2 sheets of parchment paper about ⅛-inch (3-mm) thick. Repeat with the Chocolate Cookie dough (see the recipe in this chapter). Place both sheets of dough, still in between the parchment paper, on a rimmed baking sheet, and freeze for 5 to 10 minutes until firm.

The egg wash will act as a glue for the cookie dough layers.

**Brush on egg wash on first sheet.** Remove the upper parchment paper and brush the Vanilla Cookie sheet very lightly with egg wash using a pastry brush. Make sure you don't leave any egg wash puddles, or the dough will be soggy.

Leaving the bottom parchment paper on allows for easier transportation.

**Assemble.** Remove the top parchment paper from the Chocolate Cookie sheet and flip the dough upside down onto the Vanilla Cookie sheet. Remove the parchment paper from the Chocolate Cookie sheet.

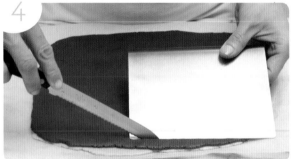

**Trim.** Using a sharp knife, trim any uneven edges of dough. For an even cleaner edge, use a ruler or bench scraper as your guide.

**5**

**Brush egg wash on second sheet.** Brush the Chocolate Cookie sheet lightly with egg wash. Again, make sure you're leaving no puddle of egg wash.

**6**

Use the parchment on the bottom of the Vanilla Cookie sheet to help with rolling.

**Roll.** Starting with the shorter edge, roll up the dough very tightly like a jelly roll. Make sure it's tight; if it's loose, the shape of the baked cookie will suffer and won't look neat. You can wrap the cylinder in parchment and refrigerate or freeze it at this point.

**7**

**Cut.** Unwrap the dough and slice it into rounds with a sharp knife. Rotate the log ⅛ turn after every slice to prevent one side of the log from flattening. If the dough softens too much, making it difficult to slice, freeze it for a couple minutes. Bake according to the cookie recipe instructions.

## Bull's-Eye Cookies

Another fun multicolored cookie is bull's-eyes. Just roll the Vanilla Cookie dough into a cylinder, and then roll out the Chocolate Cookie dough into a sheet about ½-inch (12-mm) thick. Brush egg wash lightly on top of the Chocolate Cookie dough; place the Vanilla Cookie cylinder at the edge of the Chocolate; and roll, wrapping the Chocolate tightly around the Vanilla. Slice and bake as you would with the pinwheels.

## Dyeing Cookie Dough

The Vanilla Cookie dough can be dyed with food coloring to achieve an infinite amount of hues. You can play around combining different-colored doughs to make pinwheel or bull's-eye cookies, adapting them to any theme or occasion.

**CHAPTER 5 |** ROLLED-OUT AND ICE BOX COOKIES

# Cookie Faults and Their Causes

Sometimes, despite your best efforts, your cookies won't come out the way you planned. Whether your chocolate chip cookies spread too much or your oatmeal cookies are soggy, this handy chart will help you combat the most common cookie faults.

| Fault | Causes | Fault | Causes |
|---|---|---|---|
| Hard and/or tough cookies | • Too much flour in dough<br>• Incorrect amount of sugar or butter<br>• Overmixing<br>• Baked too long or baking temperature too low | Not enough spread of cookies | • Baking temperature too high<br>• Too much flour or flour too strong<br>• Not enough sugar<br>• Not enough leavening<br>• Not preheating the oven before baking<br>• Not enough liquid<br>• Insufficient creaming |
| Uneven baking | • Cookies shaped at irregular thickness or size | | |
| Cookies too brown on the bottom | • Dark baking sheets; use heavy-gauge sheets with a dull finish instead | Cookies soggy when cooled | • Cookies left to cool overlapped |
| Cookies too brown | • Baking temperature too high<br>• Baked too long<br>• Too much sugar<br>• Oven is not calibrated | Bars are gummy | • Incorrect pan size |
| Cookies too dry | • Not enough liquid<br>• Not enough fat<br>• Too much flour<br>• Overbaked | Uneven-looking cookies from the same batch of dough | • Not scraping the bowl after mixing in the flour |
| Cookies not browned enough | • Baking temperature too low<br>• Underbaked<br>• Not enough sugar | | |
| Poor flavor for cookies | • Flavoring ingredients left out<br>• Ingredients improperly measured | | |
| Too much spread of cookies | • Baking temperature too low<br>• Not enough flour<br>• Too much sugar<br>• Too much leavening<br>• Too much liquid<br>• Baking sheet may be warm<br>• Overgreasing the pan<br>• Too much creaming, or butter is melted | | |

# Decorating
# Cookies

A large part of the pleasure people obtain from food comes from
enjoying not only how it tastes and smells, but also how it looks. In the
baking world, decorating cookies to make them look visually appeal-
ing or to match them to a theme, pattern, or palette is a great place to
start unleashing your inner pastry designer. Using icings, toppings,
food coloring, and pastry bags with special tips, decorative touches
can turn your cookies into edible works of art. Decorated cookies can
go from simple to over-the-top intricate and can be a solo project or a
family activity—it's up to you and your imagination.

# Decorative Toppings

There are plenty of choices when it comes to confectionary decorations. Decorations allow you to add a great variety of color, shapes, textures, and even themes to your cookies.

**Sugars:** As mentioned in Chapter 2, decorator's sugars—which come in many different colors and coarseness—can be used to top cookies. Decorator's sugar, also called *AA sugar,* is coarser than sanding sugar (see "Sweeteners" in Chapter 2).

**Sprinkles:** Also called *jimmies,* these small, slightly elongated pieces of colored sugar icing add fun to baked goods by bringing out everyone's inner child. They can be purchased in specific colors or mixed. Another type of sprinkles called *quins* consists of colored sugar toppings in small shapes, such as circles, flowers, and stars.

**Nonpareils:** These are similar to sprinkles but they're shaped into tiny balls. Larger versions in different colors and even some shimmer are known as *pearls,* while nonpareils filled with chocolate are called *sixlets.*

**Nuts:** While not as colorful, nuts are a natural alternative for decorating, with very interesting shapes and loads of texture. They can be used whole, sliced, or chopped.

**Decorative candy:** Brightly colored and in plenty of shapes, candies can be added to baked goods after they are baked.

## Dragees Warning

Please note that although dragees—candy shapes with a metallic coat (silver, gold, and so on)—are beautiful, they are considered nonedible decorations!

# How to Adhere Decorative Toppings to Cookies

Right before baking, you can add decorator's sugar, sprinkles, quins, nonpareils, and nuts to the cookie cut-outs when they are already on the prepared baking sheet. However, because cookie dough is soft and can't resist much handling, you might only be able to sprinkle them. For more-precise work, it's better to add the toppings after the cookies have been baked and cooled. The following walks you through how to do so.

Place each of your toppings in separate cupcake paper liners or the cavities of a muffin pan. Cover your working surface to protect it; paper, parchment, or plastic tablecloths or sheets are good options.

Cookies with a smooth surface work best.

The toppings need something sticky to keep them on the cookies, so use an "edible glue." One option is piping gel, which is a transparent sugar gel that can be piped, brushed, or spread directly onto cookies. Another option is to spread or pipe some frosting on the cookies. A third option is to melt down some jelly (with a color to match your topping) in a saucepan over low heat; once it's completely melted, you can brush a very thin layer of jelly on the parts of the cookie you want to cover with toppings.

Place the desired decorative toppings on the edible glue. If you're placing small toppings in a precise pattern, your fingers might be too big for such a detailed job. In these cases, use a pair of tweezers to hold the topping—for example 1 sugar pearl or candy—and place it on the desired position. If you'd like to cover the whole surface of the cookie, hold the cookie over a bowl and spoon on the topping, repeating as needed to cover it completely; you can reuse the sugar that falls into the bowl.

# How to Make Royal Icing

Royal icing, made from just egg whites and confectioner's sugar, is very versatile. It can be colored and it dries quite hard and smooth, so it works well as a decoration or glue for other decorations on cookies and cakes. Making it at home is quite easy.

## INGREDIENTS

3 ¼ cups (13 oz./400 g) confectioner's sugar
2 large egg whites or 2 oz. (60 g) pasteurized egg whites

You can flavor your icing with vanilla or any other extract.

**Combine the ingredients.** Beat the confectioner's sugar and egg whites or pasteurized egg whites in the bowl of a standing mixer fitted with the paddle attachment (don't use the whisk attachment—you don't want to incorporate too much air into it) on low speed until combined.

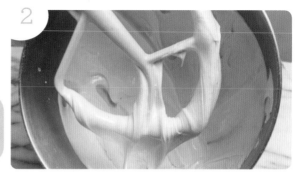

**Beat.** Increase the speed to medium-high and beat mixture until thickened and glossy and about three times the original volume, about 5 minutes.

Use the icing immediately or transfer to an airtight container, as it hardens quite quickly when exposed to air. You can refrigerate it for up to 2 weeks—just be sure to bring it to room temperature and beat it with a silicone spatula before using.

# How to Use Royal Icing

Always start with a completely cooled cookie with a smooth and dry surface. If the cookie is warm, the icing will not set and could even melt. If the surface is not smooth and dry, the royal icing will not be able to adhere. Royal icing doesn't adhere to fat, so never use it on butter-creams or other frostings with a high fat content. The following are techniques where you can take advantage of royal icing's qualities.

**Use it for tinting.** If you are adding liquid, gel, or powder food coloring (see "Edible Decorations" in Chapter 2), transfer the royal icing into small bowls, so you can make many colors from the same batch of icing and dye with a little bit of coloring (remember to add only a little at a time, as you can always add more but not take away, and food coloring tends to deepen as it sets). Using a toothpick is the best way of dispensing the color. Mix it thoroughly with a spoon or spatula and add more if needed. Cover the finished icing colors with a moistened paper towel to keep them from drying.

**Use it for piping.** Transfer the royal icing to a piping bag fitted with the desired pastry tip (see "Pastry Bags, Couplers, and Tips" in Chapter 2) and pipe borders, dots, lines, or anything you want. If you are adding any toppings on the icing, place them immediately, while the icing is still soft and sticky.

## Is Your Icing Not Flowing Correctly?

If your icing breaks easily when you pipe it, it might need thinning with a bit of water. Royal icing is very sensitive to water, so add only a few drops at a time to avoid thinning it too much. Just a little will do, as you still want it to hold a shape.

**Use it for adhering.** If you are attaching any kind of decorations to your cookies, there's no better way to keep them in place than royal icing, as it becomes very hard once completely dried! Place the items on the royal icing immediately after piping, while the icing is still soft and sticky—once dry, it won't hold anything.

**Use it for flooding.** This is a term that refers to filling in areas with a thin layer of icing. You will need to thin it down by slowly adding water by the teaspoonful, until the royal icing no longer holds a peak. There are two techniques for flooding cookies:

*Dipping:* The simplest way of flooding cookies is to hold the cookie by its edges and dip the surface of the cookie directly onto the surface of the thinned icing. Lift it up and let it drain a bit—to keep icing from dripping all over—before flipping it back up. It might take a good amount of hours for the icing to dry completely, so be careful when handling and storing the cookies.

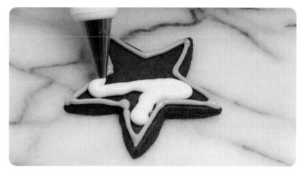

*Flooding with piped borders:* For a more professional look and intrinsic designs, pipe borders all around the inner edge of the cookie with the stiffer royal icing. You then pipe (or use a squeeze bottle or a spoon) to fill in the whole area inside the piped borders. Use a toothpick to spread the icing into corners. Let the cookies dry for a couple hours (up to overnight).

## Toothpicks

Wooden toothpicks are a great tool to have around when working with royal icing. When flooding, toothpicks can be used to push thinned royal icing into corners of the cookie the icing is not reaching by itself once piped. You can also use the toothpick tip to break icing bubbles that often form. Toothpicks are also great for unclogging pastry tips obstructed by hardened royal icing.

# part 3

# Eggs: One Ingredient, Multiple Functions

**Chapter 7:** Meringues

**Chapter 8:** Custards and Mousses

**Chapter 9:** Soufflés

# Egg Basics

Along with flour, sugar, and fat (usually butter), eggs are a component of the essential ingredient quartet for baking—and with good reason. Because they contain fat, protein, and moisture, among many other compounds and nutrients, eggs contribute to recipes in a great variety of ways. They are responsible for many acts of "magic" in the pastry kitchen that depend on the chemical reactions they are capable of achieving.

Eggs are graded depending on the thickness of their shells and egg whites. AA are the best, while B are the worst. Most eggs available in the market are A (middle grade). You can find more about egg sizes, storage info, and other specifications in Chapter 2.

When using them for baking, make sure you use fresh eggs that—unless otherwise specified in a recipe—are brought to room temperature beforehand.

## How Can You Tell If an Egg Is Fresh?

To check an egg's freshness, place it in a bowl or glass of cold water. (The water level should be at least twice the height of the egg.) If the egg is fresh, it will sink to the bottom of the bowl and probably lie on its side. A slightly older egg (about 1 week) will lie on the bottom but bob slightly. If the egg balances on its smallest tip, with the large tip reaching for the top, it's probably close to 3 weeks old. If the egg floats at the surface, it's *really* old—the egg floats because of a buildup of sulphur inside the shell. So discard it!

# Egg Functions

Whether you're baking cakes; making custards; or whipping up meringues, mousses, soufflés, or dessert sauces, recipes rely on eggs in many different ways. The following are some different functions of eggs in baking:

**Structure:** Egg protein coagulates to give structure to baked products, especially when there's low or no gluten in the recipe.

**Thickening:** Like the structure, this is given by the coagulation of the egg proteins when they are heated or in the presence of acid. Thickening is important when you're preparing custards, curds, sauces, and other products.

**Emulsification:** By having natural emulsifiers, egg yolks help produce smooth batters that combine fats and liquids that otherwise wouldn't mix. This helps give the final product the right structure and volume.

**Leavening:** As eggs are beaten or whipped, they incorporate air (such as in meringue). When a batter or mixture made with beaten eggs is baked, the trapped air expands and increases the volume of the baked good.

**Shortening:** The fat in egg yolks acts as shortening, because it shortens the gluten strands, tenderizing baked products.

**Moisture:** Eggs are mostly water, so they provide moisture to a product that would otherwise come out dry.

**Flavor:** With their natural high-glutamate content, egg yolks are rich in umami, or the fifth taste; this has been defined as the "pleasant savory taste" that expands and rounds out flavors.

**Color:** Egg yolks impart a golden hue to doughs, batters, and crusts.

**Shine:** By brushing breads and pastries with an egg wash (1 egg and 2 tablespoons water mixed together with a fork) before baking, the final product develops an attractive, shiny finish.

*chapter 7*

# Meringues

Meringues are thick, white foams made basically of whipped egg whites and sugar. They have a reputation of being technical and complicated, but meringues have been made since the early 1600s, when no electricity and obviously no standing mixers were available. In fact, Queen Marie Antoinette was said to be such a fan that she made them herself!

Nowadays, with either a handheld mixer or a standing mixer (with a whisk attachment, for more air incorporation), meringues just take a couple of minutes to whip up, requiring neither a lot of mixing nor a royal title to achieve them. Just stick to the rules and follow the techniques in this chapter, and you'll be surprised at how well you can make them. You can then use them to bake meringue cookies or shells, add volume to cakes, top pies, or make frostings.

# How to Make Meringue

A stiff foam of beaten egg whites and sugar, meringue is a versatile and essential building block in the pastry kitchen. Depending on how it's made, baked, and shaped, it can be a crust, a topping, a buttercream, and even the base for cakes and cookies. And because meringues are typically flourless, it's always good to keep them in mind when you want to bake gluten free. Two types of meringue are most commonly used:

**French meringue,** or **"common" meringue,** is made from egg whites at room temperature. The sugar is added once the egg whites are foamy or forming peaks. It's the easiest one to make.

**Swiss meringue** is made from egg whites and sugar that are warmed over a hot water bath until the sugar dissolves and the mixture is warm to the touch. The warming gives the meringue more volume and stability.

The third, less common type is **Italian meringue.** Although it is the most stable of the three, it is also the trickiest to make, as it is done by beating a hot sugar syrup into egg whites. Because most recipes use French or Swiss, I will focus on those two here.

## How to Make French Meringue

Don't worry, the vinegar will not affect the taste of your meringue!

It's best to use room-temperature eggs.

Be sure you don't have a single speck of egg yolk in your whites!

**Clean your equipment.** Even the tiniest speck of dust, fat residue, or water can prevent the egg whites from forming meringue, so it's important to make sure your equipment is spotless before you start. The best way is to wipe your mixing bowl and whisk attachment with a paper towel moistened with white vinegar.

**Foam the whites.** Place the egg whites in the mixer bowl and whisk them at medium speed until they look like sea foam. It should take about 5 minutes if the egg whites are at room temperature (a little longer if they are cool).

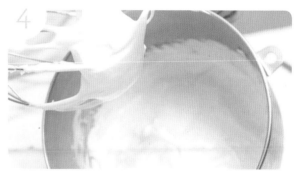

**Add the sugar.** Gradually add the sugar, 1 tablespoon at a time, waiting 30 seconds in between additions. Don't rush it! The success of the meringue depends on the slow addition of the sugar, as egg whites can only hold a limited amount of sugar without losing some volume. Once all of the sugar has been added, beat until soft peaks form.

**Increase the speed.** Turn the mixer to high and whisk the egg whites at high speed until the meringue is glossy, shiny, and stiff (yes, this is the time to increase velocity, as the structure has started developing already). Once you reach this point, turn the mixer off immediately!

## Go Slow!

For the most stable meringue, start beating the egg whites slowly, gradually increasing the speed. However, don't decrease the speed once you've increased it, as the volume might decrease as well. When you need to stop the mixer to test for consistency (soft or stiff peaks and so on), turn off the machine quickly, check it, and bring it up to speed as fast as possible.

## Don't Overbeat

Many meringues fail because they are overbeaten. The whole structure of the meringue changes once too much air is incorporated into it. Overbeating may cause the meringue to look dry and curdled, to lose volume, and to be difficult to fold into other ingredients. So the minute you see it is at the shiny and stiff stage, turn off the mixer!

# How to Make Swiss Meringue

**Clean your equipment.** Just like with French meringue, it's important to make sure your equipment is spotless before you start. Wipe your mixing bowls, whisk attachment, and wire whisk with a paper towel moistened with white vinegar.

You can also use the bowl of the standing mixer here.

**Prepare a bath.** Unlike French meringue, here the eggs and sugar are heated over a hot water bath to create a syrup. The water bath gently heats the mixture to help the sugar dissolve, but it won't coagulate the proteins of the egg whites (in other words, cook them). Set a saucepan filled $1/3$ with water on the stove and bring to a boil. Place the egg whites and sugar in a heat-proof mixing bowl and set it on top of the saucepan.

You can use the whisk attachment here instead of a whisk.

**Make the syrup.** Beat the egg white mixture by hand with a whisk until the mixture is a warm 120°F (50°C) and the sugar is completely dissolved. Remember, you're making a syrup here, not whipping the egg whites into peaks.

## Sugar Test

To test if the sugar has been completely dissolved, rub a little bit of the mixture between your thumb and first finger (make sure your hands are clean!). If you still feel sugar granules, it's not ready—keep mixing over the water bath. The mixture will be very hot to the touch, but should not burn.

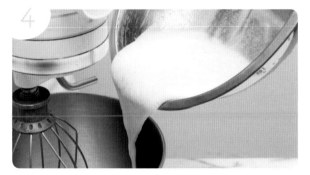

**Whip.** Transfer the egg white–sugar syrup mixture to the bowl of your mixer and whip at high speed until stiff peaks form and the meringue is completely cool. Because the sugar was previously dissolved into the egg whites and the mixture is already warm, there's no need to foam the egg whites at low speed first.

## When Is It Done?

To test whether your egg whites are the stiff-peak stage, turn the machine off, take out the whisk, and turn it upside down. The meringue peaks should hold, pointing straight up, or just collapse at the very tip.

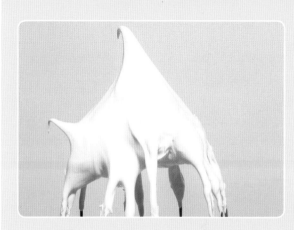

## Stages of Meringue

When reading recipes that call for beaten egg whites, the terms *foamy, soft peaks,* and *stiff peaks* are used to describe the stages of the egg white structure during beating. It's important to learn how to recognize and differentiate these stages, as they indicate when they are ready for you to add the sugar, beat faster, or stop beating to obtain the perfect, stiff, and glossy meringue.

**Foamy:** During the beginning of the whisking process, whites appear opaque and frothy, with larger and fragile bubbles that look like sea foam.

**Soft peaks:** With continued beating, the whites form peaks that drop gently when the whisk attachment is lifted. They have a less fluid consistency, and the whisk creates tracks while beating.

**Stiff peaks:** After even more beating, the egg whites resemble shaving cream and form glossy, firm peaks that hold their shape, even when the bowl is tilted. At this point, the meringue is ready; it should not be beaten anymore, or it may start losing volume.

# Pointers for Meringue Success

- As opposed to most baked goods, meringues whip better when made with older egg whites.

- When separating the eggs, do so while they are cold, and then store the separated whites uncovered in the refrigerator overnight.

- To separate eggs, it's recommended you use 2 small bowls and 1 large bowl. Catch the separated egg white in one small bowl and the yolk in the other small bowl. Once you make sure there's no yolk in the white, transfer it to the large bowl, where all the whites will be collected. This way, if there's some yolk in one white, you can reserve it for another use, but you don't spoil the whole batch of egg whites for the meringue.

- Start with egg whites at room temperature. Bring them out of the refrigerator about 1 hour before making meringue, if you are making French meringue.

- Wipe off the bowl and whisk attachment with a paper towel moistened with white vinegar, as vinegar dissolves any fat residue.

- Avoid any fat (including traces of egg yolk) from entering in contact with egg whites, as fats prevent egg whites from foaming properly.

- Add the sugar 1 tablespoon at a time and wait 30 seconds in between additions—too much sugar can sink the meringue.

- Mild acids, such as vinegar, cream of tartar, or lemon juice, give the meringue more volume and stability. Use 1 teaspoon white vinegar or lemon juice or $1/4$ teaspoon cream of tartar for every 4 egg whites.

- For best results, beat egg whites in a stainless-steel or a copper bowl. Glass can be used as well, but plastic should be avoided, as it often harbors traces of grease or fat, which inhibits the formation of the meringue.

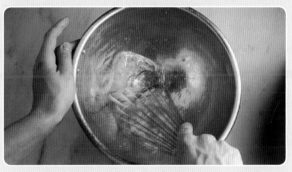

- Don't whip egg whites beyond the stiff peaks stage; otherwise, they may curdle and deflate.

- Keep meringues away from liquids and avoid making meringues in humid environments or rainy days, as sugar is hygroscopic (has a tendency to absorb water), and too much liquid inhibits the proper formation of the meringue.

- Meringues are baked on very low heat for a prolonged time. Egg proteins coagulate at a low temperature but can burn easily, so you need to develop more dehydration than actual cooking.

# How to Make Meringue Cookies

Made by following the French meringue technique, shaped into individual portions, and baked at very low temperatures, these sweet, creamy meringue clouds dry out and develop a crispy crust with a slightly chewy interior that delicately melts in your mouth. Here's how you make them.

If you're using food coloring, be sure to only add a drop or two—any more will break down your meringue.

**Make the meringue.** A basic French meringue (sugar and egg whites) is the usual base for these cookies.

**Add salt, acid, and color (if using).** Before you do the final whisk to bring the meringue to the glossy stage, salt, vinegar (or lemon juice), and vanilla (or other flavorings) are added. The salt and acid stabilize the meringue structure. For colored meringues, food coloring is added at this point as well.

**Add in any flavorings.** Once the meringue is brought to the glossy stage, flavorings—such as ½ cup mini chocolate chips, ½ cup sliced almonds or chopped hazelnuts, or 1 teaspoon citrus zest—can be folded in.

**Prep the sheets.** Because meringues are sticky, it's easy to have the parchment paper start lifting and shifting around each time you pipe a cookie. To keep the parchment sheet stable, place a small dot of the meringue on each corner of the baking sheet to help "glue" the parchment paper in place.

**Pipe the meringues.** Form the meringues and place them on the prepared baking sheet, making sure to leave space in between, because meringues expand in the oven as the air in them heats up.

## Shaping Meringues

Meringues can be shaped with a piping bag, 2 spoons, an ice cream scoop, or a $\frac{1}{4}$-cup dry measuring cup with a spoon to scrape out the meringue, depending on your desired shape and size. Usually, two large spoons—one used for scooping out the meringue and the other for scraping it out onto the line baking sheet—do a great job.

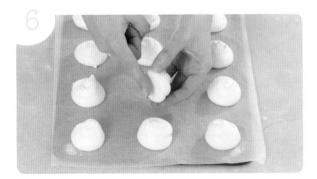

**Bake immediately.** Meringues must be baked as soon as they are shaped, as they are not stable enough to hold their shape at room temperature; if you shape them and don't put them straight into the oven, they will flatten. The heat of the oven coagulates the egg proteins, stabilizing the structure and trapping the air completely. To test for doneness, lift one meringue off the parchment—if it comes away easily, it's ready; if not, continue baking and check back a couple minutes later.

**Cool the meringues in the oven.** This is a very different way of cooling baked goods that's rarely applied to any other products. When meringues are done baking, you turn the oven off but leave the cookies in the oven to cool completely. This takes a couple hours or, even better, overnight. Keeping meringues in the oven until they cool will help with the drying process and ensure crispy meringues.

# Meringues

Eating a meringue is like biting into a crispy cloud. Besides being fat free and gluten free, they are quite versatile and go well with everything from chocolate, to nuts, to whipped cream, to fruit, to coffee! Meringue cookies also have a long shelf life, so they are great to always keep around.

## INGREDIENTS

4 large egg whites (about 4 oz./120 g), at room temperature

1 cup (7 oz./210 g) granulated sugar

Pinch salt

1 tsp. vinegar or lemon juice

½ tsp. pure vanilla extract

½ cup (3 oz./90 g) mini chocolate chips and/or sliced or chopped nuts (optional)

1 tsp. zest of any citrus fruit (optional)

Food coloring (optional)

## EQUIPMENT

2 rimmed baking sheets

Parchment paper

Standing mixer fitted with whisk attachment

Paper towel moistened with white vinegar

Silicone spatula

Piping bag, ¼ cup dry measuring cup, ice cream scoop, or 2 spoons

1. Preheat the oven to 250°F (150°C). Line the baking sheets with parchment paper. Set aside. Clean the standing mixer bowl and whisk attachment with a paper towel moistened with white vinegar.

2. Place egg whites in the bowl and whisk on medium speed until foamy, about 2 minutes.

3. Increase the speed to high and beat until stiff peaks form. The meringue peaks should hold, pointing straight up, or just collapse at the very tip when the whisk is turned upside down.

4. With the mixer still running, add sugar 1 tablespoon at a time, waiting 30 seconds in between additions. Once sugar is added, whisk for 6 more minutes or until meringue is glossy and stiff. Turn the mixer off and scrape the sides of the bowl with a silicone spatula.

5. Add salt, vinegar, and vanilla extract at once. Turn the mixer to medium speed and whisk until glossy and combined, about 2 minutes. At this point, add mini chocolate chips, sliced or chopped nuts, citrus zest, or any food coloring (if using).

6. Place meringue in a piping bag and pipe them onto the prepared baking sheets (see "How to Make Meringue Cookies"), spacing 1 inch (2.5 cm) apart. Alternately, use two spoons to scoop up a tablespoon of meringue and scrape them into mounds on the baking sheet.

7. Place the sheets in the oven and reduce the oven temperature to 200°F (93°C). Bake for 1 to 1 hour 30 minutes (time will depend on size). To test for doneness, lift one meringue off the parchment. If it comes away easily, it's ready; if not, continue baking. Check them every few minutes.

## Baking Meringues

Meringues must be baked as soon as they are shaped, as they are not stable enough to hold their shape at room temperature. Once they are baked, keeping them in the oven until they cool will help with the drying process and ensure crispy meringues.

8. When meringues are done, turn the oven off, leaving the sheets in the oven to cool completely.

9. Serve or store in an airtight container for 2 weeks. Meringues can also be frozen for up to 2 months.

**Variations:** Meringues are incredibly versatile—just about any dry ingredient can be added! For *mocha meringues,* add 2 teaspoons instant coffee or espresso powder and 1 tablespoon cocoa powder. For *chocolate chip meringues,* add 1 cup mini chocolate chips. For *chocolate meringues,* add $1/4$ cup cocoa. For *nut meringues,* add 1 cup finely chopped nuts (any kind). For *coconut meringues,* add $1/2$ cup toasted coconut. For *fruit meringues,* add $1/2$ cup finely diced candied or dried fruit. For *lemon meringues,* exchange the vanilla extract for lemon extract, and add 1 teaspoon lemon zest.

# French Macarons

Makes **20** macarons

These jewel-looking almond and meringue cookie sandwiches that adorn the windows of French bakeries are a beautiful and delicious treat. Despite their appearance and status, though, they are not hard to make.

## INGREDIENTS

½ cup plus 1 TB. (2 oz./60 g) blanched almond flour

1 cup (4 oz./125 g) confectioner's sugar

Pinch salt

2 (2 oz./60 g) egg whites, at room temperature

5½ tsp. (²⁄₃ oz./25 g) granulated sugar

2 drops food coloring (optional)

1 batch Swiss Meringue Buttercream or Chocolate Ganache (see recipes in Chapter 12)

## EQUIPMENT

2 rimmed baking sheets

Parchment paper

Standing mixer fitted with whisk attachment

Paper towel moistened with white vinegar

Sieve

Medium mixing bowl

Silicone spatula

Piping bag fitted with a ½-in. (1.25-cm) diameter plain pastry tip

Medium offset spatula

Small spoon

Plastic wrap (optional)

**CHAPTER 7 | MERINGUES**

1. Line the rimmed baking sheets with parchment paper. Set aside. Clean the bowl and whisk attachment of the standing mixer with a paper towel moistened with white vinegar.

4. Turn off the mixer and scrape down the sides of the bowl with a silicone spatula. Fold almond flour mixture into whipped egg whites with a silicone spatula.

## Sizing the Macarons

If you want to make sure you get perfectly sized macarons, make a piping guide. Draw 1-inch (2.5-cm) circles on the parchment, leaving about 2 inches (5 cm) between each circle. Make sure you place the marked side of the parchment down when lining the baking sheets so the meringues don't touch the ink.

## Testing the Batter

To test whether the batter has been sufficiently folded, place 1 teaspoon batter on a piece of parchment paper. If after 30 seconds it still holds a point on the top, the meringue still needs to be folded in further. You want to ensure the macarons have flat tops but don't spread too much.

2. With a sieve, sift together almond flour, confectioner's sugar, and salt into a medium bowl. Set aside.

3. Place egg whites in the bowl of the standing mixer and whip on medium speed until foamy, about 5 minutes. Increase the speed to high and beat until soft peaks form. Add granulated sugar 1 tablespoon at a time, waiting 30 seconds in between additions, and keep whipping until stiff, glossy peaks are formed. Add food coloring (if using).

5. Transfer batter to a piping bag. Lift a corner of the parchment paper and place a dot of meringue to "glue" the paper onto the pan. Repeat with the other three corners.

6. Pipe shallow (about $1/8$ inch/3 mm thick), 1-inch (2.5-cm) rounds of batter onto the prepared baking sheets, leaving 1 to 2 inches (2.5 to 5 cm) in between mounds. When the entire sheet is filled, tap the bottom of the pan on the countertop to release any trapped air in cookies.

## Piping Variations

There are two ways you can pipe the batter onto the sheets. Each way is acceptable; it's just a matter of preference:

Hold the bag straight up, so the tip is directly above the middle of the circle.

Hold the bag at an angle, with the tip at the edge of the circle.

7.  Evenly space two oven racks toward the center of the oven and preheat the oven to 350°F (180°C). Let macarons sit at room temperature until tops develop a thin film that doesn't stick to your finger when they're tapped, 20 to 30 minutes.

8.  Place macarons in the oven and lower the temperature to 300°F (150°C). Bake for 8 minutes. Rotate the baking sheets from top to bottom and back to front, and bake for 5 more minutes. Macarons are ready when they come freely off the parchment paper when lifted with an offset spatula. Remove from the oven immediately and let cool completely, about 5 minutes.

9.  To assemble macarons, use a small spoon to place pea-size amounts of Swiss Meringue Buttercream on flat side of half the cookies. Sandwich them with other half, squeezing them together gently. Leave at room temperature to set for a couple of hours or double-wrap in plastic wrap and freeze.

**Variations:** For *chocolate macarons*, add 2 tablespoons unsweetened cacao powder when sifting confectioner's sugar and almond flour in step 2. For *vanilla macarons*, add the seeds of 1 vanilla bean while folding dry ingredients into meringue in step 4. For *citrus macarons*, add zest of 1 citrus fruit while folding dry ingredients into meringue in step 4.

## Filling Ideas

You can fill your macarons with just about anything you like! Here are some ideas:

- Seedless jam
- Dulce de leche
- Peanut butter or any nut butter
- Swiss buttercream mixed with finely chopped nuts
- Lemon curd

If you're using a filling that has more liquid (like jams or curds), you should eat the cookies that day, as the liquid in the filling will start to break down the cookie.

# How to Make Meringue-Based Cakes

Due to meringue's capacity to trap air, meringue-based cakes don't require chemical leaveners or yeast to achieve a springy texture. Most European cakes, tortes, and traditional rolled cakes (such as jelly rolls) are often made with a meringue foundation. Of course, every cake recipe is a bit different, depending on ingredients, but here are the basic methods for making an airy, delicious meringue-based cake.

**Make the meringue.** It all starts with a good meringue and making sure it is at the right consistency—either stiff or soft peaks, depending on the recipe (see "How to Make French Meringue" in this chapter).

**Fold in the ingredients.** Folding is an integral part of a meringue-based cake. You need to incorporate your other ingredients (called the *base*) with the meringue. Whether the ingredients are wet or dry, the folding process is the same for both: add a quarter of the prepared meringue into the batter or dry ingredient mixture and stir gently to combine. This is called *lightening* the batter to make it thinner and easier to fold into the meringue.

## Folding Meringue

Be sure to do the folding gently—the point is to keep as much air in the meringue as possible! Beating the mixture will just break it down, leaving you with a flat cake.

*chapter 8*

# Custards and Mousses

*Custards* are made of a liquid mixture thickened or set by the coagulation of egg protein (which happens when that protein is heated). They can be sweet or savory, soft and pourable, or so thick they can be neatly sliced.

There are two basic kinds of custard:

1. **Stirred (or stovetop) custard** is stirred as it cooks and remains pourable when done. Crème anglaise and pastry cream are typical—and perhaps the most commonly used—examples of stirred custards in baking.

2. **Baked custard** is a liquid mixture including eggs that are prepared and baked in a baking pan or crust until firmly set. Lemon bars, flan, pecan pie, pumpkin pie, and even cheesecake are examples of baked custards.

A *mousse* is a soft and creamy preparation made light and fluffy by the addition of beaten eggs, egg whites, whipped cream, or a combination of all three. There is an enormous variety of mousses—some are made with very few ingredients, while others are complex preparations.

# How to Make Stovetop Custard

By stirring and cooking eggs, milk (or cream or half and half), and sugar until the eggs coagulate and thicken, you can make a delicious, velvety, and pourable custard. Some examples of stovetop custards are crème anglaise and pastry cream. The following guide you through how to make a great stovetop custard.

**Beat the egg yolks and sugar.** The egg yolks help to thicken the custard, so they are mixed with the sugar until light and thick. Some custards also call for another thickener, such as cornstarch, which you sift in after mixing the egg yolks and sugar.

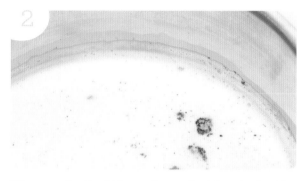

**Warm up the liquid ingredients.** Scalding the liquid ingredients shortens the final cooking time of the custard. To scald them, you bring them just below simmering. If you are infusing the liquid with a flavoring agent (such as vanilla beans or cinnamon sticks), you can add them here—just remember to strain them out.

**Temper the egg mixture.** Pouring the scalded liquid into the egg yolk mixture very gradually raises the temperature of the eggs steadily to prevent them from curdling, which would happen if you added all the hot liquid at once.

**Cook and thicken the egg mixture.** The egg mixture is now stirred constantly over a water bath set over medium-high heat to thicken further, so the custard doesn't turn out thin.

**Strain and cool.** Straining the custard through a sieve into a bowl set in an ice bath gives it a velvety texture and removes any small pieces of curdled egg that may have formed. The ice bath, which is simply a larger bowl filled with ice, speeds up the cooling process to stop any further cooking.

**Store.** Once all of the custard is in the bowl, press a piece of plastic wrap directly against the surface to prevent a skin from forming. Once completely cool, custard can be covered and stored in the refrigerator for up to 2 days.

## When Is the Custard Done?

## Pastry Cream

The custard mixture is ready when it's thick enough to coat the back of a spoon instead of running off it and has a temperature between 160°F and 185°F (71°C to 85°C).

Pastry cream should come to a boil (large bubbles form), as the thickening agent (starch) it contains stabilizes the eggs and prevents them from curdling. The thickening agent also needs to cook completely to avoid imparting a raw, starchy taste to the cream.

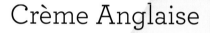

# Crème Anglaise

Also known as vanilla custard sauce, crème anglaise is made with sweetened milk slightly thickened with egg yolks. It's a great accompaniment to cakes and pastries, and if churned and frozen, can be turned into ice cream. It's very easy to make, but you must watch the temperatures carefully throughout the process to keep it from curdling.

## INGREDIENTS

½ vanilla bean, halved lengthwise
1½ cups (12 oz./360 g) whole milk
5 large egg yolks
¼ cup (1¾ oz./50 g) granulated sugar

## EQUIPMENT

Paring knife
Medium saucepan
Ice bath (large mixing bowl filled with
 ice)
Standing mixer fitted with whisk
 attachment
Silicone spatula

Instant-read thermometer
Sieve
Medium mixing bowl
Plastic wrap (optional)

1. With a paring knife, halve vanilla bean and scrape vanilla seeds from pod. Place vanilla seeds, vanilla pod, and whole milk in a medium saucepan and heat over medium heat until scalded (see the sidebar). Remove from heat, cover, and steep for 20 minutes. Uncover, and scald mixture over medium heat again. While mixture is steeping, prepare an ice bath.

2. Combine egg yolks and sugar in the bowl of a standing mixer and beat on medium speed until light and thick. With the mixer running at low speed, very gradually pour in scalded milk.

3. Fill the saucepan $1/3$ full of water and bring to a simmer over medium-high heat. Place the bowl with egg mixture over the water bath and stir constantly with a silicone spatula until it thickens. It should register 175°F to 180°F (about 80°C) on an instant-read thermometer and be thick enough to coat the back of a spoon.

4. Immediately remove from heat and pour mixture through a sieve into a medium bowl set in the ice bath. Let mixture cool in the ice bath. Serve once cool, or press a piece of plastic wrap directly against the surface to prevent a skin from forming on the sauce and store airtight in the refrigerator for up to 2 days.

## Scalding

The milk is scalded when a ring of tiny bubbles forms all around the edge where the milk touches the wall of the saucepan.

**Variations:** It's worth it to splurge on the vanilla bean, but if you prefer, you could skip the first part of step 1, go straight to scalding the milk, and just add 1 teaspoon pure vanilla extract in step 4. For *chocolate crème anglaise,* add 4 ounces (120 g) chopped chocolate in step 4 before the mixture cools (so the heat melts the chocolate into the sauce). For *coffee crème anglaise,* add 1 tablespoon instant coffee at the beginning of step 4.

# Pastry Cream

Makes a bit more than **2 cups** pastry cream

Although the ingredient list for pastry cream is longer than the one for crème anglaise, pastry cream is easier to master, as it has less chance of curdling. It contains a starch (cornstarch, all-purpose flour, or tapioca starch) that thickens and stabilizes the eggs. Pastry cream can be used as a delicious filling or topping for cakes, tarts, trifles, meringues, and pastries.

## INGREDIENTS

1 vanilla bean, halved lengthwise
½ cup (3½ oz./100 g) granulated sugar
2 cups (16 oz./480 g) half and half
3 large egg yolks
1 large egg
3 TB. cornstarch or tapioca starch
½ stick (2 oz./60 g) cold, unsalted butter, cut into 4 pieces

## EQUIPMENT

Paring knife
Medium saucepan
Standing mixer fitted with whisk attachment
Silicone spatula
Whisk

Sieve
Medium mixing bowl
Ice bath (large mixing bowl filled with ice)
Plastic wrap (optional)

1. With a paring knife, halve vanilla bean and scrape seeds from pod. Place vanilla seeds and pod, 6 tablespoons sugar, and half and half in a medium saucepan and heat over medium heat until scalded (see the Crème Anglaise sidebar). Remove from heat, cover, and steep for 20 minutes. Uncover and bring mixture to a full simmer over medium heat; the bubbles will form slowly and break apart just below the surface.

2. Combine egg yolks, egg, and remaining 2 tablespoons sugar in the bowl of a standing mixer and beat on medium speed until light and thick, about 3 minutes. Add cornstarch and beat until combined and mixture is thick and pale yellow.

3. With the mixer running at low speed, very gradually pour scalded milk mixture into egg yolk mixture and mix until just combined. Scrape down the bowl with a silicone spatula, and return mixture to the saucepan. Return to a simmer over medium heat, whisking constantly, until a few bubbles burst on the surface and mixture is thickened. Remove from heat.

4. Add butter and stir until melted. Pour mixture through a sieve into a medium bowl set in an ice bath. Let mixture cool. Serve immediately, or press a piece of plastic wrap directly against the surface to prevent a skin from forming on sauce and store in the refrigerator for up to 2 days.

## While Your Mixture Is Steeping

Prepare the ice bath and set it aside.

**Variations:** For *fruit cream,* after chilling the pastry, fold in chopped fruit (that has been drained) or a bit of your favorite flavored jam. For *chocolate cream,* add a couple ounces bittersweet or semisweet chocolate when you add the vanilla. For *liqueur cream,* add a tablespoon of flavored liqueur, such as Chambourd, Frangelico, or Kahlua. For a richer, fluffier cream, fold in some whipped heavy cream after the pastry cream has cooled.

## Other Uses for Pastry Cream

Pastry cream is incredibly versatile! Try using it as a filling for a layer cake; pipe it into eclairs, donuts or danishes; or just spoon some into a bowl and top with fresh cut fruit.

# How to Make Baked Custard

With the same basic ingredients as stovetop custards (milk, sugar, and eggs), plus some additional ingredients, baked custards are not stirred but baked until they set and become firm and sliceable. Examples of baked custard are pie fillings, quiche, flan, pots de crème, bread pudding, and cheesecake. Here are the steps to make a baked custard.

**Beat eggs and sugar.** Whisk eggs and sugar (and salt, if using) in a mixing bowl with a handheld whisk or at low speed with a standing mixer. Mix until thoroughly blended, but don't whip; you aren't looking for volume here, just incorporating ingredients.

Watch the milk carefully—if it comes to a full boil, it may curdle.

**Scald the liquids.** Scald until a ring of tiny bubbles forms all around the edge, where the milk touches the wall of the saucepan. It is not a full, rolling boil—you bring it to the point just below boiling. Scalding your liquids allows the custard to bake faster.

## Infusions

At this point you can "infuse" the scalded liquid—for instance, with a vanilla bean, fresh ginger, mint, cinnamon sticks, and so on. Just place the ingredient in the milk before scalding; once scalded, remove it from the heat, cover, and let steep for 20 minutes. Uncover the pan and scald the milk again before tossing out the infused item (unless it's ground) and pouring it into the egg mixture.

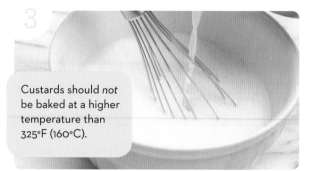

Custards should *not* be baked at a higher temperature than 325°F (160°C).

**Temper the egg mixture.** Beat the hot liquid into the egg and sugar mixture very slowly, stirring constantly with a silicone spatula or a handheld whisk. This tempers the eggs (raises the temperature of the eggs gradually) and helps prevent curdling.

**Skim.** Remove the mixture from heat immediately and use a spoon or spatula to skim off the foam on the surface of the liquid. This gives the custard a more attractive, completely smooth finish.

**Strain.** Pour the mixture through a sieve into a heat-proof, preferably spouted vessel (a large liquid measuring cup is ideal). Straining the custard gives it a velvety texture and removes any small pieces of curdled egg that may have formed.

**Pour.** Baked custards benefit from a water bath, which reduces the loss of moisture in the product and maintains a milder, steady heating temperature. If a water bath is needed, place your custard dish in a pan with sides at least 1½ to 2 inches (3.75 to 5 cm) high and then pour your custard mixture into the dish.

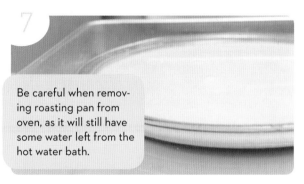

Be careful when removing roasting pan from oven, as it will still have some water left from the hot water bath.

**Make the bath.** Pour enough hot water into the large pan to reach a bit above halfway up the baking dish with the custard. This prevents cheesecakes and other custards from ending up with brown edges, uneven tops, and cracks. Although it's not strictly necessary, the end result is worth the extra effort of the water bath.

Baked custards can be stored, covered, in the refrigerator for up to 5 days.

## When Is It Done?

Because baked custards are so moist, it can be hard to tell when they're done. To test for doneness, insert the tip of a small paring knife about 1 or 2 inches (2.5 or 5 cm) from the center. It should come out clean. If the center is not set, it will set as it cools. Baked custards should not exceed an internal temperature of 185°F (85°C), as the eggs curdle beyond that point and the custards become watery; however, they are usually ready at 160°F (71°C), so use an instant-read thermometer if in doubt!

# New York Cheesecake

Makes **1** 9-in. (23-cm) cheesecake

It may be surprising to find cheesecakes in a custard section. But technically, traditional cheesecakes are a type of baked custard, as they are a liquid mixture of milk, sugar, eggs, cream cheese, and other ingredients that becomes firm when the eggs coagulate. This classic New York cheesecake is delicious by itself or can be a blank canvas for delicious toppings.

## INGREDIENTS

### Crust:

4½ TB. (2 oz./60 g) unsalted butter, melted
8 whole (4 oz./120 g) graham crackers
1 TB. granulated sugar
¼ tsp. ground cinnamon (optional)

### Filling:

5 (8-oz.) pkg. cream cheese
1½ cups sugar
¼ cup sour cream
Juice of ½ lemon (2 tsp.)
1 TB. pure vanilla extract
5 large eggs
2 large egg yolks

## EQUIPMENT

Sharp knife
Cutting board
Pastry brush
9-in. (23-cm) round springform pan
Food processor
Medium mixing bowl
Fork
Cooling rack

Standing mixer fitted with paddle attachment
Silicone spatula
Medium saucepan or kettle
Aluminum foil
Large baking pan
Instant-read thermometer
Plastic wrap

1. Preheat the oven to 325°F (170°C). With a sharp knife, cut cream cheese roughly into 1-inch (2.5-cm) cubes on a cutting board and set aside to soften. Using a pastry brush, brush the bottom and sides of a springform pan with $\frac{1}{2}$ tablespoon melted butter. Set aside.

2. To make the crust, place graham crackers in a food processor and pulse until they form fine crumbs. In a medium bowl, place graham cracker crumbs, remaining 4 tablespoons melted butter, sugar, and cinnamon (if using) and toss with a fork until combined.

## Mixing the Cream Cheese

Frequent scraping of the bowl during mixing is needed to ensure the cream cheese is completely creamed and incorporated and not left in small pieces that would affect the texture of the cheesecake.

## No Food Processor?

If you don't have a food processor, you can put the graham crackers in a zipper-lock plastic bag and use a rolling pin to crush them.

3. Pour crumbs into the springform pan and press evenly into the bottom. Place in the oven and bake until crust browns slightly, 12 to 14 minutes. Remove from the oven and cool on a cooling rack while you prepare the filling.

4. In the bowl of a standing mixer, beat cream cheese on medium-low speed until it softens. Scrape the paddle and the bowl with a silicone spatula. Add sugar, sour cream, lemon juice, and vanilla extract and mix on medium-low speed until smooth. Add eggs and egg yolks 1 at a time and beat on low speed until each ingredient is incorporated, scraping down the bowl between additions with the spatula.

5. Bring about 4 cups water to a boil in a medium saucepan. While waiting for it to boil, wrap the outside of the springform pan tightly with 3 sheets of aluminum foil in a crisscross pattern (see "Papers, Mats, and Boards" in Chapter 1). Pour cheesecake batter into the prepared pan and place in a larger baking pan. Place the pan into the oven, and add enough hot water to reach halfway up the wrapped springform pan.

6. Bake until edge is light golden brown, top is light gold, center barely jiggles, and an instant-read thermometer registers 160°F (70°C), about 50 minutes to 1 hour 10 minutes. Remove cheesecake from the water bath, remove the foil on the outside, transfer to a cooling rack, and let cool undisturbed for 2 hours.

7. Leaving cheesecake in the pan, cover loosely with plastic wrap and refrigerate until completely cold before serving, at least 6 hours to overnight. The wrapped cheesecake can be refrigerated for up to 1 week or frozen for up to 1 month.

8. To serve, release and remove the side of the springform, leaving cheesecake on the bottom of the pan, and place on a cake plate.

## Slicing Cheesecake

The best way to slice cheesecake is with a sharp straight-edge knife (not a serrated one) dipped in hot water and wiped off between slices.

## Cheesecake Toppings

Cheesecake can be eaten by itself or with delicious toppings. Some excellent options are the following:

- Fruit coulis: See the recipe in Chapter 12.

- Fresh berries macerated in sugar and lime juice (zest could be included) or balsamic vinegar: Place 1 pound (500 g) fruit (either fresh or frozen and thawed) in a large bowl. Add 3 tablespoons ($1^1/_2$ oz./45 g) granulated sugar, and let sit for at least 30 minutes. Add in the juice of $^1/_2$ to 1 lime and zest (if using) or 1 to 2 teaspoons balsamic vinegar.

- Squiggles of chocolate ganache: Ganache can be drizzled most effectively onto a chilled cheesecake while the ganache is still warm; see the recipe in Chapter 12.

- Sour cream topping: Stir together 2 cups (1 lb./500 g) sour cream, $^1/_4$ cup ($1^3/_4$ oz./50 g) granulated sugar, and 1 teaspoon vanilla extract. Spread over the cooled (but not chilled) cheesecake, and return to the oven for 12 minutes or until glossy and set.

# Lemon Bars

Lemon bars are a type of sheet cookie, as they are baked in a pan and then sliced. But they are a baked custard as well—the tart, creamy topping thickens thanks to the coagulation of the eggs it contains. This is an easy, widely satisfying cookie with a soft, melt-in-your-mouth shortbread crust greatly complemented by the smooth, tangy, citrusy, gel-like topping.

## INGREDIENTS

**Crust:**

1½ sticks (6 oz./180 g) unsalted butter
2 cups (8½ oz./255 g) all-purpose flour
½ cup (3¾ oz./115 g) light brown sugar, firmly packed
Zest of 1 lemon
½ tsp. salt
¼ tsp. pure vanilla extract

**Topping:**

4 large eggs
1½ cups (10½ oz./315 g) granulated sugar
¾ cup fresh lemon juice (about 4 lemons)
⅓ cup (1⅓ oz./40 g) all-purpose flour
Confectioner's sugar

## EQUIPMENT

13×9×2-in. (33×23×5-cm) baking pan
Parchment paper
Knife or bench scraper
Food processor
Small offset spatula
Large mixing bowl
Whisk
Instant-read thermometer (optional)
Sharp knife
Cutting board
Sieve

1. Preheat the oven to 350°F (180°C). Line a baking pan with parchment paper, leaving an overhang (see "How to Make Biscotti" in Chapter 3). Set aside.

2. To make the crust, cut butter into ½-inch (1.5-cm) pieces with a knife. Place butter, all-purpose flour, light brown sugar, lemon zest, salt, and vanilla extract in a food processor and pulse until mixture begins to form small lumps.

3. Sprinkle mixture into the prepared baking pan and press evenly onto the bottom with your hands or an offset spatula. Bake crust until golden, about 20 minutes. While crust is baking, prepare topping.

4. In a large bowl, whisk together eggs and granulated sugar until well combined. Stir in lemon juice and all-purpose flour. After removing crust from the oven, reduce the oven temperature to 300°F (150°C).

5. Pour lemon mixture over hot crust and bake until set or an instant-read thermometer registers 160°F (70°C), about 30 minutes. Remove from the oven and cool completely in the pan, about 45 minutes.

6. When cool, run a sharp knife around the edges and use the overhanging parchment to carefully lift lemon bar block out of the pan. Place on a cutting board and cut into 24 bars.

7. Using a sieve, sift confectioner's sugar over lemon bars before serving. Lemon bars keep in the refrigerator, covered, for up to 3 days.

**Variations:** Add 1 teaspoon crushed culinary-grade lavender into the lemon mixture and/or replace the lemon juice with lime juice.

# Flan

Makes **1** 8-in. (20-cm) flan

Over the years, this creamy custard—brought from Europe to the New World—has become associated with Latin American cuisine and is the typical example of a sweetened, baked custard. This version, topped with a deep caramel sauce, will conquer your heart and tastebuds!

## INGREDIENTS

**Caramel:**

¾ cup sugar
¼ cup water

**Custard:**

2½ cups (20 oz./600 g) half and half
¾ cup sugar
5 large egg yolks
⅛ tsp. salt
1 tsp. pure vanilla extract

## EQUIPMENT

8-in. (20-cm) round baking pan
Large baking pan
Large kettle or small saucepan
Small saucepan
Medium saucepan
Silicone spatula
Large mixing bowl
Whisk

Sieve
Medium mixing bowl or 8-cup-capacity
   measuring cup
Cooling rack
Plastic wrap
Small paring knife
Rimmed serving platter

1. Preheat the oven to 325°F (160°C). Place a round baking pan in a large baking pan for a water bath. Bring a large kettle of water to a boil.

2. To make the caramel, in a small saucepan over medium-high heat, mix sugar and water, stirring to combine with a silicone spatula. Cook over medium heat, swirling the pan to caramelize evenly, until sugar dissolves and caramel is light amber, about 8 minutes—do not stir. Remove from heat and pour into the round baking pan. Gently tilt the pan to coat the bottom evenly.

## Flan Warning

It is very important *not* to stir the mixture once the sugar has dissolved—if you do, the sugar will start to crystalize again and you'll end up with grainy caramel.

3. To make the custard, in a medium saucepan, heat half and half with $1/4$ cup plus 2 tablespoons sugar over medium heat until mixture is just scalded, about 5 minutes—do not let it boil! Remove from heat.

4. In a large bowl, whisk together egg yolks, remaining $1/4$ cup plus 2 tablespoons sugar, and salt.

5. Slowly pour hot half-and-half mixture into egg yolk mixture, stirring constantly with the whisk to temper yolks.

6. Strain mixture through a fine sieve into a medium bowl. Stir in vanilla extract.

7. Pour mixture into the prepared pan with caramel. Make a hot-water bath by pouring enough boiling water from the kettle into the large baking pan to come halfway up the sides of the round baking pan.

8. Bake until flan is set around the edges but slightly jiggly in the center, 40 to 45 minutes. Remove flan from water bath and set on a cooling rack. Let flan cool for about 45 minutes.

9. While still in the baking pan, cover flan with plastic wrap and place in the refrigerator for at least 6 hours up to 3 days.

10. To unmold, dip a sharp paring knife into hot water, wipe it, and run it around edge of flan. Place a rimmed serving platter upside down over the top of the pan, invert, and gently lift the pan to remove flan.

# How to Make Mousse

Mousse comes from the French term for "foam" or "lather," achieved by folding in beaten egg whites and/or whipped cream into a base. These ingredients impart a creaminess and airiness, with an end result that's always soft, light, and fluffy. Mousses can be served as a dessert by themselves or used as fillings, frostings, or toppings. Because there are many varieties of mousse, it's impossible to give a "one size fits all" technique or definition; however, these steps give you a place to start.

Don't overmix! You want the meringue to be airy and fluffy.

**Prepare the base.** A base usually involves heating for melting, softening, or cooking, followed by cooling in an ice bath; however, some recipes call for using a still-warm base, which cooks the whipped egg whites and coagulates them, making the mousse more stable. Follow the specifications in your recipe, as the way a base is made varies a lot.

**Make and fold in meringue.** The meringue is what helps make the mousse stable. Make sure to add the sugar gradually to the eggs, as you want the meringue to stay light (see "How to Make Meringue" in Chapter 7). When ready, you simply fold it into the base mixture (see "How to Make Meringue-Based Cakes" in Chapter 7), and then transfer the meringue-base mixture to a large bowl.

## Uncooked Egg Whites

The egg whites in many mousse recipes are not cooked. If you are serving mousse to someone with a compromised immune system, such as a young child or an elder, be sure to use pasteurized egg whites.

# chapter 9

# Soufflés

Soufflés are probably the most intimidating dish in both the savory and sweet kitchens. People seem to panic at reading or even thinking of the word in a recipe. In spite of their reputation, though, soufflés are not such a scary dish to prepare. Plus, the satisfaction of bringing to the table a nicely risen warm puff of steamy egg whites laced with other flavorful ingredients is incomparable.

Because a soufflé falls once it starts cooling down, it is one of those great things in life you have to enjoy at the very moment. And once you do, you'll never forget them!

# How to Make Soufflé

From the French *souffler,* which means "to blow or puff," these inflated desserts are made by beating egg whites to a meringue and folding them into a base. Baking causes the soufflé to rise, as the air in the egg foam expands when heated. The eggs coagulate toward the end of the baking process, becoming firm. Soufflés are traditionally composed of three elements: a **base** (usually a fat and starch mixture; a liquid, such as milk; and, often, egg yolks), **flavoring agents** (that are usually added into the base—for example, chocolate, cheese, fruits, liquors, purées, and so on), and **egg whites** (usually whipped with sugar to add stability). The following shows you how to use these elements to make one.

Always place the soufflé dishes on a baking sheet, in case they overflow when baking.

Add any flavoring agents, such as vanilla, at this stage.

**Prepare the dishes.** Prepare the soufflé dish(es) by greasing them with butter and coating them with sugar (and flour or cocoa powder). The dusting is very important, because if the dish is only greased, the meringue won't have anything to adhere to while rising and may slide down the walls of the dish.

**Make the base.** A soufflé base is made by heating milk and flour or another starch to make a thick mixture. It's important to stir the milk constantly in order to prevent lumps from forming. The base is thickened when you can drag your spatula across the bottom of the pan and it leaves a distinct "path."

## Setting the Oven Racks

Soufflés rise significantly, so you need to make sure the oven racks are set far enough apart to accommodate for the rise. Also, don't bake a soufflé too close to the bottom of the oven, as it could burn more easily. Once you've arranged the racks, preheat the oven.

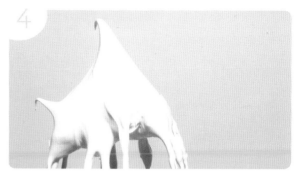

**Add the eggs and flavoring.** Once the base is made, other ingredients, such as eggs and chocolate, are added. It's important to make sure everything is well combined. (Most soufflé bases can be prepared up to this point, covered, and refrigerated for about 2 days.)

**Make the meringue.** Meringues are what give soufflés their airiness. Most soufflé recipes call for a sturdy French meringue that can hold up to having the base incorporated into it (see "How to Make Meringue" in Chapter 7). The meringue is beaten to stiff, shiny peaks.

**Fold in the meringue.** Folding in is the most delicate part of putting together a soufflé—you want to make sure the meringue is incorporated, but you don't want to mix it so much that you break down the meringue. Too much mixing will leave you with a flat soufflé. Fold the egg whites into the soufflé base as indicated in "How to Make Meringue-Based Cakes" in Chapter 7.

**Bake.** Carefully spoon the mixture into the prepared dish. The mixture should come up ½ inch (1 cm) below the rim of the dish. Bake immediately, as soufflés are not stable and will start losing volume right away.

## Save the Wreck!

Chances are, your first soufflé might not work out. But you can still serve it! If anything goes wrong with the soufflé, fill up the crater with cream, custard sauce, or ice cream; drizzle it with sauce all over; throw in some berries and a dusting of confectioner's sugar through a sieve, and it will look beautiful. If you're making a savory soufflé, add in some crème fraiche, cheese shavings, and lots of chopped fresh herbs.

# Chocolate Soufflé

Makes **1** 8-in. (20-cm) soufflé dish or
**6** 6-oz. (180-g) soufflé dishes

It may sound intimidating, but a chocolate soufflé is really not as difficult to make as its reputation suggests—and it's definitely worth it! Just follow the technique to make this warm, smooth wisp of chocolate and you'll learn how you can make the magic happen.

## INGREDIENTS

10½ oz. (315 g) best-quality bittersweet chocolate

1 TB. unsalted butter, softened

⅓ cup (1½oz./40 g) granulated sugar (plus more for the soufflé dish)

1⅓ cups whole milk

1 TB. cornstarch

3 large egg yolks, room temperature and lightly beaten

1 tsp. pure vanilla extract

6 large egg whites, room temperature

⅛ tsp. salt

Confectioner's sugar (optional)

## EQUIPMENT

1 8-in. (20-cm) soufflé dish *or* 6 6-oz. (180-g) individual soufflé dishes

Rimmed baking sheet

Sharp knife

Cutting board

Medium heat-proof bowl

Large saucepan

Medium saucepan

Whisk

Standing mixer with whisk attachment

1. Set the oven rack to the low position and preheat the oven to 400°F (204°C). Butter the inside of the soufflé dish and coat with sugar. Place on a rimmed baking sheet and set aside.

2. With a sharp knife, coarsely chop bittersweet chocolate on a cutting board. In a medium bowl set over a large saucepan $1/3$ full with simmering water, melt chopped chocolate over medium heat (don't let water touch the bottom of the bowl). Remove from heat but keep warm.

3. In a medium saucepan, whisk together whole milk and cornstarch. Bring mixture to a boil over medium heat, stirring constantly, until thick. Remove from heat, pour into melted chocolate, and stir to combine. Let mixture cool for about 2 minutes. Add egg yolks and vanilla extract, and stir until well combined.

4. In the bowl of a standing mixer, whip egg whites and salt on medium speed until foamy, about 5 minutes. Slowly add sugar, increase the speed to high, and whip until shiny and stiff peaks form, about 3 minutes.

5. Fold $1/3$ of egg white mixture into soufflé base with a whisk to lighten it. Fold in remaining egg whites until just incorporated (do not overmix). Spoon mixture into prepared soufflé dish; mixture should come up $1/2$ inch (1 cm) below the rim of the dish.

## Make Ahead

This soufflé batter can be made several hours in advance and kept in a refrigerator until just before baking. If refrigerated, bake an additional 2 to 3 minutes. Alternatively, the soufflé may rest at room temperature for up to 30 minutes before baking with no effect on the cooking time.

6. Carefully place in the oven and bake until risen, about 30 minutes for 1 dish and 12 to 15 minutes for 6 single-portion dishes, and serve immediately. Dust with confectioner's sugar (if using) and serve immediately.

# Goat Cheese Soufflé

Makes **6** ³⁄₄-cup soufflé dishes

This fluffy, savory soufflé can be served as an appetizer or even a light main dish with a bed of leafy greens and a fruity vinaigrette. This easy yet elegant dish is sure to impress!

## INGREDIENTS

¹⁄₂ stick (4 oz./120 g) butter, at room temperature

³⁄₄ cup (about 1¹⁄₄ oz./35 g) almond flour

2 TB. all-purpose flour

²⁄₃ cup (5¹⁄₄ oz./160 g) whole milk

5 oz. (150 g) goat cheese, very coarsely crumbled

2 tsp. finely chopped fresh thyme leaves

1 tsp. Dijon mustard

¹⁄₂ tsp. salt

¹⁄₄ tsp. pepper

¹⁄₈ tsp. cayenne

2 large egg yolks, lightly beaten

4 large egg whites, at room temperature

## EQUIPMENT

6 ³⁄₄-cup soufflé dishes or ramekins

Medium saucepan

Whisk

Standing mixer with whisk attachment

Small clean saucepan or kettle

Silicone spatula

Large baking pan with tall sides or roasting pan

1. Preheat the oven to 350°F (180°C). Rub the inside of the soufflé dishes with 2 tablespoons butter. Coat the insides of each with almond flour, tapping out excess to use to coat the next dish. Set aside.

2. Melt remaining 2 tablespoons butter in a medium saucepan over medium-low heat. Add all-purpose flour and cook for 2 minutes, whisking constantly. Gradually whisk in whole milk. Increase heat to medium and whisk constantly until mixture comes to a simmer and thickens, about 5 minutes.

3. Add goat cheese and whisk until melted and smooth. Remove from heat and mix in thyme, Dijon mustard, salt, pepper, and cayenne. Let cool for 5 minutes. Gradually whisk egg yolks into warm base, making sure to add them slowly to avoid curdling. Set aside.

4. In the bowl of a standing mixer, whip egg whites on medium speed until foamy; increase the speed to high and beat until whites hold firm peaks (don't overwhip; see "How to Make Meringue" in Chapter 7). While whites whip, bring 4 cups water to a boil in a small clean saucepan for the water bath.

## Roux

A mixture of flour (or starch) and fat (butter) cooked into a liquid to thicken it is called a *roux*. It is used in classic French sauces and commonly appears in soufflé bases.

5. Mix 1/3 of whites into soufflé base with a silicone spatula to lighten. Fold in remaining egg whites. Divide mixture among prepared soufflé dishes, and place dishes in a large baking pan.

6. Place the pan with the dishes in the oven and add enough hot water to the pan to come halfway up the sides of the dishes.

7. Bake soufflés until risen and golden on top and softly set in center, about 20 minutes. Serve immediately.

*part 4*

# Pies, Tarts, and Cakes

**Chapter 10:** Pies and Tarts

**Chapter 11:** Cakes and Cupcakes

**Chapter 12:** Cake Decorating

# Pies and Tarts

*Pies* come in an infinite array of flavors and ingredients. This American staple is ubiquitous in celebrations and is served in homes, cafeterias, diners, fast-food chains, and even upscale restaurants. Pie is usually cooked and served in a pie dish.

In Europe, the word *tart* is used to designate a pastry filled with fruits, jam, custard, or another filling. A tart is usually thinner and made in a tart mold or ring that's often removed before serving.

There's no exact differentiation between pie and tart dough; in fact, some can be used interchangeably. However, classic pie doughs tend to be flaky doughs made only of flour, fat, a small amount of liquid, and salt, with inventive chefs and housewives widening the repertoire by creating other crusts (such as the cracker crust). On the other hand, tart doughs are more cookielike doughs that tend to be enriched with eggs, cream, and sugar or made with a puff, sable, or brisée pastry base.

# How to Make a Basic Pie Crust

The classic flaky pie dough—made only with flour, fat, water, and salt—is easier to make than most people think. The most important part is making sure you don't overmix or overknead to prevent gluten from developing too much and to allow the fat pockets to form and produce steam in the oven. Here are the steps and tips to keep in mind to make a great pie crust.

## Start with Cold Ingredients

When making pie dough, it's essential to chill the fat (butter, shortening, and so on) and the liquid (water, milk, and so on) at least 30 minutes before using. Working with cold ingredients allows the fat to be coated by the flour instead of absorbed by it. This will keep the crust flaky. Even better: measure the dry ingredients and chill them as well.

1

Just pulse! Continuous processing might overmix the dough and melt the fat.

**Mix the dry ingredients and fats.** Pulse the dry ingredients in a food processor. Add the fat, pulsing 15 to 20 times, until the mixture resembles coarse meal, with pieces of butter no larger than a pea.

## Doing It by Hand

It's best to make your crust with a food processor to make sure the ingredients don't have time to come to room temperature. But if you don't have one, you can do it by hand with this method: Stir together the dry ingredients, and then use two forks in a slicing motion to cut in the fat. Just make sure all the ingredients are really cold, especially the fat.

The flour should not look like a powder anymore, and some parts of the dough should be clumping together.

**Add the liquid.** Add ice water by sprinkling a bit first over the flour mixture and pulsing to combine. Stop the machine and try squeezing a bit of dough in your hand. If it holds together, it's ready; if it's dry and breaks apart easily, add 1 more tablespoon of water. Pulse and test again, adding the ice water a little at a time, until it's the right consistency.

Try to work quickly and to mix the dough as little as possible.

**Work the dough.** Place the dough on a work surface, halve it by gathering and pressing (not kneading), and place each portion onto a piece of plastic wrap. Flatten and form the dough into two discs. Wrap them in the plastic wrap and chill for at least 1 hour up to 3 days or freeze for up to 3 months.

## Using the Right Amount of Liquid

Adding the right amount of liquid is crucial to obtaining the best textured crust. You don't have to use all the ice water in the recipe, as the total amount needed will depend on many factors, including how humid the environment is. Just remember, the dough shouldn't look like a smooth ball like cookie dough does—it should be moist but crumbly. Resist the temptation to overwater!

## Chilling the Dough

Dough must be refrigerated, because chilling keeps the fat from melting, which is crucial for flakiness. If you freeze the dough, don't thaw it on the counter—put the frozen dough in the refrigerator overnight before using.

## Don't Overmix!

Working the dough too much decreases the size of the fat pieces and incorporates them into the flour, which reduces the flakiness of your final product. Overworking also promotes the development of gluten, which will give you a tough crust.

Lift the parchment every few rolls to make sure the dough isn't sticking.

**Roll out.** Rolling out the dough in between two sheets of parchment or plastic is the easiest way to keep it from sticking and from needing extra flour that may affect its texture. Roll from the middle of the dough outward, rotating it 90 degrees after each stroke until you have a circle about 2 inches (5 cm) larger than the pie dish. If the dough cracks when you first start rolling, let it stand for 1 minute to warm slightly before rolling again.

**Fit the dough into the pie dish.** The easiest way to get the crust into the dish is by transferring it with the rolling pin. Lay the rolling pin on one edge of the pie crust and, lifting from the bottom sheet of parchment or plastic, begin gently rolling the pie crust around the rolling pin.

**Unroll the crust.** Position the rolling pin over the pie plate and gently unroll it into the pie pan. Position the pie dish as close as possible to the crust so you can transfer the dough quickly to the dish.

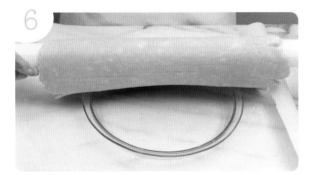

**Press the dough.** Using your fingers, gently press the dough into place. Remember to handle the dough as little as possible, to avoid warming it.

## Transferring the Dough

Another option for transferring the dough is to just use the bottom parchment or plastic sheet to lift it up and flip it into the pie dish.

To finish your pie, you have a number of options—you can make a double crust pie; make a lattice top; or add a crumb topping, and save the other half of the dough for another pie. But all pies need a nice crimped edge for that finished look. Here is how to do a nice crimp:

**Trim the excess dough.** Use scissors (or a paring knife) after fitting the dough into the pie dish. Leave a 1-inch (2.5-cm) overhang—this is key, as you need to have enough dough to tuck it under itself and allow for a proper border. Trim a little at a time, as it's always easier to trim more than to add back.

**Fold the edge of the crust.** Tuck the dough overhang under so it's even with the lip of the dish, creating a seamless, rounded border. This makes the edge thicker and easier to crimp.

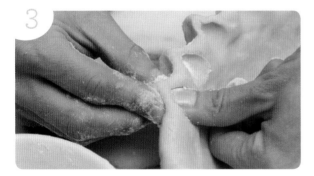

**Crimp the edge of the crust.** Pinch the edge (either internal or external) of the dough between the index and thumb of one hand, and make a dimple with the index finger of the other hand. Repeat, moving around until the entire crust has a fluted edge.

## A Tool for Crimping

Another easy option for crimping is to press the tines of a fork against the edge of the dough to flatten it against the rim of the pie dish.

## A Rounder Crimping

If you want a rounder effect, fold your index finger and use your knuckle to make the indentation. You can also use the tip of a spoon.

# Top Crust Variations

You can finish off your pie in several ways—a traditional second crust, perhaps with decorative cut-outs, a beautiful lattice top, or even a deliciously sweet crumble. Here are the various ways you can top off your pie.

## How to Make a Double Crust

To make a double crust, you employ some of the same techniques you learned in making the basic crust.

Trim the excess dough on the bottom crust.

Fill the crust with your desired filling.

Roll out the second dough in between two sheets of parchment.

Pick up the dough using a rolling pin.

Transfer the dough to the pie, gently unrolling it on top of the filling. Be careful not to drape the dough, not stretch it—if you stretch it, it will tear.

Trim the top dough to match the bottom, and press the bottom and top crusts together to seal them and prevent the filling from escaping.

Fold the pressed edges under and crimp as explained in steps 2 and 3 of "How to Crimp a Crust."

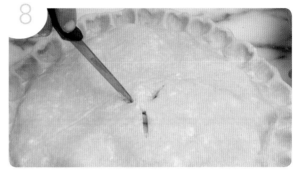

Using a paring knife, cut small, evenly spaced slits across the top crust. The vents are made not only for decorative purposes, but also to allow steam to escape, which prevents a watery filling from forming.

## Using a Pie Bird or Pie Whistle

If you own one, you can use a *pie bird* or *pie whistle*, a hollow ceramic device shaped like a funnel, chimney, or upstretched bird with an open beak. It's placed in the center of the top pie crust and allows steam to escape. You definitely don't need one, but it is sure to become a conversation piece!

# How to Do a Lattice Top

Pies with bright-colored fruit fillings look particularly beautiful covered with a lattice crust. A lattice top is made by weaving strips of pie dough, placing it on top of the filling, and securing it to the bottom crust. The open weave allows steam and excess moisture to escape during baking, which prevents a watery filling. It's not only wonderful to look at, but fun to make, too. The following walks you through how to do it.

## Thickness of the Dough

Be sure that the dough you are using is rolled out to the same thickness as the bottom crust, or your pie won't bake evenly.

**Cut the dough into strips.** You can use a paring knife, pastry cutter, or even pizza cutter along with a ruler to cut the strips. This way, the strips won't be too wide, which would lead to a higher baking time and uneven browning.

**Lay the horizontal strips.** Place 6 parallel strips of dough across the pie, leaving the same distance in between each one to promote even baking and to make the pie more attractive. Fold back strips 2, 4, and 6; this allows you to weave the strips easily and know which strip should go under and which one should go over.

## Making the Lattice on a Baking Sheet

Alternatively, you can make the lattice on a baking sheet lined with parchment paper, with the sheet acting as a working surface. You can then freeze the weaved lattice on the lined sheet until it's completely firm before sliding it over the pie filling. The freezing process prevents the dough from being too warm and melting into the filling when baked.

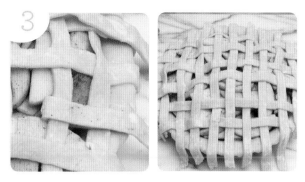

**Weave the strips.** When laying strips, make sure there's enough space for steam to escape from in between the strips to prevent a watery pie. Lay 1 strip of dough vertically across the pie. Unfold horizontal strips 2, 4, and 6, and then fold back horizontal strips 1, 3, and 5 over the vertical strip. Repeat the process until the entire pie is covered.

**Trim off the excess lattice.** Cut the ends with a knife or kitchen scissors to give the pie a finished look. It's better to trim a bit at a time to make sure you don't cut too much. You can always trim a bit more, if necessary.

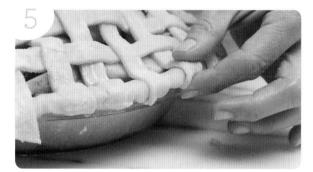

**Seal the lattice ends.** Pressing all of the lattices ends into the edge of the bottom crust to seal keeps them from shrinking during baking and detaching from the crust, which would affect the final appearance of the pie.

Make sure not to add too much egg wash, or the crust will turn out soggy.

**Apply egg wash and sugar.** The egg wash acts as a glue—keeping the lattice together and ensuring the weaved strips stay attached to the bottom pie crust—and provides a shine to the finished product. You simply "paint" the egg wash on the lattice with a pastry brush. If desired, you can also sprinkle the lattice with sugar to add more color and flavor to it.

# How to Make a Crumb Topping

Crumb toppings are less work than rolled-out pastry crusts. They are also faster to make—and quite delicious. They give a rustic look to the treat and can be used not only for pies, but for topping cheesecakes and coffee cakes as well. They are made by mixing flour; sugar; and other flavorful items, such as spices, grains, and/or ground nuts. The fat is then cut into the dry ingredients. The result is a crumbly, sweet, and delicate mixture with a melt-in-your-mouth texture. This is how it's made.

**Mix the dry ingredients.** Combine all the dry ingredients (flour, ground nuts, sugar, salt, spices, and so on) together in a bowl. You can use a whisk or silicone spatula.

Cut in the butter using two table knives or forks, a food processor, or your fingertips.

**Cut in the fat.** The crumb topping should look like coarse meal, with some bigger, pea-sized globs of butter covered in flour. You don't want the butter to be completely mixed into the dry ingredients—you just want pieces of it covered in flour. If you mix the butter in completely, it will turn into something that resembles a cookie dough.

## Cutting In

"Cut in" means to distribute solid fat (like butter) throughout dry ingredients until the flour-coated fat particles are the desired size.

## Using Your Hands

If you use your hands, don't overwork the mixture—the heat of your fingers may melt the fat. Remember, you still want coarse crumbs, not a completely incorporated dough.

Work carefully but quickly! Don't let the butter melt in your fingers.

**Refrigerate.** If you're not using the topping immediately, cover the bowl and refrigerate it until ready to use. Also, if you're working the crumb with your hands and you think the butter is getting too soft, put it in the refrigerator to firm up.

**Sprinkle the topping over the filling.** "Sprinkling" is the keyword here. Don't press the crumb topping onto the filling, as both layers could mix and turn into a messy filling-topping combination. The filling could also ooze out, so be very gentle! Make sure you cover the filling as evenly as possible, trying not to leave any empty gaps.

## Decorating the Crusts with Cut-Outs

Single- and double-crusted tarts and pies can be beautifully decorated with pastry shapes cut from rolled-out dough. You can use the method to decorate the entire top or just the edges (instead of crimping). This adds a beautiful touch that can be customized to any theme or occasion. It's easy to do, and the visual effect is quite stunning.

**Roll out the dough.** Roll out the dough in between layers of parchment paper. Put it on a baking sheet and chill it until firm. You can use the leftover trimmings from the bottom crust, if you only want to add a few cut-outs. Just make sure you reroll the dough and chill it before cutting it.

### Thickness of the Dough

Make sure the dough is not too thick. Otherwise, it will not bake at the same time as the rest of the pie and will result in underbaked pieces of pastry, while the pie will be ready or even burnt.

2

**Make the cut-outs.** Cut the dough with the cookie cutter of your choice. If you're not using the cut-outs right away, chill them on a baking sheet lined with parchment. This keeps them in shape and makes them easier to handle; dough at room temperature is too soft to hold a form and can be difficult to work with.

## Amount of Dough

If you want to cover the whole top in cut-outs, you have to cut out an entire batch of dough; covering the edges also takes about the same amount of dough.

3

**Place the cut-outs.** "Paint" the top crust with egg wash and place the cut-outs in a pattern. Make sure you don't obstruct the vents, as the pie needs to release steam. Finish by brushing the entire cut-out design with egg wash. Make sure you don't use too much wash, as it could turn the crust soggy.

## Single-Crust Pies

You can also use cut-outs instead of a traditional double crust. Just be sure to cover all the filling completely with cut-outs, overlapping each cut-out slightly but making sure there's space in between cut-outs to allow for the steam to escape and to avoid a watery pie.

# Apple Pie

Makes **1** 9-in. (23-cm) pie

A good apple pie smells, tastes, and feels like a grandmother's hug. This American dessert icon is a wonderful way of enrobing apples and spices in flaky dough. Nothing beats a completely homemade apple pie! Plus, it actually takes less time to prepare a crust at home than to run to the store to purchase one.

## INGREDIENTS

**Crust:**

2½ cups (10⅔ oz./320 g) unbleached all-purpose flour
1 TB. granulated sugar (plus more for sprinkling)
1 tsp. salt
10 TB. (5 oz./150 g) chilled unsalted butter, cut into ½-in. (1.25-cm) cubes
6 TB. (3 oz./90 g) chilled nonhydrogenated shortening, cut into ½-in. (1.25-cm) cubes
3 to 4 TB. (or more) ice water
Egg wash (see "How to Make a Basic Pie Crust")

**Filling:**

5 cups (about 5 to 6) apples, peeled, cored, and cut into ¼-in. (6-mm) slices
2 TB. fresh lemon juice (from 1 lemon)
2 TB. cornstarch or tapioca starch
½ cup (3½ oz./100 g) light or dark brown sugar, firmly packed
1 tsp. ground cinnamon
½ tsp. ground cloves (optional)
¼ tsp. ground nutmeg (optional)
¼ tsp. ground allspice (optional)
¼ tsp. ground ginger (optional)
⅛ tsp. salt

## EQUIPMENT

Food processor
Plastic wrap
Large mixing bowl
Wooden spoon or silicone spatula
Cutting board
Parchment paper

Rolling pin
9-in. (23-cm) pie baking dish
Sharp knife
Pastry brush
Rimmed baking sheet
Cooling rack

**CHAPTER 10 | PIES AND TARTS**

## What Kind of Apples?

The best baking apples are a bit denser and sturdier so they keep a bit of their crunch after baking and can hold their flavors against all of the other spices. Granny Smith, Jonagold, Pippin, Braeburn, Fuji, and Pink Lady are all excellent baking apples. Stay away from Golden Delicious, Red Delicious, Gaia, and Cortland, though—these varieties become mealy and mushy when baked.

1. To make the crust, place all-purpose flour, sugar, and salt in a food processor and process for a few seconds to combine. Add butter and shortening, and process, pulsing 15 to 20 times, until mixture resembles coarse meal, with pieces of butter no larger than a pea.

2. Remove the processor lid and sprinkle 3 tablespoons ice water over flour mixture. Pulse 4 to 5 times to combine. Stop the machine and try squeezing a bit of dough in your hand. If it holds together, it's ready; if it's dry and breaks apart easily, add 1 more tablespoon ice water. Pulse and test again, adding 1 tablespoon ice water at a time, until ready.

## Consistency of Crust

Pie crust dough doesn't come together as cohesively as other kinds of dough, but the flour should not seem like a powder anymore and some parts of the dough should be clumping together.

3. Turn pie crust dough out onto a work surface and cut in half. Working quickly, gather and press each portion onto a piece of plastic wrap. Flatten and form 2 discs. Wrap crust dough and refrigerate at least 1 hour before using.

4. To make the filling, place apple slices in a large bowl and sprinkle with lemon juice. Add cornstarch, brown sugar, cloves (if using), nutmeg (if using), allspice (if using), ginger (if using), and salt and stir gently with a wooden spoon to combine.

5. Remove one disk of crust dough crust dough from the fridge. Roll out the dough with a rolling pin (see "How to Roll Out Pie Dough") until you have a circle roughly 12 to 13 inches (30 to 33 cm) in diameter. Try to work dough as little as possible.

6. Transfer crust to the pie pan and trim all but 1 or 2 inches (2.5 or 5 cm) of pie dough from around the edge with a sharp knife; use trimmings to patch up any holes or tears. Place crust in the refrigerator and chill for at least 15 minutes.

7. Preheat the oven to 400°F (200°C) with a rack in the middle position.

8. Pour filling into prepared crust. Roll out second disk of dough, making the circle smaller than the first by 1 or 2 inches (2.5 or 5 cm). Transfer top crust onto pie, and trim edges.

9. Gently press top and bottom crusts together and crimp edges to seal. Brush entire crust with egg wash using a pastry brush. With a sharp knife, cut at least 4 vents in top crust. Sprinkle top of pie with a bit of granulated sugar.

10. Place the pie dish on a rimmed baking sheet and bake for 15 minutes. Lower the heat to 350°F (180°C) and bake for a 30 to 40 more minutes until top is browned and filling bubbles.

11. Remove from the oven, cool on a cooling rack about 2 minutes so pie isn't too hot, and serve. Pie keeps well covered at room temperature for 2 days.

## Getting Dough into the Pan

Instead of rolling dough around the rolling pin, you could use the bottom parchment or plastic sheet to lift it up and flip it into the pie dish.

## Pie Crust Baking Tip

If the edges of the crust brown too quickly, cover them with foil.

# How to Make a Cracker Crust

At some point, someone—perhaps in a rush or lacking the ingredients needed for a traditional crust—discovered that grinding graham crackers, cookies, or wafers and binding them with melted butter into a crust results in a delicious, quick, easy, and functional solution to modern-day pie-making. The following shows you how to prepare this type of pie crust.

**Grind the crackers.** You want the crackers to be fine crumbs so the crust can stick together well and bake evenly. By pulsing the crackers in a food processor or placing them inside a zipper-lock bag and rolling them over with a pin, you can grind them to the consistency you need.

**Add melted butter and sugar (if using).** The melted butter helps bind the crumbs, while the sugar is just an optional sweetener for the crust. You can pulse these ingredients in a food processor or mix them by hand with a silicone spatula or fork until the mixture resembles wet sand.

## Cracker Substitutes

You can substitute the graham crackers with chocolate or vanilla wafers or even gingersnaps—any dry but soft cookie will work.

**Remove the weights.** Remove the weights by carefully lifting the foil or parchment, and return the crust to the oven to finish baking. This allows the crust to brown and caramelize in the oven, which will develop its flavor further.

## Cooling the Crust

When a recipe calls for blind baking a crust and then cooling it completely before filling it, make sure the crust has indeed reached room temperature; otherwise, the heat of the warm crust might melt or cook the filling, making it unpleasant in appearance and even flavor—or even ruining it completely.

# Fresh Fruit Tart in Almond Crust

Makes **1** 9-in. (23-cm) tart

This recipe uses an easy-to-make crust with a classic pastry cream topped with the fruit of your choice. It's beautiful to look at and very delicious. This is a recipe that you can easily adapt to the seasons, using whatever fresh fruit is available.

## INGREDIENTS

**Crust:**

1½ cups (6⅓ oz./190 g) unbleached all-purpose flour

½ cup (1½ oz./45 g) blanched, sliced almonds

⅓ cup (1⅓ oz./40 g) confectioner's sugar

⅛ tsp. salt

1 stick (4 oz./120 g) unsalted butter, cold and cubed

2 large egg yolks

2 tsp. almond liqueur, such as Amaretto (optional)

**Topping:**

½ cup (6 oz./180 g) red currant or apricot jelly (no chunks, seeds, or fruit pieces)

½ to 1 lb. (250 to 500 g) assorted fruit, such as berries, grapes, sliced kiwis, peeled and cubed mango, pitted and sliced stone fruit, and so on

**Filling:**

1 recipe Pastry Cream (see the recipe in Chapter 8)

## EQUIPMENT

Food processor

Plastic wrap

Parchment paper

Rolling pin

9-in. (23-cm) tart pan

Aluminum foil (optional)

2 16-oz. (450-g) bags dry beans or rice or pie weights

Cooling rack

Medium saucepan

Silicone spatula

Pastry brush

Small offset spatula

Serving platter (optional)

1. To make the crust, place $\frac{1}{4}$ cup all-purpose flour and almonds in a food processor and pulse until almonds are finely ground, about 1 minute. Pulse in remaining $1\frac{1}{4}$ cups all-purpose flour, confectioner's sugar, and salt. Add butter and pulse until a coarse meal forms. Add egg yolks and almond liqueur (if using) and pulse until dough comes together; it will look moist, like cookie dough.

2. Press dough into a disk, wrap in plastic wrap, and chill in the refrigerator for 4 hours or up to a week. (You can also freeze the dough up to 3 months—just thaw it overnight before using.)

3. When ready to bake tart, place dough between 2 sheets of parchment paper. Using a rolling pin, roll out dough until you have a circle roughly $1\frac{1}{2}$ to 2 inches (4 to 5 cm) larger than the diameter of the tart pan.

4. Remove the parchment paper from top of dough, lift dough from the bottom sheet of parchment paper, and carefully flip dough into the tart pan. Remove the parchment paper and lightly press dough into the pan, using any excess to patch up holes or tears or to even thickness around the edges. To remove excess dough around the edges, run the rolling pin over the top of the tart pan. Chill in the refrigerator for 30 minutes.

5. Preheat the oven to 325°F (160°C). Line the tart pan with a parchment paper round slightly larger in circumference than the pan. Fill the tart pan with the bags of dry beans or rice, making sure to spread them out evenly.

6. Place crust in the oven and bake for 20 minutes. Take crust out of the oven and remove the weights by carefully lifting the parchment paper. Put crust back in the oven and continue baking, uncovered, until it is pale golden, about 5 to 10 minutes. Transfer to a cooling rack to cool completely, about 30 to 40 minutes.

7. To make the topping, in a medium saucepan, bring red currant jelly to a boil over medium-high heat, stirring occasionally with a silicone spatula, until completely melted, about 2 minutes. Remove from heat and set aside.

8. Spoon chilled Pastry Cream into cooled tart shell. Arrange fruit over top of tart. With a pastry brush, brush fruit with melted jelly topping to glaze it.

9. Remove the outer ring from the tart pan, slide a thin offset spatula between bottom of crust and the tart pan bottom to release, and slip tart onto a serving platter (or just skip this step and transfer it on the tart pan bottom!). Tart should be served within 30 minutes for best texture.

*chapter 11*

# Cakes and Cupcakes

*Cakes* are symbols of merriment, fun, and happiness. They tend to be the dessert of choice to celebrate a birthday and to commemorate a wedding, an anniversary, or many other holidays. Cakes come in many varieties, including layer cakes, coffee cakes, carrot cakes, chocolate cakes, sophisticated tiered cakes, and flourless cakes. Modern-day cakes are usually prepared with a combination of the typical baking quartet of flour, sugar, eggs, and butter or oil and decorated with icings, nuts, fondant, sprinkles, cream, ganache, and many other items.

Cakes that are baked in individual portions or "cups" and then frosted and decorated are known as *cupcakes* in the United States, *fairy cakes* in the UK, and *patty cakes* or *cup cakes* in Australia. Because they are baked in paper (or other material) liners, cupcakes are easy to transport, hold, and eat.

# How to Make Layer Cakes
## Using the Creaming Method

For most butter-based cakes, the creaming method—also known as the conventional method—is used for mixing the ingredients together into the batter. This allows for an emulsion (a uniform mixture of two unmixable substances, such as fat and water) to form. Creaming also combines all the ingredients smoothly and uniformly, which allows air to be incorporated and helps the cake develop the proper texture. The following walks you through the process.

**Allow the ingredients to come to room temperature.** Emulsions form best when the ingredients are not cold, so after you measure out your ingredients, let them sit until they are room temperature.

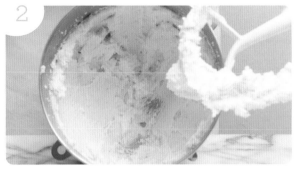

**Mix the butter.** To achieve the desired emulsion, place the butter in the bowl of a standing mixer and mix it at low speed until it is smooth and creamy. Don't set the mixer at full speed; the air cells form better when not mixed too quickly.

**Add the sugar, salt, and any flavorings.** These ingredients mix easily with the fat of the butter and don't interrupt the development of the emulsion. Mixing the sugar with the creamed butter is a non-negotiable step; otherwise, the emulsion and the volume of the cake may be compromised. You simply cream the mixture on medium speed until light and fluffy.

**Add the eggs.** The eggs should be added one at a time, mixing after each addition, until each egg is absorbed before adding the next one. If they are added too quickly, the emulsion breaks and they can't be absorbed properly. After the eggs are beaten in, mix until light and fluffy, scraping down the sides of the bowl to ensure even mixing.

**Add the dry and liquid ingredients.** The dry and liquid ingredients should be added alternately, because the flour helps the batter absorb the liquid. Do this by adding ¼ of the dry followed by ⅓ of the liquid (such as milk, juice, and so on), mixing after each addition until blended. Repeat until all the ingredients are used.

> Scrape down the sides of the bowl occasionally for even mixing.

**Divide the batter.** This makes the process very easy, as you'll automatically end up with one separate layer per pan. Pour the batter evenly among 2 or 3 prepared pans of the same shape and size.

**Bake.** Don't let the pans touch each other in the oven—otherwise, the air won't circulate and the cakes will rise unevenly. The layers are done when they shrink away slightly from the sides of the pan, spring back when pressed lightly in the center, or a toothpick inserted in the center comes out clean.

**Cool.** Because cakes are fragile while still hot, place the pans on cooling racks and let cool for about 15 minutes. Once that's done, turn out the layers onto a rack by placing a cooling rack on top of the cake pan and then carefully flipping the cake pan upside down to release the cake onto the rack. Let the cakes cool completely before icing or decorating. If you aren't using them right away, wrap them in plastic wrap and freeze so they stay moist.

# Moist Chocolate Cake

Makes **1** two-layer 8-in. (20-cm) cake

This is my go-to chocolate cake recipe. It's put together in a cinch, it's always reliable, and it produces a moist and delicious cake. The secret ingredient in this cake recipe is mayonnaise, which may be making your nose wrinkle; however, mayo is an emulsion of oil, eggs, and an acid, which are common ingredients in many cake recipes.

## INGREDIENTS

1 cup water

Nonstick cooking spray

2 cups (8 1/2 oz./250 g) all-purpose flour

1 cup (7 1/2 oz./225 g) light or dark brown sugar, firmly packed

1/2 cup (1 1/2 oz./45 g) natural unsweetened cocoa powder (preferably nonalkalized)

1 1/2 tsp. baking powder

1/2 tsp. baking soda

1 cup (8 oz./240 g) full-fat mayonnaise

2 tsp. vanilla extract

## EQUIPMENT

2 8-in. (20-cm) round baking pans

Parchment paper

Medium saucepan *or* kettle

Large mixing bowl or 8-cup-capacity liquid measuring cup

Whisk

Silicone spatula

Toothpick

2 cooling racks

Small offset spatula

Plastic wrap (optional)

1. Place the rack in the middle position and preheat the oven to 350°F (175°C). Lightly coat baking pans with nonstick cooking spray. Line bottoms with parchment paper and spray again with nonstick cooking spray. Set aside.

2. In a medium saucepan, bring water to a boil over medium heat. While waiting, in a large bowl, whisk together all-purpose flour, brown sugar, cocoa powder, baking powder, and baking soda.

3. Switch to a silicone spatula and add mayonnaise and vanilla extract to dry mixture, mixing until mayonnaise is completely incorporated.

4. Add boiling water and switch back to the whisk, mixing until well combined. Divide batter between both baking pans, using a silicone spatula to scrape the bowl.

5. Bake cakes, rotating halfway through, until a toothpick inserted into the centers come out clean and cakes spring back when pressed lightly in the center, about 20 to 30 minutes.

6. Transfer baking pans to cooling racks and let cool 10 minutes. Loosen sides of cakes with an offset spatula and turn out onto cooling racks. Remove the parchment paper and let cool completely, about 30 minutes.

7. Once cake is completely cooled, decorate it with your favorite frosting (see "How to Frost a Cake" in Chapter 12) or tightly double-wrap cake layers in plastic wrap and freeze for up to 1 month.

## Batter Warning

Don't let the batter sit after the hot water has been added, as the leaveners are activated with the heat and moisture and will start reacting. You want that to happen inside the oven!

# Vanilla Velvet Cake

Makes **1** three-layer 9-in. (23-cm) cake

This golden, buttery cake goes well with frostings, fruit, and buttercream or is satisfying just by itself. It turns beautifully into cupcakes as well and is mixed by the textbook creaming method for cakes. This is the perfect cake for birthday parties, bake sales, or any time a delicious dessert is needed.

## INGREDIENTS

2 sticks (8 oz./240 g) unsalted butter, softened (plus more for pans)

1$^3/_4$ cups granulated sugar

1 tsp. pure vanilla extract

4 large eggs, at room temperature

2$^3/_4$ cups (11$^2/_3$ oz./350 g) all-purpose flour (plus more for pans)

2$^1/_4$ tsp. baking powder

$^3/_4$ tsp. fine salt

1 cup whole milk

Frosting (optional; see Chapter 12 for recipes)

## EQUIPMENT

3 9-in. (23-cm) round cake pans

Parchment paper

Standing mixer fitted with paddle attachment

Silicone spatula

Medium mixing bowl

Whisk

Toothpick

3 cooling racks

Small offset spatula

Plastic wrap (optional)

1. Place 2 racks in the middle position of the oven and preheat the oven to 350°F (175°C). Grease and lightly flour the cake pans and line the bottoms with parchment paper. Set aside.

2. In the bowl of a standing mixer fitted with a paddle attachment, cream butter, sugar, and vanilla extract on medium speed until light and fluffy, about 3 minutes.

## Butter for Mix

Make sure to start with softened butter (at room temperature); see "Dairy" in Chapter 2.

3. Add eggs one at a time, beating well on medium speed after each addition. Scrape the sides of the bowl with a silicone spatula after all eggs are added.

4. In a medium bowl, whisk together all-purpose flour, baking powder, and salt. Add flour mixture to egg-butter mixture in 4 separate additions, alternating with whole milk and beating well at low speed after each addition.

5. Divide batter equally among the cake pans, smoothing out tops with an offset spatula. Place the pans in the oven, 2 pans on one rack and 2 on the other. Bake, rotating the pans halfway through, until a toothpick inserted into centers comes out clean and cakes spring back when pressed lightly in centers, about 20 to 25 minutes.

6. Transfer the cake pans to cooling racks and let cool 10 minutes. Loosen the sides with an offset spatula and turn out cakes onto the racks. Remove the parchment paper and let cool completely, about 30 minutes.

7. Once cake layers are completely cooled, stack and decorate with your favorite frosting (if using; see "How to Frost a Cake" in Chapter 12) or tightly double-wrap cake layers in plastic wrap and freeze for up to 1 month.

# Carrot Cake

Makes **1** two-layer 9-in. (23-cm) cake

This classic cake is moist and full of spice. I particularly love how all the ingredients come together wonderfully but still preserve some of their individual character and texture. Its ideal topping is, of course, a tangy cream cheese icing (see the sidebar).

## INGREDIENTS

Nonstick cooking spray

¾ cup (75 g) pecans or walnuts, plus more for decoration (optional)

2 cups (8½ oz./260 g) all-purpose flour

1 tsp. baking soda

1½ tsp. baking powder

½ tsp. salt

1 tsp. ground cinnamon

1 tsp. ground ginger (optional)

¼ tsp. ground nutmeg (optional)

4 large eggs

1½ cups (8¾ oz./265 g) dark brown sugar, firmly packed

1 cup (8 oz./240 g) neutral-tasting oil (see "Other Fats and Oils" in Chapter 2)

½ cup (4 oz./120 g) unsweetened applesauce

2 tsp. pure vanilla extract

2½ cups (12 oz./340 g) finely grated raw carrots

½ cup (2 oz./60 g) unsweetened grated coconut (optional)

Cream Cheese Frosting (see recipe in Chapter 12)

## EQUIPMENT

2 9-in. (23-cm) round cake pans

Parchment paper

Rimmed baking sheet

Cutting board

Sharp knife

2 medium mixing bowls

Whisk

Silicone spatula

Toothpick

2 cooling racks

Small offset spatula

Plastic wrap (optional)

1. Place the rack in the middle position of the oven and preheat the oven to 350°F (180°C). Lightly coat the cake pans with nonstick cooking spray. Line the bottoms with parchment paper and spray again with nonstick cooking spray. Set aside.

2. Line a rimmed baking sheet with parchment paper. Place pecans on the baking sheet and place in the oven. Toast until lightly browned and fragrant, about 8 minutes. Remove pecans and let cool for a few minutes. Once cool, coarsely chop nuts on a cutting board with a sharp knife.

3. In a medium bowl, whisk together all-purpose flour, baking soda, baking powder, salt, cinnamon, ginger (if using), and nutmeg (if using).

4. In a separate medium bowl, whisk together dark brown sugar, neutral-tasting oil, eggs, applesauce, and vanilla extract until combined. Add to flour mixture, switch to a silicone spatula, and stir until smooth. Add carrots, chopped pecans, and coconut (if using) and mix to combine.

5. Divide batter equally between the prepared pans and smooth tops with an offset spatula. Place in the oven and bake until a toothpick inserted into centers comes out clean and cakes spring back when pressed lightly in centers, about 25 to 30 minutes.

6. Transfer the pans to cooling racks and let cool 15 minutes. Loosen sides of cakes with an offset spatula and turn out onto cooling racks. Remove the parchment paper and let cakes cool completely, about 40 minutes.

7. Once cake layers are completely cooled, stack and decorate with Cream Cheese Frosting (see "How to Frost a Cake" in Chapter 12) and decorate with extra nuts (if using), or tightly double-wrap cake layers in plastic wrap and freeze for up to 1 month.

# Molten Chocolate Cake

Makes **6** ½-cup (4-oz./120-g) cakes

Chef Jean-Georges Vongerichten created these individual chocolate cakes that became the rage in the 1990s. The secret to these easy cakes is to take them out of the oven at the right stage of the baking process and serve them immediately. If you ever need to impress anyone, use this recipe, which I've adapted slightly from the original.

## INGREDIENTS

Nonstick cooking spray (optional)

4 oz. (120 g) best-quality bittersweet chocolate, coarsely chopped

½ stick (2 oz./60 g) unsalted butter (plus more for greasing)

3 large eggs, at room temperature

¼ cup (1¾ oz./50 g) granulated sugar

1 tsp. pure vanilla extract

⅛ tsp. salt

2 tsp. all-purpose flour (plus more for dusting)

Ice cream, Crème Anglaise (see the recipe in Chapter 8), Fruit Coulis (see the recipe in Chapter 12), or confectioner's sugar (optional)

## EQUIPMENT

6 4-oz. (110-g) ramekins or self-standing cupcake liners

Rimmed baking sheet

Cutting board

Sharp knife

Medium saucepan

Medium heat-proof mixing bowl

Medium mixing bowl

Whisk

Ice cream scoop or ¼-cup-capacity dry measuring cup

Medium silicone spatula

6 serving plates

## Alternative Baking Cups

You can also make these cakes in oven-safe coffee cups.

1. Preheat the oven to 450°F (230°C). Butter and lightly flour the bottoms and sides of the ramekins and place on a rimmed baking sheet. Set aside.

2. Fill a medium saucepan $1/3$ full of water and bring to a simmer over medium heat. Place bittersweet chocolate and butter in a medium bowl, set over the saucepan, and cook until melted. Remove from heat and let cool slightly.

## Melting Chocolate Caution

Make sure no water or steam gets into the chocolate mixture!

3. In a separate medium bowl, whisk eggs, sugar, vanilla extract, and salt until thick and slightly pale. Slowly whisk in melted chocolate mixture and beat until smooth. Add all-purpose flour to chocolate mixture, whisking until incorporated (batter will become thicker).

## Equipment Tip

You can use the same whisk for the whole procedure—no need to wash in between.

4. Scoop batter into the prepared ramekins, filling them all the way to the top. Bake until sides of cakes are firm but centers are still quite soft, liquid, and wobble when jiggled, about 6 to 7 minutes.

## Storing the Cakes

The cups of batter can be made ahead and refrigerated for up to 24 hours. Bring them up to room temperature 30 minutes to 1 hour before baking.

5. Let cakes cool for 1 minute. Gently loosen sides with an offset spatula. Cover each with an inverted serving plate and flip over. Let stand for 10 seconds and then unmold very carefully by lifting the ramekins straight up.

6. Serve immediately with ice cream or Crème Anglaise (see the recipe in Chapter 8) on the side and some Fruit Coulis (see the recipe in Chapter 12), or just dust with sifted confectioner's sugar.

# Russian Sour Cream Coffeecake

Makes **1** 9×13-in. (22×32-cm) cake

Coffeecakes get their name not because they are made with coffee, but because they are a great accompaniment to it. They are very comforting, sweet, moist, and rich but not heavy. This explains why they are eaten not only as dessert, but as breakfast or a snack at any time of the day.

## INGREDIENTS

### Topping:

½ cup (3½ oz./100 g) light brown sugar, firmly packed
¾ cup (3 oz./90 g) all-purpose flour
½ tsp. ground cinnamon
⅛ tsp. salt
½ stick (2 oz./60 g) unsalted butter, softened
½ cup (2 oz./60 g) coarsely chopped walnuts, almonds, or pecans

### Cake:

Nonstick cooking spray
2 cups (9½ oz./285 g) all-purpose flour
1 tsp. baking powder
1 tsp. baking soda
½ tsp. salt
1 stick (4 oz./120 g) unsalted butter, softened
1 cup (7 oz./210 g) granulated sugar
1 tsp. pure vanilla extract
3 large eggs
1 cup (8 oz./240 g) sour cream or plain yogurt

## EQUIPMENT

9×13-in. (23×33-cm) baking pan
Parchment paper
Medium mixing bowl
Silicone spatula
2 table knives or pastry blender
Sieve
Large mixing bowl

Standing mixer fitted with paddle attachment
Toothpick (optional)
Cooling rack
Plastic wrap (optional)

1. Preheat the oven to 350°F (180°C). Spray a baking pan with nonstick cooking spray. Line the bottom with parchment paper, leaving an overhang. Set aside.

2. To make the topping, in a medium bowl, combine light brown sugar, all-purpose flour, cinnamon, and salt with a silicone spatula. With 2 table knives, cut in butter until mixture resembles coarse crumbs. Stir in walnuts and set aside.

## Cutting In the Butter

No pastry blender or knives? Use your fingers! Just don't overwork the mixture, as the heat of your fingers may melt the fat. You still want coarse crumbs, not a completely incorporated dough.

3. To make the cake, using a sieve, sift together all-purpose flour, baking powder, baking soda, and salt into a large bowl.

4. In the bowl of a standing mixer fitted with a paddle attachment, cream butter, sugar, and vanilla extract on medium speed until light and fluffy, about 3 minutes. Beat in eggs one at a time. Scrape the bowl with the silicone spatula.

5. Add flour mixture to egg mixture in 4 separate additions, alternating with sour cream and beating well on low speed after each addition.

6. With the silicone spatula, spread batter in the prepared pan. Sprinkle with topping.

7. Bake until cake is golden and pulls away from the sides or when a toothpick inserted into the center comes out clean and cake springs back when pressed lightly in the center of the pan, about 35 to 40 minutes.

8. Set cake pan on a cooling rack to cool for at least 10 minutes. Unmold cake by pulling up on the parchment overhangs. Serve warm or at room temperature. You can also double-wrap in plastic wrap and store at room temperature for up to 2 days or in the freezer for up to 3 months.

**Variations:** For a different presentation, make this cake in a Bundt pan! Spread $1/3$ of batter in the bottom of the pan, sprinkle with $1/3$ of filling, and repeat these layers twice. Bake until golden, about 50 minutes.

# Chocoflan

This is chocolate cake and flan all in one; it's rich, quite luxurious, and a fascinating magic trick. The cake batter is poured in the pan first and then topped with the custard (flan) mixture. While in the oven, the two layers mysteriously switch places, and when the cake is unmolded, the flan ends up on top!

## INGREDIENTS

**Sauce:**

Nonstick cooking spray

½ cup (8 oz./240 g) dulce de leche (or cajeta)* or caramel sauce

**Cake:**

1¾ cups (7⅓ oz./220 g) all-purpose flour

1 cup (7 oz./210 g) granulated sugar

⅓ cup (1 oz./30 g) unsweetened cocoa powder

¾ tsp. baking powder

¾ tsp. baking soda

½ tsp. salt

1 large egg, at room temperature

½ cup (4 oz./120 g) neutral-tasting oil (see "Other Fats and Oils" in Chapter 2)

1¼ cups (10 oz./300 g) buttermilk

**Flan:**

1 (12-oz.) can evaporated milk

1 (14-oz.) can sweetened condensed milk

4 large eggs

1 TB. pure vanilla extract

½ tsp. salt

**Topping:**

¼ cup chopped pecans, toasted

*Sold in Latin American markets or online.*

## EQUIPMENT

12-cup-capacity Bundt pan

Roasting pan *or* pan that easily fits Bundt pan

Large mixing bowl (2 if using an immersion blender)

Whisk

Silicone spatula

Medium saucepan or kettle

Blender (regular or immersion)

Aluminum foil

Toothpick (optional)

Cooling rack

Serving platter

1. Preheat the oven to 350°F (180°C). Generously coat the inside of a Bundt pan with nonstick cooking spray. Pour dulce de leche in the bottom of the pan and place the pan in a roasting pan. Set aside.

2. To make the cake, in a large bowl, whisk all-purpose flour, sugar, cocoa powder, baking powder, baking soda, and salt until well incorporated. Switch to a silicone spatula and add egg and neutral-tasting oil, mixing until blended. Add buttermilk and mix until thoroughly combined. Pour cake batter into the prepared Bundt pan. Set aside.

3. Put water in a medium saucepan and bring to a boil over medium-high heat. (This is for the water bath.)

4. To make the flan, in a blender, combine evaporated milk, condensed milk, eggs, vanilla extract, and salt and blend on high for 30 seconds. Slowly pour flan mixture over cake batter.

5. Cover the Bundt pan loosely with aluminum foil and add hot water into the roasting pan to reach a bit over halfway up the Bundt pan. Place the entire setup in the oven.

6. Bake until surface of cake is firm to the touch or a toothpick inserted into center comes out clean, about 50 to 60 minutes. Remove the Bundt pan from the water bath and transfer to a cooling rack to cool completely, about 4 hours, or refrigerate overnight.

7. To unmold, invert a large, rimmed serving platter over the Bundt pan, hold together tightly, and flip over. Remove the pan and top with chopped pecans. Serve cold, at room temperature, or warmed up. Cake can also be covered and kept for 1 day at room temperature or for up to 2 days in the refrigerator.

## Can't Find Dulce de Leche?

Make your own! The process takes a little patience, but it's super easy. Take a can of sweetened condensed milk and put it in your slow cooker. (Don't open the can!) Add water until the can is completely covered. Set the cooker to low and cook for 8 hours (or up to 10 hours if you like darker caramel). After cooking, set the can in cold water to bring it to room temperature, making sure not to open it until it's cool. Once cool, open the can, and *voilà*—dulce de leche! The sauce can be stored in an airtight container for several weeks (if it lasts that long!).

You can cook more than one can at once, if you like—just make sure the cans aren't touching each other in the cooker.

## Pan Safety Precautions

If you're worried about transferring the roasting pan with the hot water to the oven, place the roasting pan with the Bundt pan in it in the oven first. You can then pour the water into the roasting pan.

# Adapting Cake Recipes for Cupcakes

Nearly any recipe that is suitable for a layer cake can be used to make cupcakes. People love munching on these ready-made, individual portions that can be frosted and decorated any way you like. The following walks you through what you need to do to adapt.

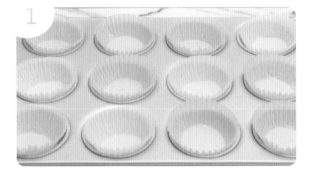

**Line the muffin tins.** It's much easier to release cupcakes out of the muffin pan when the pan is lined with paper or foil cupcake liners. Self-standing cupcake liners are available and work well when placed on a baking sheet.

**Distribute the batter evenly.** Try to fill up the muffin pan as evenly as possible, as doing so promotes even baking. Ice cream scoops, piping bags, and ¼-cup dry measure cups are all good for dispensing cupcake batter and make the job easier and neater.

## Having Trouble Pouring?

If you make cupcakes often but have a hard time pouring the batter without a mess, you might think of investing in a batter dispenser. These practical tools are specially made for cupcakes and/or pancakes.

**Compensate for empty space in the pan.** If you don't fill up all the cavities in a pan with batter, fill the remaining ones with water. This distributes the heat and ensures even baking, so some aren't done or burnt while others are not baked through.

## Cupcake Cautions

The following are a couple common issues you should avoid when making cupcakes:

- **Avoid overfilling the pans:** Don't fill up cupcake molds more than $^3/_4$ full, unless specified in the recipe. You don't want the batter to overflow!

- **Don't bake too long:** Due to their small size, cupcakes conduct heat more efficiently, so they bake much faster than full-size layered cakes.

- **Cool before decorating:** Never frost a cupcake while it's still warm; otherwise, the frosting or icing will turn into a milklike substance and lose its shape and texture. Be patient!

# Save the Wreck!

Unless the cake is completely burnt (and I mean carbonized), there's almost always a solution, even if the baking process didn't go as smoothly as planned. If the cake is underbaked (and you only realized when it was too late to keep it longer in the oven), if it collapsed when you unmolded it, if it overbaked or baked unevenly, and sometimes if an ingredient was omitted or measured wrong, there are some tricks you can use to still be able to serve a less-than-perfect cake and impress your guests. Try to keep at hand one or more (ideally three) of the following:

**Let fruit save you.** Fruit can cover up some mistakes or imperfections, adding flavor and color. You can macerate frozen fruit (preferably of different kinds) in a bit of sugar until the juices come out and use them as a sauce or a topping. Fresh fruit of as many colors as possible (dry fruit works, too) can also be sliced in different shapes and thicknesses. You can also prepare a fruit coulis (see the recipe in Chapter 12).

**Whip it up.** A dollop or a layer of whipped cream or coconut whipped cream (see the recipes in Chapter 12) can cover many imperfections and act as a filling or a topping, offering great texture, contrast, and volume. If you have no whipping cream or canned coconut milk, use your breakfast Greek yogurt! Sweeten it to taste with sugar and add a bit of vanilla extract; it will add an extra-tangy quality to the dessert.

**Add some booze.** Dessert wine or any liquor (even brewed coffee or tea, if you don't want to add any alcohol) brushed onto layers of dry cake or pastry can add back some of the lost moisture.

**Get help from what you've got at home.** Store-bought ice cream and/or sorbet, cookie crumbs or crushed cookies, chopped nuts, cacao nibs, shaved chocolate or chocolate chips, and shaved coconut are helpful in preparing a composed dessert out of a recipe gone wrong! They can add texture and cover up imperfections.

**Get fancy.** Wrecked (and nonwrecked) desserts taste amazing with sauce(s). Use the recipes provided in this book to make pastry cream, crème anglaise (see the recipe in Chapter 8), and/or chocolate ganache (see the recipe in Chapter 12) to make a sauce for your dessert. No time? You can use store-bought chocolate sauce (although it won't be the same, it can still save your wreck!).

**Cut and serve smartly.** You can turn wrecked cake rounds into individual trifles. A large round cookie cutter, a pastry brush (if using wine or liquor), small Mason jars or wine glasses, and spoons can help you work some magic. Cut the cake layers into rounds with a cookie cutter (they don't need to come out as perfect circles) so they fit into the Mason jar or wine glass. Alternate layers of cake (that you can brush with wine or liquor before placing in the jars) with one or more of the ingredients mentioned previously (ideally, use three of them), mixing and matching with the ones you have available. If you forgot to add sugar to the cake, make sure you include a very sweet element. If the cake turned out too dry, make sure you add a creamy and a moist element, such as crème anglaise and fruit coulis, and brush the cake with liquor or honey or maple syrup diluted in water. Cover with plastic wrap (or jar lids) and refrigerate for 30 minutes or overnight. Serve with spoons.

## Serving Portions

Use spoons to serve individual tasting portions of a composed dessert. Just layer it up the same way as described previously, but in tiny individual portions.

*chapter 12*

# Cake Decorating

Cakes are edible canvases where anyone can let their creative juices flow. Decorated cakes can be turned into complex pieces of art or architecture or made into simple, eye-pleasing desserts. There's an innumerable amount of styles, techniques, and ingredients to decorate cakes, which is the subject of this chapter.

You're working with ingredients that change consistency and color with temperature and other conditions you can't completely control, which can be frustrating at times. However, the results are worth it. Go with the flow and have items to cover up your mistakes, such as sprinkles, fondant cut-outs, store-bought sugar decorations, baked cookies, and even extra frosting. Even professional cake designers have to improvise sometimes, so don't worry! Plus, you'll get more familiar with the motions and textures of buttercream, icing, chocolate, fondant, or anything else you decide to use. So start with simple projects, and as you gain confidence, challenge yourself.

# How to Frost a Cake

A frosting or icing is a sweet coating for cakes and other baked goods. It adds flavor and richness; enhances appearance; and forms a protective coat, keeping the cake fresh for a longer time. Buttercream, royal icing, glaze, fudge, ganache, boiled icing, and fondant are all examples of frosting, and all have different uses and characteristics. In general, buttercreams are the most widely used kind of frosting in cake decorating, so the following steps use this frosting to illustrate the assembly and frosting of a layer cake.

Brush loose crumbs from the cake with a pastry brush, as they make icing difficult.

If using a serving plate, place sheets of parchment paper under the edges of the cake to keep the plate clean.

**Get the cake layer ready.** Turning your baked cake layer onto a cardboard cake circle (see "Papers, Mats, and Boards" in Chapter 1) will put it upside down, giving a flat surface to the frosting. Frozen cake is the easiest to cut, crumbles the least, and is less delicate and easier to handle; therefore, you should wrap the cooled layers individually in plastic wrap and freeze them overnight.

**Spread the frosting.** To give it some height and allow you to turn it, place the first cake layer of cake—still on the cake board but unwrapped—in the center of a cake turntable or on a serving plate. Spread the frosting with an offset spatula on the bottom layer from the center out to the edges; you always want to push rather than pull the filling when spreading.

## Watch the Temperatures!

Cake layers must be completely cooled before assembling and frosting; otherwise, the icing melts. If you can't freeze the cooled cake before assembling, make sure you spread a dab of frosting in the center of the cake circle to hold the cake layer in place.

When ready to frost, use buttercream at room temperature in order to have the right consistency. If the buttercream has been refrigerated, remove it from the refrigerator at least 1 hour before using.

## Piping the Frosting

Alternatively, you could pipe the frosting in a spiral starting in the center of the cake, until the whole surface is covered. If you do it this way, use a large, plain pastry tip.

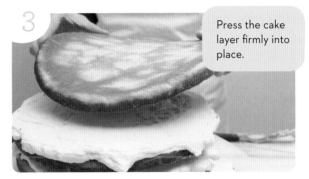

3 Press the cake layer firmly into place.

**Add the next layer.** Remove the next layer from the wrapping and very carefully scrape the bottom of the cake away from the cake board using an offset spatula; you want it to stay together. Place the cake on top of the frosted bottom layer of cake flat side up so frosting it is smoother. Frost as described in step 2 and repeat with the other layers, if applicable.

4 Push rather than pull or drag to prevent pulling up crumbs and getting them all mixed with the icing.

**Frost the whole cake.** The first frosting layer is called the *crumb coat,* because it holds all the crumbs. Place a good amount of icing on the center of the cake, and then spread it to the edges and down the sides. Once you're finished, hold the spatula at an angle and, with a very light hand, smooth the ridges toward the center, rotating and smoothing until they disappear. Refrigerate or freeze the cake a few minutes to harden the layer a bit.

5 Don't overdo the amount of frosting—it's easier to add than to take away.

**Add the second layer of frosting.** The second "hand" of frosting gives the cake a clean, crumbless finish. Dipping the spatula in hot water will help create a smooth coat. You can smooth the icing or give it texture or swirls. You can also pipe designs or—taking advantage of the stickiness of the frosting—adhere decorative sprinkles, fondant cut-outs, candy, and so on.

# How to Decorate a Cake in Simple Ways

There are many simple ways of beautifying cakes and cupcakes to the max. When decorating, it's always important to keep in mind color and texture, as contrast guides the eye and makes a strong impact. The following are some great techniques to take your baked goods to the next level.

**Masking:** Apply a coating of chopped or sliced nuts, coconut, chocolate shavings, sprinkles, cake crumbs, or any other ingredient in small pieces to the sides of a cake. Hold the frosted cake (always on a cake board or serving plate; otherwise, the bare cake may break) in your hand over a sheet of parchment paper. Lightly press a handful of the selected ingredient with your dominant hand against the side of the cake, letting the excess fall onto the parchment paper. Turn the cake a quarter turn and repeat until the sides are completely (or partially, if you prefer) covered. Feel free to reuse the pieces on the parchment.

**Stenciling:** Designs can be made on a cake by masking part of the top with either a store-bought stencil, parchment paper cut-outs, or a paper doily and then dusting the cake with Confectioners' sugar, cocoa powder, shaved chocolate, nut flour, or another ingredient in very fine form (passed through a sieve). Parchment paper cut-outs can also mask a cake to be sprayed with food coloring, revealing patterns or designs after the cut-outs are carefully peeled off.

## Confectioners' Sugar Caution

Note that confectioners' sugar dissolves into the frosting, so apply it right before serving the cake; otherwise, it will get absorbed into the surface of the cake and the design will disappear.

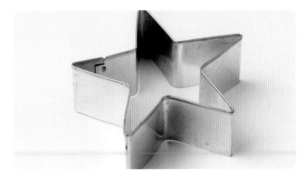

**Using cookie cutters as stencils:** This is a variation of stenciling. It allows you to use two different decorating elements at the same time, giving you great results when using decorator's sugar or sprinkles in different colors. Select a cookie cutter (you can use more than one) and place it on top of a cake or cupcake. Place one type of colored sugar or sprinkles all over the inside of the outline of the cutter and another color (you can skip the second color, if you want) outside the outline. Carefully lift the cutter to reveal the design on the icing.

**Drizzling:** Melted white, dark, and/or colored chocolate can be drizzled on top of a cake with the back of a wooden spoon (or a fork) into a squiggle design. This is a very easy way of adding color and contrast. Just make sure you let the chocolate set before handling it!

**Making patterns:** Take advantage of the shapes and colors of nuts, fruits, and small molded chocolates and arrange them at the same intervals all around the perimeter of a frosted cake.

## Get Creative!

You can arrange any of the aforementioned ingredients in patterns and specific sequences, or you can do random, free-form designs. Just make sure you don't do a bit of patterns and a bit of free designs together—a mix of the two will be confusing to the eye and will lack harmony. Choose one or the other.

## Great Ingredients for Cake Decorating

Nuts; fresh and dried fruit; melted, ground, shaved, or molded chocolate; marzipan shapes and fondant cut-outs; baked cookies and meringues; nonsprayed edible flowers (either candied or fresh); decorator's sugar; and sprinkles are all very good for creating edible designs with different shapes and textures. However, never underestimate the effect of dusted cocoa powder or Confectioners' sugar!

# Swiss Meringue Buttercream

Makes about **3 cups** (24 oz./675 g) frosting

## INGREDIENTS

4 large (4 oz./120 g) egg whites

1 cup plus 3 TB. (8 oz./240 g) granulated sugar

⅛ tsp. salt

3 sticks (12 oz./360 g) unsalted butter, softened

2 tsp. pure vanilla extract

## EQUIPMENT

Small saucepan (smaller than the base of the bowl of the standing mixer)

Standing mixer fitted with whisk attachment

Silicone spatula

1. In a small saucepan, add egg whites, sugar, and salt and follow technique on "How to Make Swiss Meringue" (see Chapter 7).

2. Pour Swiss meringue into the bowl of a standing mixer, add butter several tablespoons at a time, beating well on medium-low speed after each addition. At some point, the mixture will look curdled; that's normal. Add vanilla extract and beat until incorporated, scraping down the sides of the bowl with the spatula as necessary.

3. Buttercream can be kept refrigerated in an airtight container for up to 1 week or frozen for up to 1 month. Bring to room temperature before using.

# Classic American Buttercream

Makes about **3 cups** (24 oz./675 g) icing

## INGREDIENTS

1 stick (8 oz./240 g) unsalted butter, softened

3 to 4 cups (24 to 32 oz./375 to 500 g) confectioner's sugar

¼ cup (2 oz./60 g) whole milk

1 tsp. pure vanilla extract

⅛ tsp. salt

## EQUIPMENT

Standing mixer fitted with paddle attachment

Silicone spatula

1. In the bowl of a standing mixer, beat butter on medium speed until soft and creamy, about 2 to 3 minutes. Add 3 cups confectioner's sugar, whole milk, vanilla extract, and salt, and mix over low speed until light and fluffy and the icing is thick enough to spread, about 5 minutes. Scrape down the sides of the bowl with the spatula as necessary.

2. If icing is still too loose, add remaining confectioner's sugar ¼ cup at a time to desired consistency.

3. Use, or store at room temperature in airtight container for up to 3 days.

# Chocolate Ganache

Makes **2 cups** (16 oz./500 g) ganache

Chocolate ganache is the fancy name of a densely rich chocolate cream that can be used as a frosting or glaze or a base for truffles, popsicles, mousses, and even hot chocolate. The best news is that it's made with only two ingredients—chocolate and heavy cream—although other flavors can be added as well.

## INGREDIENTS

8 oz. (240 g) bittersweet chocolate
1 cup (8 oz./240 g) heavy cream

## EQUIPMENT

Cutting board
Serrated knife
Medium heat-proof
   bowl
Small saucepan
Silicone spatula

Standing mixer fitted
   with whisk attach-
   ment (if making
   whipped ganache)

**Variations:** The ingredient proportion to make basic ganache is 1:1 (chocolate to cream); however, it can be made firmer or softer. For a firmer product, the ratio can be changed to 2:1. If you want a soft-textured ganache, the ratio can be changed to 1:2. If you want to intensify the chocolate flavor, add salt flakes or a bit of fine salt.

1. On a cutting board, chop bittersweet chocolate with a serrated knife into pieces no larger than $1/4$ inch (5 mm) and place in a medium bowl. Set aside.

2. Bring heavy cream to a boil in a small saucepan over medium heat. Cream will rise up in the pan, but don't let it boil over. Remove from heat and immediately pour cream over chocolate. Let stand for 2 minutes.

3. Stir with a silicone spatula in a circular motion, from the center of the bowl and moving outward, until chocolate is completely melted and mixture is smooth.

4. To use as a cake filling or for truffles: Let ganache sit at room temperature to cool, about 15 minutes. Once cool, it can be covered and refrigerated for up to 2 weeks.

   To use as a glaze for cakes, cookies, and so on: Use warm ganache immediately, pouring it over cake or dunking cookies into it. Reheat for a few seconds if it starts to harden.

   To use as a frosting: Place cooled ganache in the bowl of a standing mixer fitted with a whisk attachment, and whip on medium speed until ganache is light, thick, and creamy. Spread on desired item immediately, as it sets when cold.

# Whipped Cream

Makes about **2 cups** (8 oz./240 g)
whipped cream

## INGREDIENTS

1 cup (8 oz./240 g) heavy
cream

1 TB. granulated sugar or
more to taste

1 tsp. pure vanilla extract (or
seeds of ½ vanilla bean)

## EQUIPMENT

Standing mixer fitted with whisk attachment or medium
metal mixing bowl and a handheld mixer or whisk

1. Chill the mixing bowl and whisk attachment in
   the freezer for at least 15 minutes.

2. In the chilled bowl, place heavy cream, sugar,
   and vanilla extract and beat at low speed until
   small bubbles form, about 30 seconds. Increase
   the speed to medium and beat until the beaters
   leave a trail, about 30 seconds. Continue beating on medium speed until cream is smooth,
   thick, and almost twice its initial volume. Stop
   once the desired consistency is reached (either
   soft or stiff peaks).

3. Use and store any leftover whipped cream in
   an airtight container in the fridge for up to 10
   hours. When ready to use, rewhip for 10 to 15
   seconds.

# Coconut Whipped Cream

Makes about **2 cups** (12 oz./360 g)
whipped cream

## INGREDIENTS

1 (13.5-fl-oz./398-ml) can
full-fat unsweetened
coconut milk, chilled
overnight

1 TB. granulated sugar or
more to taste

1 tsp. pure vanilla extract (or
seeds of ½ vanilla bean)

## EQUIPMENT

Standing mixer fitted with whisk attachment or medium
metal mixing bowl and a handheld mixer or whisk

1. Chill the mixing bowl and whisk attachment in
   the freezer for at least 15 minutes.

2. While equipment chills, remove coconut milk
   from the fridge very carefully and without
   shaking. When you open the can, the milk
   should have separated while chilling (you want
   that!). Scoop off cream that has risen to the top
   and place in the chilled bowl. Add sugar and
   vanilla extract and beat on medium speed until
   mixture looks like whipped cream, about 1 to 2
   minutes.

3. Use and store any leftover whipped cream in
   an airtight container in the fridge for up to 10
   hours. When ready to use, rewhip for 10 to 15
   seconds.

# Cream Cheese Frosting

Makes about **2¹/₂ cups**
(17 oz./510 g) frosting

This classic creamy, tangy, rich frosting is great on carrot cake; cakes with fruits, nuts, and vegetables (such as pumpkins); or on its own by the spoonful! In my opinion, it's best when the amount of sugar is kept on the lower range, as this lets all the other flavors come through.

## INGREDIENTS

8 oz. (240 g) cream cheese, at room temperature
   for about 1 hour
1 stick (4 oz./120 g) unsalted butter, softened
2 tsp. pure vanilla extract
2 TB. lemon juice (optional)
1 cup (4 oz./120 g) confectioner's sugar

## EQUIPMENT

Standing mixer fitted with paddle attachment
Silicone spatula

1. In the bowl of a standing mixture fitted with a paddle attachment, place cream cheese, butter, vanilla extract, and lemon juice (if using) and mix on medium-high speed until fluffy, about 3 minutes. Scrape down the bowl with a silicone spatula. Add confectioner's sugar and beat until creamy and smooth, about 1 to 2 minutes.

2. Frost desired items at room temperature. Frosting can be stored covered and refrigerated for up to 5 days, but it should be brought to room temperature and rewhipped before using.

## Chilling the Equipment

It's essential to work with cream and equipment that are cold to make sure the emulsion (air suspension) is successful.

# Fruit Coulis

A coulis (pronounced *koo-LEE*) is a sweetened fruit purée used as a sauce for desserts. From cheesecake, to molten chocolate cakes, to coffeecake, a coulis can enhance and add a colorful touch to pretty much any sweet treat.

Yields about **3¹/₄ cups** (26 oz./780 g) fruit coulis

## INGREDIENTS

1¹/₂ pt. (18 oz./500 g) fresh or frozen fruit, pitted, hulled, and peeled as necessary

¹/₂ cup water

¹/₂ to ³/₄ cup sugar or to taste

2 tsp. lemon or lime juice (from about 1 fruit)

## EQUIPMENT

Medium saucepan

Blender or immersion blender *or* food processor

Sieve

Small mixing bowl

Silicone spatula

Plastic wrap

## Fruit You Can Use

Strawberries, raspberries, blueberries, blackberries, mango, kiwi, and peaches all make good coulis. No fresh fruit? Frozen fruit can be used with great results.

**CHAPTER 12 |** CAKE DECORATING

1. In a medium saucepan, combine fruit, water, and ½ cup sugar. Cook over medium-high heat, stirring occasionally, until sugar is dissolved and fruit has heated through. If needed, add more sugar.

## Save the Wreck!

If you're in a rush or trying to cover a baking wreck, purée the fruit with water and sugar without even cooking or straining it. The uncooked purée won't be as thick, but it will still add color and flavor and will get you out of trouble!

## Decorating with Coulis

Get creative by putting coulis of different fruits into squeeze bottles and decorating plates or desserts with a variety of colors, shapes, and flavors.

2. Remove from heat, transfer mixture to a blender (leave in the saucepan if you're using an immersion blender), and purée until smooth.

3. Pass mixture through a sieve into a small bowl, pressing with a silicone spatula to extract as much liquid as possible. Discard solids and stir in lemon juice.

4. Cover with plastic wrap and refrigerate until cold. Stir before using. Coulis can be kept covered and refrigerated for up to 4 days. If it's too thick when you're ready to use it, thin with a bit of water.

*part 5*

# Breads

**Chapter 13:** Quick Breads

**Chapter 14:** Yeast-Risen Breads

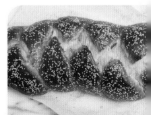

*chapter 13*

# Quick Breads

If yeast scares you; if you have an urge but little time to bake; or if you are looking for something fresh, delicious, and super easy to come out of your oven, you are in the right chapter.

Although quick breads have many ingredients in common with breads (of any kind), yeast is not one of them. Quick breads rise thanks to the predictable and fast-acting powers of chemically produced baking powder and/or baking soda, as opposed to a living organism. Because they don't require fermentation and are tender products with no need for gluten development, whipping up a batch of quick breads usually takes only a few minutes—hence the name.

There's a great diversity of quick breads in terms of texture, size, presentation, and flavor. For example, *muffins*—which are individual-sized quick breads—could be savory and have cheese and/or vegetables in them, or they could be sweet and made with fresh fruit. *Biscuits* and *scones* can also be savory or sweet and eaten with dinner or as breakfast.

# How to Make Muffins

Some recipes call for making muffins using the creaming method, but most use the actual *muffin method*. The main aspect of the muffin method is that you don't actually mix the batter too much, so you never want to use an electric mixer when making muffins. Here's how it's done.

**Prepare the pan.** Although you don't have to use them, muffin liners do make cleanup and transport of your muffins much easier. They are a matter of preference—if you'd rather not use liners, just be sure to grease the pan well with cooking spray.

**Prepare the dry ingredients.** Because you want to stir the batter as little as possible, sifting the dry ingredients makes sure they're well incorporated before adding them to the wet ingredients.

## Run Out of Liners?

Use parchment paper! Just cut the parchment paper into 5-inch (12.5-cm) circles and press into the tin, smoothing out the creases until they fit. Parchment paper creates a crispier outside to your muffins, which some people prefer!

## When Are They Done?

Test your muffins for doneness by either inserting a toothpick in the center (which should come out clean when ready) or by touching gently the top of the muffin or loaf in the center to see if it springs back.

**Prepare the liquid ingredients.** Most muffins use eggs and oils for the liquids. In a separate bowl from the dry ingredients, just whisk the eggs, oils, and all other liquids until well combined.

**Combine.** Add the liquid ingredients to the dry ones and mix with a silicone spatula just until the flour is moistened. The batter will look lumpy, but that's okay; it doesn't need to be smooth. *Don't overmix!* You'll end up with tough, irregular-shaped muffins or elongated holes inside the muffins. The less you mix, the less gluten is developed and the more delicate the muffin will be.

**Include add-ins.** If you're using chocolate chips, chopped nuts, herbs, shredded cheese, fruit, and so on, add them right after the dry and liquid ingredients have been combined. Do it gently and with as few strokes as possible to avoid overmixing.

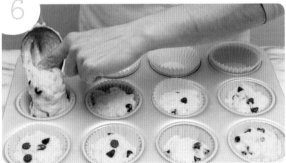

**Pan and bake.** Pour the batter into prepared pans and bake immediately. This is key, as the baking soda starts reacting the moment it gets exposed to moisture, and you want it to generate gas in the oven (not before baking). If you let the batter sit, the leavening won't work properly and the volume will be lost.

Muffins and quick breads freeze beautifully—just double-wrap them after they have cooled completely.

# Yogurt Muffins

makes **12** muffins

These delicious, easy, and simple muffins are moist, sweet, and lightly scented with vanilla. Once you've gained confidence with the basic recipe, you can add different flavors and textures with foolproof results, as long as you stick with the basic ingredients and proportions.

## INGREDIENTS

2 cups (10 oz./300 g) unbleached all-purpose flour
3/4 cup (5.5 oz./165 g) granulated sugar
2 tsp. baking powder
1/4 tsp. salt
1 cup (8 oz./240 g) plain Greek yogurt
1/3 cup (2 2/3 oz./80 g) neutral-tasting oil (see "Other Fats and Oils" in Chapter 2)
2 large eggs
1 tsp. pure vanilla extract

## EQUIPMENT

12-cup muffin pan
12 muffin paper liners
2 medium mixing bowls
Sieve or sifter
Whisk
Spoon or ice cream scoop
Toothpick or cake tester
Cooling rack
Plastic wrap (optional)

1. Preheat the oven to 350°F (180°C). Line the muffin pan with paper liners and set aside.

2. In a medium bowl, sift together all-purpose flour, sugar, baking powder, and salt with a sieve. Set aside.

3. In a separate medium bowl, whisk together Greek yogurt, neutral-tasting oil, eggs, and vanilla extract until combined and smooth. Whisk liquid mixture into flour mixture until just combined (all flour should be moistened). If any other ingredients are used, they should be added at this point.

4. Spoon mixture into the cups of the prepared pan, filling the cups 3/4 full.

5. Bake until a toothpick inserted into centers comes out clean and muffins spring back when pressed lightly in the center, 25 to 30 minutes.

6. Remove from the oven and let cool on a cooling rack, about 5 minutes. Take muffins out of the pan and serve warm or at room temperature. Muffins keep well for 1 day in an airtight container at room temperature or double-wrapped in plastic wrap and frozen for up to 1 month.

# Banana Muffins

makes **12** muffins

These muffins are ultra-moist, sweet, delicious, and easy. They are also the best way to use those overripe bananas hanging at the kitchen countertop. The darker the peel, the sweeter the muffins will be.

## INGREDIENTS

3 small to medium very ripe bananas

1 large egg

¼ cup (2 oz./60 g) neutral-tasting oil (see "Other Fats and Oils" in Chapter 2)

1 tsp. pure vanilla extract

1 cup (7 oz./210 g) granulated sugar

1 cup (4¼ oz./120 g) all-purpose flour

1 tsp. baking soda

¼ tsp. salt

## EQUIPMENT

12-cup muffin pan

12 muffin paper liners

Blender, food processor, immersion blender, or standing mixer fitted with whisk attachment

Silicone spatula

Spoon or ice cream scoop

Toothpick or cake tester

Cooling rack

Plastic wrap (optional)

1. Preheat the oven to 350°F (180°C). Line the muffin pan with paper liners and set aside.

2. In a blender, blend bananas on high speed until completely mashed. Add egg, neutral-tasting oil, and vanilla extract and blend on high again until combined. Scrape down the sides with a silicone spatula.

3. Add sugar, all-purpose flour, baking soda, and salt and pulse 3 to 5 times until well combined without overmixing.

4. Spoon mixture into the cups of the prepared pan, filling the cups ²/₃ full.

5. Bake until a toothpick inserted into centers comes out clean and muffins spring back when pressed lightly in the center, 18 to 22 minutes.

6. Remove from the oven and let cool on a cooling rack, about 5 minutes. Take muffins out of the pan and serve warm or at room temperature. Muffins keep well for 1 day in an airtight container at room temperature or double-wrapped in plastic wrap and frozen for up to 1 month.

# How to Make Biscuits and Scones

Deliciously soft, dense, and flaky, biscuits and scones owe most of their texture to their high fat content. This lubricates the gluten strands in the dough, acting as a tenderizer that prevents gluten from developing more than necessary. Again, avoid handling the dough as much as possible, as gluten develops through kneading. Biscuits and scones are mixed through the *biscuit* or *pastry method,* which is done with the following steps.

**Measure the ingredients.** Measure and sift your dry ingredients. The best way to measure your ingredients is by using a scale so you don't get too much flour in your biscuits, which could make them tough.

Pulse, don't process! Overmixing the dough will melt the fat, and you'll lose the flakiness.

**Cut in the fat.** Because you want your fats to stay as cold as possible, it's best to cut in the fats using a food processor (recommended) or your hands. Pulse together the dry ingredients. Add the fat and pulse again until the mixture resembles coarse meal, with pieces of butter no larger than a pea.

## Mixing by Hand

If mixing it by hand, try to work as quickly as possible using 1 mixing bowl and 2 forks to do the mixing. Make sure all the ingredients are really cold, especially the fat (you could even freeze the flour-sugar-salt mixture for 15 minutes while you cut the butter).

The dough should look crumbly.

**Add the liquids.** Mix the liquid ingredients into the fat-flour mixture, just until the ingredients are combined and a soft dough is formed. Don't overmix, or the fat pieces, which are needed for texture, can get incorporated into the rest of the dough and gluten may develop.

**Knead the dough.** Knead the dough lightly on a work surface or just press the dough together into a mass. Because the dough will be a bit sticky, use a bench scraper to lift and fold the dough over on itself. Don't overwork the dough—you just want to get it to where it's sticking together, not a smooth ball.

**Roll out.** Roll out the dough with a rolling pin to the thickness specified in the recipe. If your dough is still sticky, you can flour the surface a bit or place the dough between sheets of parchment paper.

**Cut the dough.** Use a knife, a bench scraper, or round cutters, depending on what shape you want your biscuits to be. If the dough is too sticky, dip the cutters in flour to make a sharper cut. Space the cuts as closely as possible to minimize scraps.

**Brush.** Place the scones or biscuits on the prepared pans, leaving space in between. Brush the tops with egg wash or milk and sprinkle with sugar or toppings, depending on the recipe. Bake immediately until slightly golden and fragrant.

## Make Ahead!

Biscuits and scones are best the day they are made, so it's ideal to bake them fresh every time. To make them ahead, follow the steps up to step 5, place them on a pan, and freeze until firm. Once frozen, you can just put them in a zipper-lock freezer bag and keep them in the freezer until you're ready to bake. The baking time will be longer, but there's no need to thaw them ahead.

# Biscuits

Biscuits are traditional quick breads from the American South, and fresh out of the oven, they are pure flaky glory! Although traditionally made with buttermilk, I've adapted this recipe to use yogurt instead, as buttermilk isn't easy to find in some places.

## INGREDIENTS

2¼ cups (9⅓ oz./280 g) all-purpose flour

1 TB. granulated sugar (for sweet biscuits, increase the sugar to 2 TB.)

1 TB. baking powder

¾ tsp. baking soda

¾ tsp. salt

1 stick (4 oz./120 g) unsalted butter, chilled

1 cup (8 oz./240 g) plain yogurt (not Greek)

## EQUIPMENT

Rimmed baking sheet

Parchment paper

Large mixing bowl

Whisk

Cutting board

Sharp knife

Pastry blender (optional)

Silicone spatula

Ice cream scoop or ¼-cup dry measuring cup (optional)

1. Preheat the oven to 400°F (200°C). Line a rimmed baking sheet with parchment paper and set aside.

2. In a large bowl, whisk together all-purpose flour, sugar, baking powder, baking soda, and salt.

3. On a cutting board, cut butter into about ½-inch (1-cm) cubes with a sharp knife. Add cubes to the bowl with dry ingredients and, using a pastry blender or your fingers, cut butter into flour mixture until it resembles coarse meal.

4. Using a silicone spatula, stir in yogurt until large, moist clumps form. While it's still in the bowl, use your hands to briefly knead mixture just until it holds together.

5. Using a standard-size ice cream scoop, scoop portions of dough onto the prepared baking sheet, leaving about 2 inches (5 cm) between each mound. Lightly pat top of each mound to flatten slightly.

## Alternative to Scooping Dough

Instead of scooping the dough out, transfer the dough to a lightly floured surface and pat to a ³/₄-inch (8-mm) thickness. Using a round cookie cutter, cut out biscuits and place on the prepared baking sheet, leaving 2 inches (5 cm) in between each.

6. Bake until golden brown, 12 to 14 minutes depending on size. Cool for 5 minutes and serve as soon as possible.

## Freezing Biscuit Dough

Biscuits don't keep well once baked, but the dough can be shaped into portions and frozen for up to 1 month or until ready to bake (just add a couple more minutes to the baking time).

**Variations:** For savory biscuits, add ½ cup (2 oz./60 g) ground Parmesan cheese or 1 tablespoon chopped fresh herbs after the butter has been cut into the flour. You can also use these biscuits to make the American classic, strawberry shortcake—just split the biscuits and fill with fresh strawberries and whipped cream.

# Oat Scones

makes **12** scones

Cream of tartar, together with baking soda and the moistness of the milk, make the oats rise and give these delicious scones their characteristic dense but still light consistency—a crusty exterior and a soft, flaky interior. The oats add a lovely bite and an even, more complex texture.

## INGREDIENTS

1½ cups (6⅓ oz./190 g) all-purpose flour (plus more for dusting and covering hands)

½ tsp. salt

1 tsp. baking soda

2 tsp. cream of tartar

½ cup (1¾ oz./50 g) rolled oats

2 TB. (1 oz./30 g) granulated sugar or evaporated cane juice (plus more for sprinkling)

3 TB. (1½ oz./45 g) unsalted butter, chilled

¾ cup (6 oz./ 180 g) whole milk

## EQUIPMENT

Rimmed baking sheet

Parchment paper

Sieve

Large mixing bowl

Whisk

Pastry cutter (optional)

Cutting board

2-in. (5-cm) round cutter

Pastry brush

Cooling back

## What Is Evaporated Cane Juice?

Evaporated cane juice, also called *turbinado,* can be found in higher-end or specialty supermarkets. Don't worry if you can't find it—granulated sugar works just as well.

1. Preheat the oven to 425°F (215°C). Line a rimmed baking sheet with parchment paper and set aside.

2. With a sieve, sift all-purpose flour, salt, baking soda, and cream of tartar into a large bowl. Whisk in oats and sugar, mixing until well distributed.

3. Using a pastry cutter or your fingertips, cut in butter pieces until mixture looks like coarse meal or wet sand. Add all but 2 tablespoons whole milk and mix very briefly.

4. Turn out mixture onto a floured cutting board. With lightly floured hands (you'll need this because dough is very sticky), clump dough together to form a rough ball. Pat dough to about 1- to 1$\frac{1}{4}$-inch (2.5- to 3.2-cm) thickness. Dip the round cutter into flour and cut dough into circles. Place cut rounds on the prepared baking sheet, leaving 1 inch (2.5 cm) in between each. Gather together remaining dough, pat it down again, and cut.

5. Using a pastry brush, brush tops of scones with remaining 2 tablespoons whole milk and sprinkle each with about $\frac{1}{4}$ teaspoon sugar.

6. Bake until risen and golden, about 10 minutes. Let cool slightly on a cooling rack and serve warm.

**Variations:** Add $\frac{1}{2}$ cup (3 oz./90 g) dried fruit—such as raisins, sour cherries, cranberries, diced apricots, or caramelized ginger—when adding the oats and sugar in step 2. You can also add citrus zest at that time.

## Dough Warning

Don't knead the dough—it should be handled as little as possible.

## Storing Scones

Leftover scones can be stored in an airtight container at room temperature for 1 to 2 days or double-wrapped in plastic wrap and frozen for up to 1 month. If you don't want to make an entire batch at once, you can freeze the dough. After you cut out the rounds, place the unbaked scones on a parchment-lined baking sheet and put in the freezer. Once frozen solid, double-wrap them in plastic wrap and put them in a freezer bag. You can then just pull out a couple and bake!

# *chapter 14*

# Yeast-Risen Breads

Made of flour, water, yeast, and a little salt (sometimes with the additions of fats, eggs, sugar, and flavoring agents) yeasted bread is perhaps the simplest of baked goods—in terms of ingredients, that is. Bread is actually a very complex, even scientific, food; there are several chemical reactions that occur to turn these few ingredients into a delectable, chewy, and satisfying bite.

Breads with crisp, thin crusts (such as baguettes and Italian loaves) are made with little or no sugar and fat, very low moisture, and steam, while rich dough breads (such as brioche and challah) are made with higher proportions of fat and, sometimes, sugar and eggs.

# An Introduction to Yeast-Risen Breads

Imagine that first bite into a piece of French bread—that crunchy crust with a whisper of caramel revealing a chewy, slightly fermented interior. Or imagine that soft, buttery, still-warm piece of slightly sweet brioche with a bit of jam and your morning coffee. Although these two types of bread have a completely different texture and taste, they are actually made the same way—with yeast. While bread can be intimidating for the first-time baker, it doesn't need to be. In fact, bread is fairly simple; there are very few ingredients, and aside from the mixing and shaping, it doesn't require much attention at all. Making bread takes a little practice, but even your mistakes will still be tasty!

There are two types of yeast-risen breads: crisp, crusted breads and rich dough breads. The general method for making both types is the same. But before I get into the how-to of making the breads, let's look at what makes these breads different.

# Crisp, Crusted Bread

Breads with crisp, thin crusts—such as baguettes (French bread), kaiser rolls, pizza crusts, and Italian loaves—tend to be made purely of flour, yeast, water, and a bit of salt (with maybe a very sparse addition of sugar and/or oil) and are baked using steam. People covet these breads' crust, which is why they are often shaped into long loaves that increase the proportion of crust in them.

# Rich Dough Breads

Yeasted breads that are made with higher proportions of fat and, sometimes sugar and eggs as well—such as brioche, panettone, challah, croissants, and Danish pastries—are categorized as rich yeast doughs. They are baked in pans, free formed or rolled out, and cut and shaped in a variety of ways. Their dough tends to be softer and stickier than crisp, crusted bread dough, and their gluten structure is not as strong due to the presence of fats, making them a bit more delicate to handle. The fat also slows down the fermentation process; therefore, they often contain more yeast than lean doughs. Depending on the recipe, the fat or sugar are sometimes added later to prevent the fermentation from being affected by those ingredients. Not all rich dough breads are sweet; some don't have sugar or just contain very little of it. On the other hand, others contain a lot of sugar and are sometimes filled or topped with sweet ingredients, such as preserves, glazes, creams, or chocolate.

# The Main Events in Yeasted Bread

There are two main reactions that go into making bread: the fermentation of the yeast and the development of gluten. As yeast feeds itself with the sugars and starches present in the dough, it produces carbon dioxide gas and alcohol, generating volume and flavor. The formed gases need a stretchable network within the dough to keep them trapped as they expand with the heat of the oven. This structure and strength is given by gluten (and sometimes eggs in bread dough), a substance made of proteins present in wheat and other grains.

With all this in mind, bread baking requires not only the precise measuring of ingredients, but also the proper process to put it all together. The following are several key steps:

- Combining all the ingredients evenly to develop the gluten
- Letting the dough rest at the temperature necessary for fermentation
- "Punching" the dough to redistribute the yeast and relax the gluten
- Proofing the dough, a second fermentation that increases the volume of the shaped dough
- Baking the bread, where the final rising occurs—the proteins coagulate and the starches gelatinize, giving it a sturdier structure and crust

Following all of these steps may seem daunting at first, but it doesn't take long to understand the techniques and the hows and whys of bread baking. And with a little practice, you'll be filling your home with the wonderful aroma of fresh-baked bread in no time.

# Quick Breads

If you want to ease into making bread, quick breads are the way to go. Quick breads—such as banana or zucchini bread—are not as complex as yeasted breads, as the chemical leaveners used to produce volume in them can be easily controlled, and there are no pesky kneading or proofing stages. They are also really fast and easy to prepare, as well as quite delicious and versatile.

Before I show you how to prepare both yeasted and quick breads, I want to go over the most important part of the bread-baking process: kneading.

# Kneading Bread

Kneading bread dough plays a key role in the bread-making process. The kneading process combines all the ingredients into a uniform, smooth dough; distributes the yeast evenly throughout the dough; and develops the gluten. In order for gluten to develop, the proteins in the flour must first absorb water; then, as the dough is kneaded, the gluten forms long, elastic strands. In general, the more a dough is mixed, the more the gluten develops. However, this doesn't mean that bread dough should be overmixed—that could lead to the gluten strands breaking.

## By Hand or by Machine?

Kneading dough by hand is the preferred way of making bread; not only can you feel the texture to make sure it is right, but it also feels great! However, kneading can also be done in a standing mixer fitted with a dough hook attachment or even in a food processor. Still, even if you do use a machine, the final kneading (after the bread has risen) should be done by hand. Here is how to do it:

Sprinkle your work surface with flour. (It's nice to knead on a silicone mat.) Scrape the dough out onto it.

Press the dough down and out, stretching it with the heels of your hands, which in turn will stretch the gluten strands in the dough.

## Too Sticky?

If the dough is too sticky, sprinkle it with flour, being careful not to add too much. Another option is to let the dough rest for about 5 minutes; this will give the flour time to absorb some water, which will make the dough less sticky.

## Stickiness Test

The dough will start feeling less sticky about halfway through the kneading process, with a smoothness that indicates it might not need any more flour sprinkled on it. To determine if you should keep adding flour to your dough, squeeze the dough gently with your entire hand. If the dough is too sticky, pieces will come away on your hand; if it has enough flour, your hand will pull away cleanly.

This dough is still too sticky.

A clean hand means good dough!

Fold the top half of the dough back toward you and press down and out again.

Rotate the dough a quarter turn and repeat the kneading motion.

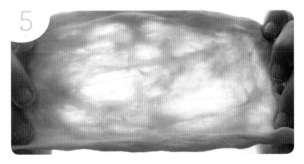

Keep kneading until the dough is smooth, about 10 to 15 minutes. Near the end of the kneading process, do the "windowpane test" to see if the dough's gluten has been developed enough: Cut off a piece of dough about the size of a golf ball and carefully spread it between your thumbs and first two fingers. If the dough stretches into a thin, translucent membrane without tearing, the gluten is where you need it to be. If the membrane breaks, continue kneading the dough a bit longer and test again.

# Working with Yeast

As discussed earlier, fermentation is one of the two most important processes in bread making. Fermentation is produced by the yeast. Because yeast is a live microorganism, you need to create the circumstances for it to feed and grow so it can produce the carbon dioxide gas and alcohol needed for your bread to rise and develop flavor. Basically, you need to understand yeast and keep it happy! The following is what yeast needs to thrive:

- **Warm (not hot) liquids.** Yeast dies at about 140°F (60°C), so to avoid yeast murder, liquids should be 110°F (43°C) or below before being added to the yeast. If you don't have an instant-read thermometer, feel the liquid with the inside of your wrist; if you were to bathe a baby in a liquid at that temperature, then it's good for the yeast. Also keep in mind that yeast grows faster in warm (but not hot) environments, which is why you should let dough rise in a warm place in the kitchen.

- **Nourishment.** Yeasts eat sugar and flour starches, which is why it's usually activated with a bit of sugar or honey in a warm liquid.

- **No salt.** Salt kills yeast when in direct contact, so don't add salt directly into a yeast starter. When making bread dough, add the salt together with the flour and mix well immediately to disperse. But don't skip the salt altogether; it not only flavors the dough, but also develops its texture (by strengthening the structure of the gluten) and helps control the fermentation process. It keeps yeast in line!

- **Time.** You can't rush the natural fermentation process. Yeast needs to eat and metabolize the sugars and starches in the dough at a certain rate—in other words, you can't make it "stuff its face"! It's a slow process, but in return, you get a deep flavor that can only be developed with time.

- **Temperature control.** Cold temperatures slow yeast down. If you use a very cold liquid when mixing bread dough, the yeast will take longer to activate than when you use a warm liquid (which it prefers). However, this is something you can take advantage of. For example, if you mix a batch of bread dough at night and leave it in the fridge, it will rise while you sleep, and you'll be able to punch it down and shape it the following morning, as opposed to waiting for it to rise for about 1 hour and 30 minutes at room temperature. Now if you left the dough overnight at room temperature, it would get out of control, as the yeast would keep fermenting further than the capacity of the gluten to hold the structure together, and you'd end up with a messy dough explosion.

# Freezing Dough

Cold temperatures retard the fermentation process, and freezing temperatures stop it completely; however, freezing dough doesn't kill the yeast. Once the temperature of the prepared frozen dough starts rising, the yeast gets back into action.

You can use this practical piece of knowledge to mix a dough and freeze it before it rises. When you want to bake it, you bring it back to room temperature to let it rise. This process takes longer, but it will give you the flexibility of not having to spend 5 to 6 hours in a row at it.

You can also freeze the dough after you have shaped the loaves, right before proofing, for months before you want to bake the bread. Just freeze the dough until it is firm, and then double-wrap it in plastic, making sure the wrap is airtight (air can damage the dough and add an unpleasant flavor). When you're ready to bake, just thaw it. Be sure to unwrap it as soon as the dough comes to room temperature—you don't want the wrap to impede the rising process or get stuck in the dough.

## Freezing Bread

Baked bread can also be frozen up to 6 months with good results. To do so, wrap the bread tightly in plastic wrap and then wrap it again in foil or freezer paper or put it in a zipper-lock freezer bag. You can write the date and label your bread before sticking it in the freezer in order to know how long you've had it. You can also slice your loaves once cool but still fresh and then wrap and freeze the slices separately, so you only thaw the servings you need when you want them.

When you're ready to thaw the bread, simply bring it out of the freezer and leave it on the countertop for a couple hours (the thaw time depends on the size of the loaf, roll, or slices).

## Making a Sponge

Some bread recipes call for making a sponge, a mixture of water, flour, and yeast that is allowed to ferment before making the dough. The sponge method can yield breads with increased flavor and requires less yeast, because it multiplies greatly during the sponge fermentation period. These doughs are prepared in two stages, which give the yeast action a head start. Here's how you do it:

1. Mix the liquid, the yeast, and part of the flour (and in some cases, part of the sugar) into a thick batter. Leave it to ferment for some hours and up to many days, depending on the type of bread.

2. Punch down the sponge and knead in the remaining flour, turning it into a dough.

# How to Make Yeast-Risen Bread

With so few ingredients, the secret to making crisp, crusted, yeast-risen breads relies on the method itself. The proper fermentation and gluten development are crucial, so keep this in mind while mixing, kneading, waiting, handling, and baking. The following are the steps to take to achieve a successful loaf of bread with a crispy crust.

**Mix the ingredients.** The most important part of assembling the ingredients for bread is the temperature of the water that will be combined with the yeast. Remember, it has to be warm, not hot (see "Working with Yeast"). Mix the salt with the flour; never directly mix it into the yeast mixture, or it will kill the yeast.

**Knead.** Knead the dough as indicated in "Kneading Bread" to develop the gluten optimally. Once the dough has been kneaded, shape it into a round.

## Shaping Challah

For the yeast-risen bread challah, the three-stranded braid is the easiest to make, but it can also be braided into four-, five-, or even six-strand braids. It can even be shaped into one large rope and coiled into itself (a traditional Jewish New Year round challah). It can also be portioned into small ropes and knotted for individual challahs.

One beautiful presentation of challah is made by separating the initial dough into one larger and one smaller portion. Each of them is then divided into three ropes and turned into three-strand braids. The smaller braid is glued on top of the large one with egg white, and the challah is baked as a double-tier braid.

**Ferment.** Oil the dough by coating the bowl with cooking spray and dragging the dough around the sides to completely coat it. Cover the dough and leave it undisturbed in a warm spot of the kitchen to ferment. During this process, the yeast acts on the sugars and starches in the dough, producing carbon dioxide gas and alcohol. The microorganism grows, which makes the dough expand. The gluten will become smoother and more elastic, so it will be able to stretch further and hold more gas.

**Punch down the dough.** This doesn't mean hitting the dough! Instead, you deflate the dough by pulling it up on all sides, folding it over the center, and pressing it down. To finish the action, turn the dough upside down in the bowl. Punching down the dough expels some of the carbon dioxide and redistributes the yeast for further growth. It also relaxes the gluten and evens out the temperature of the whole dough.

**Shape the dough.** Follow the directions of the recipe and place the formed dough on baking sheets lined with parchment paper (some recipes call for a dusting of cornmeal or other ingredients). If you are making more than one loaf or roll with the batch of dough, divide the dough into portions. Scaling the portions yields loaves or rolls of the same size and promotes even baking.

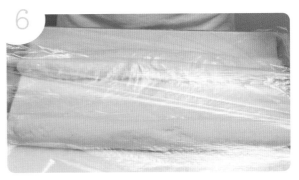

**Proof the dough.** This is a fancy name for a second rising, or fermentation, that increases the volume of the shaped dough (*fermentation* is the term applied for the mixed dough, and *proofing* is for the shaped dough). Not all bread recipes require proofing, but if your recipe calls for proofing, don't skip this step—it's needed to develop the volume, texture, and flavor even further.

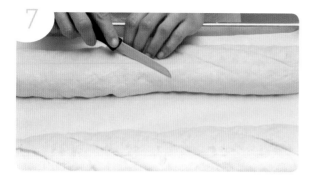

**Wash and/or score.** Some bread recipes call for the loaf or rolls to be scored with a knife or blade right before baking. This doesn't only have an aesthetic purpose, it also allows for a continued expansion of the loaf even after the crust has formed. Other breads are brushed with egg wash or water before baking, and some are sprinkled with seeds or other ingredients for an attractive presentation.

**Bake in a steam bath.** Due to their leanness, crispy crusted breads require very high temperatures to achieve the desired crust color; therefore, they are baked in a steam bath. The steam helps keep the crust soft during the first part of baking and distributes the heat in the oven, so the bread can expand rapidly and evenly. It is at this point that the bread rises for a third and last time, as the trapped gases expand even more with the heat. The yeast dies after the temperature reaches 140°F (60°C), the proteins coagulate, and the starches gelatinize, making the bread firm and allowing it to hold its shape. This is when the crust forms.

Of course, you can eat bread warm, but you shouldn't eat hot bread—it needs to cool a bit to allow the excess moisture and alcohol from the fermentation to escape (cooling it on wire cooling racks is best). Freshly made bread can be kept at room temperature for 1 day or double-wrapped airtight with plastic wrap and frozen once completely cooled.

## When Is It Done?

To know when the bread is done, check its internal temperature with an instant-read thermometer (on the side, so the surface of the loaf doesn't perforate); it should be at least 190°F (85°C). You can also tap the bread on the bottom—it should make a hollow sound.

# How to Shape Baguettes

Crisp on the outside, chewy on the inside—what's not to love about baguettes? In order to get that light, airy interior, follow these steps for shaping the dough.

Form the dough into a log. Starting at one end, gently press the top of the dough between your thumb and palm.

Take the part between your thumb and palm and fold it over, covering your thumb.

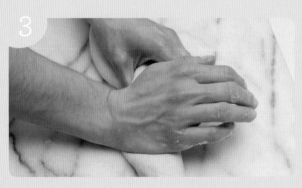

With the heel of your other hand, press down on the dough where your thumb was to "seal" the fold you just made.

Repeat the action up the length of the bread. Place the dough seam-side down on the tray.

# French Bread (Baguette)

Makes **2** 14-in. (35-cm) loaves bread

This recipe is a shorter and easier but very tasty version of the traditional method, ideal if you're just learning to make bread. Once you get the hang of working with yeast and kneading dough and discover the pleasure of biting into an ultra-fresh, still-warm, homemade piece of bread, you'll keep coming back for more.

## INGREDIENTS

1½ cups (12 oz./345 g) warm (about 110°F/43°C) water

2 envelopes (1½ TB.) dry active yeast

2 TB. granulated sugar or honey

3½ to 4 cups (15.5 to 17.5 oz./437.5 to 500 g) all-purpose flour

1½ tsp. salt

Nonstick cooking spray

## EQUIPMENT

Medium glass mixing bowl or 4-cup or more capacity liquid measuring cup

Silicone spatula

Large mixing bowl

Whisk

Plastic wrap

Bench scraper

Parchment paper (optional)

Very sharp (nonserrated) knife or razorblade

Rimmed baking sheet

Heat-proof baking pan

Small saucepan or kettle

Cooling rack

## Baguette Baking Tip

The steam produced by the boiling water is what gives the bread a crispy crust. Therefore, make sure you close the oven quickly once you put it in to avoid any steam escaping.

1. Pour ½ cup (4 oz./115 g) warm water in a medium glass bowl, add dry yeast and sugar, and stir with a silicone spatula to combine. Set aside to let yeast activate, about 5 minutes; mixture will foam.

## Yeast Not Activating?

If yeast mixture doesn't foam or bubble, see tips in "Leavening Agents" in Chapter 2.

2. In a large mixing bowl, whisk together all-purpose flour and salt. Make a well in center of mixture and pour in activated yeast liquid, stirring with the spatula. Gradually add remaining 1 cup (8 oz./230 g) warm water and mix until dough comes together into a ball but is not too wet (you may not need all of water). If dough is sticky, add a little bit more flour.

3. Using your hands, knead until dough is smooth and elastic. Dough is done when you poke it with a finger and it bounces back. (If it's uncomfortable to knead in the bowl, turn dough onto a surface covered with parchment paper or flour.) Form dough into a ball by rounding dough and tucking in edges under bottom, and spray top with nonstick cooking spray. Turn ball upside down into the bowl and spray other side. Cover the bowl with plastic wrap and let rest in a warm place until doubled in size, about 25 to 30 minutes.

4. Cut dough in half with a bench scraper and place on a floured surface. Pat each portion into a large rectangle about ¾-inch (1.5-cm) thick. Roll up dough, beginning with the short side and stopping after each full turn to press edge of roll firmly into flat part of dough to seal. Tuck and roll so any seams disappear into dough (see "How to Make Crusted Bread"). Each roll should be about 12 to 14 inches (30 to 35 cm) long and 2 inches (5 cm) wide. Fold and seal each end. Flip seam side down and place on the prepared baking sheet 3 inches (7.5 cm) apart.

5. Using a very sharp knife, score tops of loaves, making equidistant, diagonal slits ½ inch (1 cm) deep. Loosely cover loaves with plastic wrap and let rise in a warm place until they double in size, about 25 minutes.

6. Place one oven rack on the bottom and the other in the middle position. Put a baking pan on the bottom rack. Preheat the oven to 450°F (230°C). Bring about 1 quart (1 liter) water to a boil in a saucepan.

7. Remove the plastic wrap from loaves. Working quickly, fill the baking pan ½ full with hot water, and then place the baking sheet with loaves on the middle rack in the oven, making sure to quickly shut the oven door so no steam escapes. Bake baguettes until golden brown, about 15 minutes. Loaves are ready when they make a hollow sound when tapped on the bottom.

8. Let cool 5 minutes on a cooling rack and serve the same day. Baguettes can be double-wrapped in plastic wrap and frozen for up to 2 weeks.

# Walnut-Raisin Bread

Makes **2** 10-in. (25-cm) loaves bread

Crusty breads made with nuts and dried fruits are great for sandwiches or for serving along with cheese platters and cold cuts. They are not really sweetened; instead, they just have slight hints of fruitiness and the crunch from the nuts. This easy-to-make recipe produces loaves with extra-crispy crusts and a soft, flavorful interior.

## INGREDIENTS

⅓ cup (1⅔ oz./50 g) raisins
½ cup (4 oz./115 g) boiling water (212°F/100°C)
¾ cup (6 oz./180 g) lukewarm water (not more than 86°F/30°C)
1½ tsp. active dry yeast
2½ TB. pure maple syrup

1½ cups (6⅓ oz./190 g) bread flour (plus more for dusting)
1 cup (4 oz./120 g) whole-wheat flour
1 tsp. salt
½ cup (1⅔ oz./50 g) walnuts, coarsely chopped
Nonstick cooking spray

## EQUIPMENT

Small mixing bowl or 2-cup-capacity liquid measuring cup
Plastic wrap
Medium glass bowl or 4-cup or more capacity liquid measuring cup
Silicone spatula
Standing mixer fitted with hook attachment or large mixing bowl
Sieve

Rimmed baking sheet
Parchment paper
Bench scraper
Heat-proof baking pan
Small saucepan or kettle
Very sharp (nonserrated) knife or razorblade
Cooling rack

1. In a small bowl, place raisins and cover with boiling water. Cover the bowl with plastic wrap and let raisins rehydrate for 10 minutes.

2. In a medium glass bowl, pour $^2/_3$ cup (5 oz./ 150 g) lukewarm water and add dry yeast and maple syrup, stirring with a silicone spatula to combine. Set aside to let yeast activate, about 5 minutes; mixture will foam.

3. In the bowl of a standing mixer fitted with a dough hook, place bread flour, whole-wheat flour, and salt and mix on low speed until combined.

4. Pour yeast mixture into flour mixture and knead dough until everything comes together in a rough ball, about 5 minutes. If mixture is too dry, add remaining 2 tablespoons lukewarm water.

5. Stop the mixer and scrape the sides of the bowl with the silicone spatula. Turn the mixer back on and knead for 4 additional minutes; by then, dough should be more elastic and smoother.

6. Drain raisins through a sieve and add them to dough along with chopped walnuts. Knead for another 1 to 2 minutes to fully incorporate fruit and nuts.

7. Turn dough onto a floured surface and knead by hand, until dough bounces back when poked with your finger. Form dough into a ball by rounding dough and tucking in edges under bottom. Spray top of dough with non-stick cooking spray. Turn ball upside down and place back into the bowl to spray the other side. Cover the bowl with plastic wrap and let rest in a warm place until dough has doubled in size, about 1 hour 30 minutes.

8. Line a rimmed baking sheet with parchment paper and set aside.

9. Halve dough with a bench scraper (do not punch it down). Put half of dough back in the bowl and cover with plastic wrap. On a floured surface, gently pat other half of dough into a 1-inch (2.5-cm) thick rectangle. Beginning with the short side, roll up dough (see "How to Make Crusted Bread"). Fold and seal either end. Flip dough seam side down and place on the prepared baking sheet 3 inches (7.5 cm) apart. Cover loosely with plastic wrap and let rise in a warm place for an additional 45 minutes.

10. Place one oven rack on the bottom and the other in the middle position. Put a baking pan on the bottom rack and preheat the oven to 425°F (220°C). Bring about 1 quart (1 liter) water to a boil in a small saucepan.

11. Remove the plastic wrap from loaves. With a very sharp knife, score tops of loaves, making equidistant, diagonal slits $^1/_2$-inch (1-cm) deep.

12. Working quickly, fill the baking pan $^1/_2$ full with the boiling water, then place the baking sheet with loaves on the middle rack in the oven, making sure to quickly shut the oven door so no steam escapes. Bake loaves until golden brown, about 20 to 25 minutes. Loaves are ready when they make a hollow sound when tapped on the bottom.

13. Let cool 5 minutes on a cooling rack and serve the same day. Loaves can be double-wrapped in plastic wrap and frozen for up to 2 weeks.

**Variations:** Instead of raisins, try dry cherries, cranberries, or sultanas. Pecans or almonds can be substituted for the walnuts.

# Brioche

Makes **1** 9- or 10-in. (23- or 25-cm) loaf

Brioche is a classic French bread that, due to the presence of eggs, butter, and liquid, is almost like a cake. It is a favorite for breakfast and snack time and goes really well with fruit, preserves, and chocolate. However, that doesn't mean it can't be paired with foie gras and other savory main dishes.

## INGREDIENTS

⅓ cup (2.5 oz./76.5 g) warm milk (not hotter than 86°F/30°C)

1 envelope (2¼ tsp.) active dry yeast

2 TB. granulated sugar

1⅔ cups (8¾ oz./250 g) all-purpose flour (plus more for covering hands)

½ tsp. salt

2 large eggs, at room temperature

1 large egg yolk

2 TB. unsalted butter, softened

## EQUIPMENT

Medium glass bowl or 4-cup or more capacity liquid measuring cup

Silicone spatula

Standing mixer fitted with hook and paddle attachments or large mixing bowl and whisk

Plastic wrap

9- or 10-in. (23- to 25-cm) loaf pan

Parchment paper

Bench scraper

Small mixing bowl

Fork

Pastry brush

Toothpick

Cooling rack

1. In a medium glass bowl, pour warm milk and stir in dry yeast and 1 teaspoon sugar with a silicone spatula. Set aside to let yeast activate, about 5 minutes; mixture will foam.

2. In the bowl of a standing mixer fitted with the hook attachment, place all-purpose flour, remaining 5 teaspoons sugar, and salt and mix (or whisk, if using the large bowl) until well combined. Slowly pour in warm yeast-milk mixture and beat on low speed (or use your fingertips) to incorporate.

3. Add eggs and mix until fully incorporated, about 3 minutes; dough will be smooth and sticky. Scrape the sides of the bowl and switch to a paddle attachment, if using the standing mixer.

4. Take small (about 1 tablespoon) portions of softened butter with your fingertips (from the hand that's not mixing, if kneading by hand) and add one by one into dough, mixing on medium speed after each addition. Work dough until it's elastic, shiny, and has no butter lumps. Dough should now separate more easily from the sides of the bowl—or your fingers—while mixing without having to scrape it.

5. Cover the bowl with plastic wrap and let dough rise in a warm place until doubled in size, about 1 hour 30 minutes.

6. Prepare the loaf pan by laying long, wide strips of parchment paper across the length and width of it, so the paper overhangs the edges.

7. Using the standing mixer with the hook attachment or your hands and a lightly floured surface, knead dough again for about 10 minutes. (If you're using a mixer, you will hear the dough "slap" against the sides of the bowl—that means it's ready.) The dough will be shiny but still somewhat loose. Using a bench scraper, divide dough into 8 approximately equal pieces. Dust your hands with flour and on a lightly floured surface, roll pieces into balls, place on the prepared pan, and cover again loosely with plastic wrap. Let rise again until doubled, about 1 hour.

## Using Flour

Don't use too much flour on your work surface or on your hands—if you introduce too much flour to the dough, you will end up with a tough brioche.

8. Preheat the oven to 400°F (200°C) with the rack in middle position. In a small bowl, beat egg yolk with a fork and brush on top of brioche with a pastry brush. Place loaf in the oven and bake for 10 minutes. Lower the temperature to 350°F (180°C) and bake for another 20 to 30 minutes, or until a toothpick inserted into the center comes out clean.

9. Remove from the oven and let cool on a cooling rack, about 5 to 10 minutes. Unmold by lifting the paper overhangs and eat warm or finish cooling. Brioche keeps well in an airtight container at room temperature for 1 day or double-wrapped in plastic wrap and frozen for up to 1 month.

**Variations:** Brioche can be baked in individual brioche molds. To do so, make small balls of dough, place into the molds, and brush with egg yolk. Bake for 5 minutes at 400°F (200°C), and then lower the temperature to 350°F (180°C) and bake for about 10 more minutes.

# Challah

Makes about **2 lb.** (900 g) dough, enough for **1** very large loaf or **2** smaller loaves

Challah is a rich, braided bread lightly sweetened with either sugar or honey. Challah is traditionally made for the Jewish Sabbath and holidays, but you don't have to be Jewish to enjoy this beautiful, glossy bread any day of the week. Plus, leftover challah makes the best French toast ever!

## INGREDIENTS

1 cup (8 oz./240 g) lukewarm water (not hotter than 86°F/30°C)

½ cup (6 oz./180 g) mild-tasting honey (see "Sweeteners" in Chapter 2)

1 envelope (2¼ tsp.) active dry yeast

4½ cups (19 oz./570 g) all-purpose flour

2½ tsp. salt

3 large eggs, divided

¼ cup (2 oz./60 g) neutral-tasting oil (see "Other Fats and Oils" in Chapter 2)

Nonstick cooking spray

2 tsp. sesame or poppy seeds (optional)

## EQUIPMENT

Medium glass mixing bowl or 4-cup or more capacity liquid measuring cup

Silicone spatula

Standing mixer fitted with dough hook or large mixing bowl and whisk

Plastic wrap

Rimmed baking sheet

Parchment paper

Bench scraper

Pastry brush

Instant-read thermometer (optional)

Cooling rack

1. In a medium glass bowl, combine lukewarm water, mild-tasting honey, and dry yeast, stirring with a silicone spatula to dissolve. Set aside to let yeast activate, about 5 minutes; mixture will foam.

2. In the bowl of a standing mixer fitted with a dough hook, place 4 cups (17.5 oz./500 g) all-purpose flour and salt and mix on low speed until combined (if using the large bowl, mix with a whisk). Add 2 eggs plus 1 egg yolk (reserving the remaining egg white for the glaze) and neutral-tasting oil and mix until combined (use a spatula, if mixing by hand).

3. Pour in activated yeast mixture and mix at medium-low speed until a dough forms. If making challah by hand, use your hands for kneading, or continue working dough in the standing mixer a couple more minutes. If dough is too sticky, add ¼ cup (1 oz./31 g) all-purpose flour.

4. Turn dough onto a surface and knead until it is smooth, elastic, and holds its shape. If dough is still sticky, add a bit more flour, but don't overdo it; you want challah to be moist! Dough is ready when you poke it with a finger and it bounces back.

5. Form dough into a ball by rounding dough and tucking in edges under bottom. Spray top with nonstick cooking spray. Turn ball upside down back into the bowl and spray other side. Cover the bowl with plastic wrap and let rest in a warm place until doubled in size, about 1 hour 30 minutes.

6. Line a rimmed baking sheet with parchment paper. Set aside.

7. Remove plastic wrap and punch down dough. With a bench scraper, divide dough into 3 approximately equal portions. Working with one piece at a time (and keeping the rest loosely covered with plastic in the bowl), turn portion of dough onto a lightly floured surface and roll it with the palms of your hands into a rope about 14 inches (35 cm) long and about 1-inch (2.5-cm) thick. Place the rope on the prepared sheet.

8. Repeat the shaping process with remaining 2 portions and place the 3 ropes next to each other so they line up. Pinch their top ends together. Take the rope on the right and lay it over the center rope. Take the rope on the left and lay it over the center rope.

9. Repeat the braiding process (which is exactly the same as braiding hair) until the whole ropes are used. Pinch the ends together and tuck both ends under the braid. Cover the braid loosely with plastic wrap and let it rise in a warm place until doubled in size, about 40 to 60 minutes.

10. Preheat the oven to 400°F (200°C) with the oven rack in middle position. Brush surface of challah loaf with reserved egg white and sprinkle with sesame or poppy seeds (if using).

11. Bake until surface browns, about 20 minutes. Reduce temperature to 350°F (180°C) and bake for an additional 15 to 20 minutes. Loaf is ready when it makes a hollow sound when tapped on the bottom or an instant-read thermometer registers 190°F (90°C) internal temperature.

12. Remove loaf from the oven, transfer to a cooling rack, and allow to cool for at least 20 minutes. Challah can be wrapped airtight in plastic wrap and kept at room temperature for up to 2 days or kept in the freezer for up to 1 month.

# Glossary

**baking powder**   A dry ingredient used to increase volume and lighten or leaven baked goods.

**beat**   The process of rapidly stirring a batter to incorporate the ingredients, along with air.

**blind baking**   The process of baking a pie crust or tart shell before it's filled, usually with pie weights on top. *See also* pie weights.

**caramelization**   The result of heating carbohydrates—such as sugar and other sweeteners—to temperatures of 300°F (150°C) or higher, causing them to turn brown and develop a distinct flavor.

**coagulation**   The process by which proteins become firm, usually when heated.

**cream**   The process of beating fat (butter, shortening, and so on) and sugar against the sides of a bowl until the texture is softened and lumps are eliminated. This action forms tiny air pockets in the fat, making the finished product light and airy.

**cut in**   The process of rubbing cold fat and dry ingredients together by hand, with a food processor, with two table knives or forks, or using a pastry blender. This is done until the fat is broken down into small pea-, walnut-, or cornmeal-size pieces and surrounded (but not incorporated) by the dry ingredients. This action produces flakiness in the dough.

**drizzle**   To lightly sprinkle drops of a liquid over food, often as the finishing touch to a dish.

**egg wash**   A glaze made of lightly beaten eggs, often with the addition of sugar and/or water, that's brushed on goods before baking to add a shiny finish. A common formula is 1 large egg and 2 tablespoons water, which are beaten with a fork.

**emulsion**   A mixture of liquids that would normally be incapable of mixing. Eggs often act as emulsifiers in recipes (for example, in cake recipes to mix the fat with the liquid ingredients), facilitating this mixture.

**fermentation**   The process in which a microorganism (in baking, usually yeast) metabolizes the sugar and starches present in a mixture and produces carbon dioxide gas and alcohol. This gives airiness to the dough and develops flavor.

**foam**   The process of whipping eggs to incorporate air.

**fold in**   The process of combining one ingredient with another by gently turning the mixture with a spatula or whisk to minimize the loss of air.

**gluten**   A substance formed from proteins present in wheat and other grains that develops with moisture and kneading. It gives dough elasticity, strength, and structure.

**knead**   To work dough to make it pliable so it holds gas bubbles as it bakes. Kneading is fundamental in the process of making yeast breads.

**lattice crust**   A top crust for a pie made of weaved strips of pastry.

**leavening**   An agent that makes baked goods rise, such as yeast, baking powder, and baking soda.

**meal**   Coarsely ground grain.

**oven spring**   The rapid (and often final) rise of yeasted baked goods that takes place in the oven due to the production and expansion of trapped gases (mainly carbon dioxide) through the heat.

**pie weights**   Small weights made of a heat-proof material used to weigh down a pie shell or pie crust that is being blind baked. *See also* blind baking.

**proof**   The fermentation process that bread dough goes through after it's been shaped.

**punch down**   The process of deflating yeast dough to expel some of the carbon dioxide, redistribute the yeast, relax the gluten, and even out the temperature.

**roll out**   The process of extending dough using a rolling pin.

**room temperature**   A temperature that is neither cold nor hot—ideally between 65°F (18°C) and 75°F (24°C). It is usually the best temperature for stirring, spreading, creaming, and folding in ingredients, unless indicated in a recipe.

**scaling**   The process of weighing ingredients on a scale.

**steam bath**   A method in which boiling water is added into a vessel on the bottom rack of the oven when the oven is very hot. The product to be baked is then placed on the top oven rack and the door is shut very quickly to avoid steam escaping. The steam distributes the heat in the oven, helping bread form a crispy crust.

**stir**   The process of using a spoon, whisk, or beater to move ingredients around in a circular motion. Stirring is a more gentle form of beating.

**temper** (eggs)   The process of adjusting the temperature of eggs before they are added to hot ingredients to prevent them from curdling. A small amount of the hot mixture is added to the eggs to warm them; the egg mixture is then added into the hot ingredients.

**water bath**   A method for cooking an ingredient with diffused heat. The ingredient is placed in a separate bowl above or within a saucepan with boiling or simmering water, so it cooks gently without reaching the boiling point. This is used for very heat-sensitive baking projects, such as melting chocolate, cooking custards and cheesecake, or preparing Swiss meringue.

**whip**   The process of incorporating air into a mixture of ingredients (usually egg whites or heavy cream) by stirring them by hand with a wire whisk or with an electric mixer.

# Index

## Numbers

8-cup liquid measures, 14
10X sugars, 22

## A

adhering toppings, decorating cookies, 109
agave nectar, 25
all-purpose flours, 32
allspice, 39
Almond-Cranberry Biscotti, 74-75
alternatives
    cooling racks, 9
    muffin pan, 13
    nondairy milk, 26
    pastry bags, 18
aluminum foils, 15
anise, 39
Apple Pie, 188-191
apples, baking, 189
arrowroot starches, 35

## B

bagged cookies, 77
bags, piped cookies, 84-87
baguettes, shaping, 261
baked custards, 141
    Flan, 156-157
    Lemon Bars, 154-155
    New York Cheesecake, 150-153
    preparation, 148-149
baking cups, Molten Chocolate Cake, 212-213
baking pans, 12-13
baking powders, 37
Banana Muffins, 241
bar cookies, 54, 59
    Almond-Cranberry Biscotti, 74-75
    biscotti, 72-73
    Granola Bars, 64-65
basil, 39
basket-weave pastry tips, 19
batter dispensers, 218

bench scrapers, 6
biscotti, 54-55
    Almond-Cranberry Biscotti, 74-75
    bar cookies, 72-73
biscuits, 54, 237
    preparation, 242-243
    recipe, 244-245
bittersweet chocolates, 45
bleached flours, 33
blenders, 10
blind baking crusts, 198-199
Blondies, 70-71
boards, 15-16
bowls, 15
bread flours, 32
breads, 235
    freezing, 256
    quick breads, 237, 251
        Banana Muffins, 241
        biscuits, 242-245
        muffin preparation, 238-239
        scones, 246-247
        Yogurt Muffins, 240
    sweets, 39
    yeast-risen, 249
        Brioche, 266-267
        Challah, 268-269
        crisp, crusted, 250
        freezing dough, 256
        French Bread, 262-263
        kneading, 252-253
        preparation, 258-260
        reactions, 251
        rich dough, 250
        sponge, 257
        Walnut-Raisin Bread, 264-265
        yeast fermentation tips, 254
Brioche, 266-267
brown sugars, 23
Brownies, 68-69
brushes, pastry, 7
bull's-eye cookies, 103-104
bundt pans, 13
buttercreams
    Classic American Buttercream, 228
    Swiss Meringue Buttercream, 228

buttermilk, 27
butters, 28-29
  cake mixes, 209
  creaming, 56
  cutting in, 215

# C

cake boards, 16
cake flours, 32
cakes, 173, 203
  adapting recipes for cupcakes, 218-221
  Chocoflan, 216-217
  decorating, 223
    basics, 224-225
    Chocolate Ganache, 229
    Classic American Buttercream, 228
    Coconut Whipped Cream, 230
    Cream Cheese Frosting, 231
    Fruit Coulis, 232-233
    simple methods, 226-227
    Swiss Meringue Buttercream, 228
    Whipped Cream, 230
  layer
    Carrot Cake, 210-211
    Moist Chocolate Cake, 206-207
    preparation, 204-205
    Vanilla Velvet Cake, 208-209
  meringues, 134-135
    Chocolate Cloud Cake, 136-137
    Pavlova, 138-139
  Molten Chocolate Cake, 212-213
  Russian Sour Cream Coffeecake, 214-215
  troubleshooting, 220-221
candies, decorating cookies, 108
cane juices, evaporated, 246
cardamom, 39
Carrot Cake, 210-211
caster sugars, 22
Celtic sea salts, 41
Challah, 268-269
challah, shaping, 258
cheesecakes
  New York Cheesecake, 150-153
  slicing, 152
cheeses, 27-28
chef's knives, 8

chemical leaveners, 37
chili spice, 39
chilling dough, 63, 177
chives, 39
Chocoflan, 216-217
chocolate, 45-47
  Blondies, 70-71
  Brownies, 68-69
  Chocolate Chip Cookies, 80
  chocolate chip meringues, 129
  Chocolate Cloud Cake, 136-137
  Chocolate Cookies, 100-101
  Chocolate Ganache, 229
  Chocolate Soufflé, 168-169
  macarons, 132
  melting, 213
  meringues, 129
Chocolate Chip Cookies, 80
chocolate chip meringues, 129
Chocolate Cloud Cake, 136-137
Chocolate Cookies, 100-101
Chocolate Ganache, 229
Chocolate Soufflé, 168-169
chopping
  chocolates, 46
  nuts, 42
cinnamon, 39
clarifying butters, 29
Classic American Buttercream, 228
closed-star pastry tips, 19
cloves, 39
cocoa, 45-47
coconut oils, 31
coconut palm nectars, 25
coconut palm sugars, 25
Coconut Whipped Cream, 230
coffee grinders, 11
coffeecakes, Russian Sour Cream Coffeecake, 214-215
colors, egg function, 117
condensed milk, 26
confectioners' sugars, 22
cookie cutters, decorating cakes, 227
cookie presses, 11, 87
cookie scoops, 6
cookies, 54-55
  bar, 59
    biscotti, 72-75
    Granola Bars, 64-65

decorating, 107
    adhering topping, 109
    royal icing, 110-113
    toppings, 108
dropped, 76
    Chocolate Chip Cookies, 80
    Mexican Wedding Cookies, 83
    Oatmeal-Raisin Cookies, 82
    Peanut Butter Cookies, 81
    preparing, 78-79
ice box, 91
    Chocolate Cookies, 100-101
    pinwheels, 102-104
    preparation, 96-97
    Vanilla Cookies, 98-99
meringue, 126-129
mixing methods, 56-57
piped, 76
    basics, 84-87
    Spritz Cookies, 88-89
rolled-out, 91
    Gingerbread Cookies, 94-95
    preparations, 92-93
sheet, 59
    Blondies, 70-71
    poured, 66-69
    pressed, 60-63
troubleshooting common faults, 105
cooling racks, 9
corn syrup, 25
cornstarches, 35
couplers, 19
cracker crusts, 192-193
cream, 26-27
Cream Cheese Frosting, 231
cream cheeses, 27
creaming
    layer cake preparation, 204-205
    mixing cookies, 56
Crème Anglaise, 144-145
crimping dough, 179
crisp, crusted breads, 250
crumb toppings, 184-185
crusts
    basic preparation, 176-179
    blind baking, 198-199
    cracker
        Key Lime Pie, 194-195
        preparation, 192-193
    nut, 196-197

tops
    crumb topping, 184-185
    decorative cut-outs, 185-187
    double crust, 180-181
    lattice, 182-183
cultured dairy products, 27
cupcakes, 203
    adapting cake recipes, 218-221
custards, 141
    baked
        Flan, 156-157
        Lemon Bars, 154-155
        New York Cheesecake, 150-153
        preparation, 148-149
    stovetop
        Crème Anglaise, 144-145
        Pastry Cream, 146-147
        preparation, 142-143
cutters, 6, 227
cutting boards, 16

# D

dairy, 26-29
dark brown sugars, 23
date syrup, 24
decorating
    cakes, 223
        basics, 224-225
        Chocolate Ganache, 229
        Classic American Buttercream, 228
        Coconut Whipped Cream, 230
        Cream Cheese Frosting, 231
        Fruit Coulis, 232-233
        simple methods, 226-227
        Swiss Meringue Buttercream, 228
        Whipped Cream, 230
    cookies, 107
        adhering topping, 109
        royal icing, 110-113
        toppings, 108
    Gingerbread Cookies, 95
    Spritz Cookies, 89
decorative cut-outs (crusts), 185-187
decorator's sugars, 22
demerara, 23
digital scales, 11, 50
dill, 39
dip measuring, 48
double crusts, 180-181

dough
    chilling, 63, 177
    dyeing, 104
    freezing, 79
dragees, 108
dried milk, 26
drizzling, decorating cakes, 227
dropped cookies, 55, 76
    Chocolate Chip Cookies, 80
    Mexican Wedding Cookies, 83
    Oatmeal-Raisin Cookies, 82
    Peanut Butter Cookies, 81
    preparing, 78-79
dry measures, 48
dry measuring cups, 14
dulce de leche, preparation, 217

## E

edible decorations, 44
egg whites
    uncooked, 158
    whipped cream, 159
eggs, 36, 115
    basics, 116-117
    cracking, 78
    custards, 141
        baked, 148-157
        stovetop, 142-147
    freshness, 116
    meringues, 119
        cakes, 134-135
        Chocolate Cloud Cake, 136-137
        cookies, 126-127, 126-129
        French Macarons, 130-133
        Pavlova, 138-139
        preparation, 120-125
    mousses, 141
        Mascarpone Mousse, 162-163
        Praline Mousse, 160-161
        preparation, 158-159
    soufflé, 165
        Chocolate Soufflé, 168-169
        Goat Cheese Soufflé, 170-171
emulsification, egg function, 117
equipment, 5
    baking pans, 12-13
    boards, 15-16
    bowls, 15
    couplers, 18-19
    machinery, 10-11
    mats, 15-16
    measuring tools, 14-15
    paper, 15-16
    pastry bags, 18-19
    rolling, 92
    tips, 18-19
    utensils, 6-9
evaporated cane juices, 23, 246
evaporated milk, 26
exotic salts, 41
extracts, 40

## F

fairy cakes, 203
fats, 30-31
fennel, 39
fermentation
    sponge, 257
    yeast tips, 254
    yeast-risen breads, 251
fillings, macarons, 133
fine-mesh sieves, 7
Flan, 156-157
flavor, egg function, 117
flavoring agents, 38-41
flavors, 40
flours, 32-33
    making homemade nut, 42
folding meringue, 134
food color markers, 44
food color sprays, 44
food coloring, 44
food processors, 11
freezing
    biscuit dough, 245
    breads, 256
    dough, biscuit, 245
    dropped cookie dough, 79
    yeast-risen dough, 256
French Bread recipe, 262-263
French breads, 250
French meringues, 120-121
Fresh Fruit Tart in Almond Crust, 200-201
Fruit Coulis, 232-233
fruit meringues, 129
fruits, 40

## G

gel food coloring, 44
gelatins, 35
ginger, 39
Gingerbread Cookies, 94–95
Goat Cheese Soufflé, 170–171
Granola Bars, 64–65
granulated sugars, 22
grinders, 11

## H

half-and-half, 27
handheld mixers, 10
Hawaiian sea salts, 41
hazelnut praline pastes, 160
heavy creams, 27
herbs, 38–41
    sweets, 39
Himalayan salts, 41
honey, 24

## I

ice box cookies, 55, 91
    Chocolate Cookies, 100–101
    pinwheels, 102–104
    preparation, 96–97
    Vanilla Cookies, 98–99
icing sugars, 22
immersion blenders, 10
infusions, 150
ingredients, 21
    chocolate and cocoa, 45–47
    dairy, 26–29
    decorating cakes, 227
    edible decorations, 44
    eggs, 36
    fats, 30–31
    flavoring agents, 38–41
    flour, 32–33
    gelatins, 35
    leavening agents, 37
    nonwheat flour, 34
    nuts, 42–43
    oils, 30–31
    starches, 35

sweeteners
    brown and unrefined sugars, 23
    nectars, syrups, and non-cane-derived sweeteners, 24–25
    white sugars, 22
instant-read thermometers, 8

## J–K

jelling agents, 35

kettles, 9
Key Lime Pie, 194–195
Key limes vs. Persian Limes, 195
kneading, yeast-risen breads, 252–253
knives, 8
koekje, 54
kosher salts, 41

## L

lards, 30
lattice crusts, 182–183
lavender, 39
layer cakes
    Carrot Cake, 210–211
    Moist Chocolate Cake, 206–207
    preparation, 204–205
    Vanilla Velvet Cake, 208–209
leavening agents, 37
    egg function, 117
    yeast-risen breads, 249
        Brioche, 266–267
        Challah, 268–269
        crisp, crusted, 250
        freezing dough, 256
        French Bread, 262–263
        kneading, 252–253
        preparation, 258–260
        reactions, 251
        rich dough, 250
        sponge, 257
        Walnut-Raisin Bread, 264–265
        yeast fermentation tips, 254
Lemon Bars, 154–155
lemon meringues, 129
light brown sugars, 23
liners, muffins, 238
liqueurs, 40

liquid egg whites, 36
liquid food coloring, 44
liquid measures, 48
liquid measuring cups, 14
liquid sweeteners, 24
little cakes, 54
low-fat milk, 26
luster dusts, 44

# M

mace, 39
machinery, 10-11
making homemade nut flours, 42
mandelbread, 59
mandelbrot, 59
margarines, 30
mascarpone, 28
Mascarpone Mousse, 162-163
masking, decorating cakes, 226
mats, 15-16
measuring, basics, 48-50
measuring spoons, 15
measuring tools, 14-15
melting
    butters, 28
    chocolates, 46
meringues, 119
    Chocolate Cloud Cake, 136-137
    cookies, 126-129
    French Macarons, 130-133
    Pavlova, 138-139
    pointers for success, 125
    preparation
        French, 120-121
        Swiss, 122-123
    stages, 124
metal cutters, washing and drying, 6
Mexican Wedding Cookies, 83
microplane zesters, 8
microwaves, melting chocolates, 47
milk, 26-27
    scalding, 145
milk chocolates, 46
milk solids, 26
mint, 39
mixers
    handheld, 10
    standing, 10

mixing, cookies, 56-57
mocha meringues, 129
Moist Chocolate Cake, 206-207
moisture, egg function, 117
molasses, 24
    brown sugars, 23
Molten Chocolate Cake, 212-213
mousses, 141
    Mascarpone Mousse, 162-163
    Praline Mousse, 160-161
    preparation, 158-159
muffin pans, 13
muffins, 237
    Banana Muffins, 241
    preparation, 238-239
    Yogurt Muffins, 240
muscovado, 23

# N

natural cane sugars, 23
nectars, 24-25
neutral-tasting oils, 31
New York Cheesecake, 150-153
nibs, 45
non-cane-derived sweeteners, 24-25
nondairy milk alternatives, 26
nonpareils, decorating cookies, 108
nonstick cooking sprays, 31
nonsugar sweeteners, 24
nonwheat flours, 34
nut butters, 43
nut pastes, 43
nutmeg, 39
nuts, 42-43
    crusts, 196-197
    decorating cookies, 108

# O

Oatmeal-Raisin Cookies, 82
offset spatulas, 7
oils, 30-31, 40
olive oils, 31
one stage mixings, 57
open-star pastry tips, 19
oven racks, soufflé, 166
oven thermometers, 8

# P

pans, 9
  baking, 12-13
papers, 15-16
parchment papers, 15
paring knives, 8
pastry bags, 18
pastry brushes, 7
Pastry Cream recipe, 146-147
pastry creams, 143, 147
pastry flours, 32
pastry tips, 19
  piped cookies, 85-87
patterns, decorating cakes, 227
patty cakes, 203
Pavlova, 138-139
Peanut Butter Cookies, 81
peelers, vegetable, 7
Persian limes vs. Key limes, 195
petal pastry tips, 19
petit-four pastry tips, 19
pie birds, 181
pie pans, 13
pie whistles, 181
pies, 173, 175
  Apple Pie, 188-191
  crusts
    basic preparation, 176-179
    blind baking, 198-199
    cracker, 192-193
    nut, 196-197
  Fresh Fruit Tart in Almond Crust, 200-201
  Key Lime Pie, 194-195
  tops, 180-187
pinwheels cookies, 102-104
piped cookies, 55, 76
  basics, 84-87
  Spritz Cookies, 88-89
piping
  French Macarons, 132
  frosting, 225
  royal icing, 111
plain pastry tips, 19
plastic wraps, 15
pots, 9
powdered food colors, 44
powdered sugars, 22
  decorating cakes, 226
Praline Mousse, 160-161

pressed cookies, 76
pressed sheet cookies, 54
presses, cookie, 87
pressing, cracker crusts, 193
pure maple syrup, 24

# Q

quick breads, 237, 251
  Banana Muffins, 241
  biscuits
    preparation, 242-243
    recipe, 244-245
  muffin preparation, 238-239
  scones, 246-247
  Yogurt Muffins, 240

# R

raisins
  Oatmeal-Raisin Cookies, 82
  Walnut-Raisin Bread, 264-265
rectangular baking pans, 12
refrigerator cookies, 55, 91
  Chocolate Cookies, 100-101
  pinwheels, 102-104
  preparation, 96-97
  Vanilla Cookies, 98-99
rendered fats, 30
rich dough breads, 250
ricottas, 28
rimmed baking sheets, 12
rock salts, 41
rolled fondant, 44
rolled oats
  Granola Bars, 64-65
  Oatmeal-Raisin Cookies, 82
rolled-out cookies, 55, 91
  Gingerbread Cookies, 94-95
  preparations, 92-93
rolling equipment, 92
rolling pin bands, 92
rolling pin rings, 92
rolling pins, 6
rolling strips, 92
rosemary, 39
round baking pans, 12
round pastry tips, 19

roux, 171
royal icing, decorating cookies, 110–113
Russian Sour Cream Coffeecake, 214–215

## S

saffron, 39
sage, 39
salts, 41
sanding sugars, 22
scalded milk, 145
scallions, 39
scones, 237, 246–247
scoops, cookie, 6
scrapers, 6
sea salts, 41
seized chocolates, 47
self-rising flours, 32
semisweet chocolates, 46
serrated knives, 8
sheet cookies, 54–55, 59
    Blondies, 70–71
    Brownies, 68–69
    Shortbread, 62–63
sheets, rimmed baking, 12
shine, egg function, 117
Shortbread, 62–63
shortening, 30
    egg function, 117
sifting, 49
silicone mats, 15
silicone spatulas, 7
single-crust pies, 186
skim milk, 26
soufflé, 165
    Chocolate Soufflé, 168–169
    Goat Cheese Soufflé, 170–171
sour creams, 27
spatulas
    offset, 7
    silicone, 7
specialty pastry tips, 19
spelt flours, 33
spice grinders, 11
spices, 38–41
sponge mixing, 57
sponges, yeast-risen breads, 257
spooning measures, 48
spoons, measuring, 15

springform pans, 12
sprinkles, decorating cookies, 108
Spritz Cookies, 88–89
square baking pans, 12
standing mixers, 10
star anise, 39
starches, 35
stenciling, decorating cakes, 226
stevia, 25
stirred custards, 141
storage
    brownies, 69
    cakes, 213
    chocolates, 47
    Key Lime Pie, 195
    scones, 247
stovetop custards, 141
    Crème Anglaise, 144–145
    Pastry Cream, 146–147
    preparation, 142–143
stovetops, melting chocolates, 47
structures, egg function, 117
substitutes, crackers, 192
sucanat, 23
sugar alcohols, 25
sugars, 22
    decorating cookies, 108
superfine sugars, 22
sweep measuring, 48
sweeteners
    brown and unrefined sugars, 23
    nectars, syrups, and non-cane-derived sweeteners, 24–25
    white sugars, 22
Swiss Meringue Buttercream, 228
Swiss meringues, 122–123
syrups, 24–25

## T

table salts, 41
tapioca starches, 35
tart pans, 13
tarts, 173, 175
    crusts
        basic preparation, 176–179
        blind baking, 198–199
        cracker, 192–193
        nut, 196–197

Fresh Fruit Tart in Almond Crust, 200–201
    Key Lime Pie, 194–195
thermometers
    instant-read, 8
    oven, 8
thickening, egg function, 117
thyme, 39
timers, 8
tinting, royal icing, 111
toasting nuts, 42
toothpicks, 16
    decorating cookies, 113
toppings
    cheesecakes, 153
    decorating cookies, 108
troubleshooting
    cakes, 220–221
    cookie common faults, 105
turbinado, 23
turntables, 16

## U

uncooked egg whites, 158
unrefined sugars, 23
unsweetened chocolates, 45
unsweetened cocoa powders, 45
utensils, 6–9

## V

vanilla, 38–39
Vanilla Cookies, 98–99
Vanilla Velvet Cake, 208–209
vegan butter substitutes, 30
vegetable peelers, 7
verbena, 39

## W-X-Y-Z

Walnut-Raisin Bread, 264–265
weighing, 49
weights, blind baking crusts, 198–199
Whipped Cream, 230
whipping creams, 27
whisks, 7
white chocolates, 46
white sugars, 22
whole cane sugars, 23
whole milk, 26

whole-wheat flours, 33
wooden skewers, 16
wrapping, springform pans, 12

yeast, 37
yeast-risen breads, 249
    Brioche, 266–267
    Challah, 268–269
    crisp, crusted, 250
    freezing dough, 256
    French Bread, 262–263
    kneading, 252–253
    preparation, 258–260
    reactions, 251
    rich dough, 250
    sponge, 257
    Walnut-Raisin Bread, 264–265
    yeast fermentation tips, 254
Yogurt Muffins, 240
yogurts, 27

zests, 38–39

Photo Credits

All photos by Kotaro Kawashima, with the exception of the following:

**Photography © Dorling Kindersley:** Edward Allwright: 227 top right; Clive Bozzard-Hill: 17 (cake board); Paul Bricknell: 8 (timer), 12 (cookie sheet); Martin Cameron: 13 (bundt pan), 40, 46 bottom; Angela Coppola: 3, 10 (mixer); Andy Crawford: 13 (tart pan), 44, 226 right; Steve Gorton: 3, 45 (chocolate); Will Heap: 6 (scoop), 3, 7 (whisk), 7 (sieve), 16 (foil), 18, 19, 51, 56; Sian Irvine: 22, 31; Ruth Jenkinson: 6 (scraper), 8 (thermometer), 10 (immersion blender), 11 (scale), 16 (parchment), 16 (wrap), 17 (skewers), 42; Dave King: 3, 6 (rolling pin), 8 (knives), 9 (rack), 9 (kettle), 10 (blender), 11 (processor), 13 (muffin), 14 (dry measure), 17 (board), 21, 35 (cornstarch), 35 (gelatin), 36, 37, 43, 88, 116, 119, 121, 124 middle, 124 right, 127 bottom left, 127 top right; David Murray: 9 (pots), 11 (grinder), 41; Ian O'Leary: 15 (bowl), 27 top, 46 top; Gary Ombler: 7 (offset), 8 (zester), 8 (knives); Roger Phillips: 8 (oven thermometer); Susanna Price: 223, 226 left; William Reavell: 221; Tina Rupp: 3, 5, 7 (spatula), 10 (hand mixer), 26, 48 top; William Shaw: 3, 32, 34, 152; Howard Shooter: 6 (cutter), 7 (brush), 13 (pie pan), 15 (spoons), 23, 27 bottom, 48 bottom, 127 bottom left, 227; Simon Smith: 24, 27 middle; Steve Tanner: 14 top; Philip Wilkins: 7 (peeler); Paul Williams: 30; Jerry Young: 125 right. **Coleman Yuen, Pearson Education Asia Ltd:** 28.